RATED X

RATED X

How Porn Liberated Me from Hollywood

MAITLAND WARD

ATRIA BOOKS

New York   London   Toronto   Sydney   New Delhi

An Imprint of Simon & Schuster, Inc.
1230 Avenue of the Americas
New York, NY 10020

Names and identifying characteristics of some individuals have been changed.
Some dialogue has been re-created.

First Atria Books hardcover edition September 2022

ATRIA B O O K S and colophon are trademarks of Simon & Schuster, Inc.

For information about special discounts for bulk purchases, please contact Simon &
Schuster Special Sales at 1-866-506-1949 or business@simonandschuster.com.

The Simon & Schuster Speakers Bureau can bring authors to your live event.
For more information or to book an event, contact the Simon & Schuster Speakers
Bureau at 1-866-248-3049 or visit our website at www.simonspeakers.com.

Interior design by Hope Herr-Cardillo

Manufactured in China

1   3   5   7   9   10   8   6   4   2

Library of Congress Cataloging-in-Publication Data

Names: Ward, Maitland, 1977- author.
Title: Rated X : how porn liberated me from Hollywood / Maitland Ward.
Description: First Atria Books hardcover edition. | New York : Atria Books, 2022.
Identifiers: LCCN 2021057349 (print) | LCCN 2021057350 (ebook) |
ISBN 9781982195892 (hardcover) | ISBN 9781982195908 (paperback) |
ISBN 9781982195915 (ebook)
Subjects: LCSH: Ward, Maitland, 1977- | Actors—United States—Biography. |
LCGFT: Autobiographies.
Classification: LCC PN2287.W413 A3 2022 (print) | LCC PN2287.W413 (ebook) |
DDC 791.4502/8092 [B]—dc23/eng/20220217
LC record available at https://lccn.loc.gov/2021057349
LC ebook record available at https://lccn.loc.gov/2021057350

ISBN 978-1-9821-9589-2
ISBN 978-1-9821-9591-5 (ebook)

To my husband, who has encouraged and stood by me every step of the way. And to my mother and father, who raised me to be the independent spirit that I am.

RATED X

CHAPTER 1

I USED TO HIDE IN my room and imagine David Hasselhoff and I would one day get married, probably after a fast chase and definitely after we solved some crime with KITT, his talking car. Who knew that KITT was played by Bill Daniels and that he would one day be my teacher? David would wear his leather Knight Rider jacket when we wed, with his curly chest hair exposed, and I would wear a gown with ribbons and hoopskirt, and my dogs would be my flower girls. I thought he might smell like the baking vanilla or maybe gasoline straight from the pump. KITT would marry us, and we would drive off to a place where we could make babies. But the fantasy always abruptly ended there. I knew that in order for any of that to happen, I would have to grow up and leave my parents. And that would disappoint everyone.

I was acutely aware that if I could remain around the age of seven for the rest of my life, I would make my family proud. Seven, I thought, would be an age where when you danced around the living room in a Cinderella dress, they'd applaud you, but the glass slippers wouldn't yet pose any real threat. It's an odd thing to realize no one wants you to grow up when you're actively doing that.

I was a sheltered only child, raised in Long Beach, a suburb of Los Angeles that people nicknamed Iowa by the Sea because of the simple small-town vibe and also because in the postwar years, it was said that "you couldn't swing a cat in this town without leaving a patch of fur on a Hawkeye." We weren't Iowans, though. My people came from Texas and Saskatchewan, somewhat respectively.

I walked home from school with the same kids in the first grade as I did in the eighth, and I could smell what was cooking for dinner the second my mother greeted me at the door. In the afternoons, my mother and I would watch soap operas, and then I'd play *Star Wars* with my dogs and cats in a big yard with a little frog pond that was shaded with avocado trees. Our springer spaniel was always Chewie, and I was always Princess Leia. At dusk, I'd sit at the front window and wait for my father's car to turn into the driveway. Those headlights and that turn and my dad's footsteps walking up our porch were predictable. Every girl should take for granted that her dad will always come home.

I spent a lot of time alone. I didn't have any siblings or first cousins or much family at all around, but I was loved—so much so that I felt guilty whenever I played away from home too long. Family consisted of my mom and dad and my grandmother on my father's side, whose love of gardening and her obsession with the Rapture always had her at odds with the natural elements. "They say Jesus is coming this year," she'd say. "I wonder if my grapefruits will have come in." So much casual planning for the end of the world made me feel at home in a controlled state of chaos.

"Don't give it up to any man who won't commit to paying your bills," my grandmother once said after giving me the talk about the cows and the mooching pervert who drank all that free milk from the fast titties. She thought this was encouragement for me to uphold my virtue; it turns out it was a solid business model for OnlyFans.

My grandmother was always worried about everything, but mostly about God punishing her for doing something wrong. And when she was worried, she cleaned. She was in constant zigzag motion trying to avoid a lightning strike. It all stemmed from her father who took her out of school in the eighth grade. She said he didn't like the teacher, and she said it like that was a valid reason. "He was a man of God's word," she would say as she washed each dish by hand in her sink. "And he brought us up right to obey." And she never had a good night's sleep because of it.

Jesus watched over me through my childhood—not from some place of peace on a cloud but from a miniature gold-plated frame that my grandmother one day propped up on my dresser. Like, *poof*, all of a sudden there was a blond, blue-eyed Jesus right next to my David Hasselhoff lunch box and they were at odds. She said that this picture would bring me comfort. In fact, much like her father did for her, it kept me up at night.

"Talk to him," my grandmother said, pointing to the frame. "Just tell him whatever you did bad today, and you'll be forgiven." I looked away fast from David Hasselhoff. "Unless it's drugs or premarital sex," she said. "Then you'll have to be burned at the stake by the Beast because you'll never get up in the Rapture."

"Bad" felt like such a broad-ranging topic. Did she mean bad because I ate too many cookies or bad because I could feel my breasts coming in and I noticed a boy at school looking at my shirt? Bad got more complicated as I grew up.

I put an elastic bandage around my breasts at various points in my upbringing (I had gotten the bandage for an ankle sprain), depending on how guilty I felt for growing and how much I thought Jesus's eyes were following me from inside the frame. I thought that maybe I could stop myself from having to develop boobs—or at least they wouldn't poke out of my shirt and have that boy looking at me anymore. I was already so tall for my age that I thought if I squished myself down with something heavy on my head every night—like a book or a water jug or anything else I could find that felt satisfactorily oppressive but wouldn't actually crack my bones—then my spine would get the hint that it had already grown enough. Maybe word would travel down to my breasts and also my vagina, which was now tingling with pre-pubescence. But every time I measured myself on the inside of my closet door, I found that I was losing my battle at remaining a child. And there was that tingling.

My family believed I had a weak constitution—that I was constantly under the threat of sickness and needed to be protected. They never tried to get me diagnosed with strange diseases for attention or put me in a wheelchair like Munchausen by proxy victims, but there was a constant undertone that I couldn't handle some things—most things—simply because I nearly died at birth.

My mother, who had suffered miscarriage after miscarriage, was told I wouldn't make it. That she would keep bleeding and all of me would eventually flush right out, just like all the others had. She looked for me in the toilet every morning. She was on bed rest for weeks, the doctors amazed that I still had a heartbeat. "You and me, we stuck it out and you came out so beautiful," she said. When my mother was cut open as she lay on a metal slab and I was presented to the world, I was over eight pounds and screamed the moment I breathed air. But my screams or my breath were never proof enough of my strength to survive.

And that's really where it comes from—the feeling that I should never grow up. I felt if I did, then I'd grow away from the story of my weakness and that special connection with my mom.

I believed in this fable that I was weak for some time. Though I was never unusually sick as a child and I had a strong throwing arm, I still believed that I was less able than other kids because of some trauma I suffered in the womb. Finally, when I was grown-up, it dawned on me that I hadn't escaped death by a lottery ticket or a Hail Mary pass. I'd survived because I was determined enough to hold on.

When I was about six, I came to the shocking realization that Barbie doesn't have a vagina. I had run straight from my bath to play with my dollhouse, towel falling off me, when I looked down and saw that I had a slit and Barbie did not.

"Grandma," I said, running to her in horror. She was baking something in the kitchen, and I caused her to jump and burn her pinky.

"Why doesn't she have any girl parts?" I asked. I was terrified that Barbie couldn't pee. When she saw me pointing to her flat, plastic crotch, she stopped what she was doing, kneeled down squarely in front of me, and said, "You don't need those parts until you're married." When she saw that I was standing there naked, she said, "And put your towel back on, so nobody sees yours right now."

I went back to my room, dropped my towel, and sat in a hunch with my belly rolls looking up at me, and I stared down at my vagina. I wasn't supposed to have it until I was married, but there it was, like a sickness or something to hide. I wondered if I should sew it, like the doctor did when I cut my chin open after I fell off my gymnastic rings in the yard. Then I thought about how much I didn't like needles or even sewing at all. Maybe I could just hide it my whole life, get married, and when my husband discovered it, he'd think it just magically appeared because we were so in love. Then I thought how I never wanted a boy to see my vagina at all.

"HAVE YOU EVER FELT good funny down there?" my friend Alison asked me as we swam in the aboveground pool my parents had just put up in our yard. "You mean in the deep end?" I asked, pointing to the bottom of the pool. There wasn't any deep end; it was all just three feet, but perhaps I was being metaphorical. "No, I mean in your panties," Alison said, then dipped her hair back into the water.

In my panties? I was nearly twelve and didn't know anything about my vagina except that I peed from it and one day soon I'd bleed from it too.

"I don't really have any fancy panties," I said, thinking she meant those satin ones from Victoria's Secret I'd seen in the catalogs. They looked smooth and decadent and like they did something I didn't know about yet. They looked like the kind of panties the girls on *As the World Turns* wore.

"No," she said, her laugh bubbling the water as she waded. "I mean when you touch it. My mom says it's completely natural as long as you do it for yourself and don't show anyone."

She proceeded to explain how she did it, which involved wide, circular hip movements and some Nivea pump lotion. I just watched as the water whirlpooled around her as she demonstrated motions that looked less erotic and more like something that would earn fish at Sea World. "Next week," she said, "I may try inserting a tampon."

Alison's mom married her third husband when we were in the first grade, and quickly thereafter, they moved up north. After that, we'd mostly see each other on holidays and in the summers when she'd come back down to visit her dad, who it seemed to me was out of work most of the time because he was always home and lived with his own mother. She was wilder than my other friends, who were mostly considered good church kids who lived with both parents under a thirty-year-mortgaged roof. I liked that she was daring. I didn't have to be such a good girl with her, because no matter what I did, she was always worse than me.

We didn't do anything more than talk about sex or masturbation until we were thirteen and had already been inserting tampons for some months. We were in my grandmother's guest room when something happened. She was sleeping over, and we wanted to feel what a real French kiss was like. We had bought some good panties at the mall, and we finally discovered what they did. They were scratchy, they rode up your butt, and we spent so much money on them we couldn't go to a movie. But I liked the way she kissed me and how tingly I felt when her body was pressed to mine.

I liked the fact that I could be sexual with her and exploratory, and no one suspected us. We could be locked away in my room and nobody would be the wiser as to what we were up to. Being gay or bisexual or having any sort of attraction to the same sex wasn't something my family ever thought or talked about. No one was homophobic; it just never occurred to them—like snow couldn't happen in Los Angeles but it's lovely in Vermont. Although I knew I wasn't gay—primarily because of David Hasselhoff—and I didn't even know what bisexual really was, I knew that I liked girls, and I used the fact that my parents thought it was completely innocent for me to be in bed with them at night as a loophole. I always hid the Jesus photo when Alison came over. I didn't want him spying on us, though I still apologized to him later.

I didn't have a real orgasm until I was fourteen and had a mouth full of metal and neon rubber bands. It was entirely by accident on my Strawberry Shortcake canopy bed.

"France is like nine hours ahead," my nerdy friend, Daniel, said as we talked on the phone. I lay back on my mattress, wondering why I hadn't replaced the canopy top like I had my bedsheets. I had grown-up flowers on my duvet and Strawberry Shortcake with a watering can pouring down on me—an image that both glued me to my childhood and simultaneously dared me to grow.

"What's your point?" I asked him.

"Well," he said, "if we got on a plane now, we'd be in France in like no time. We could have lunch at the Eiffel Tower and then fly back and be home by dinner. Your parents couldn't get you in trouble because they wouldn't know you've been gone, and we'd have an international romance."

I rolled my eyes and threw a sock up at Strawberry Shortcake.

I had met Daniel in the second grade, when his grandmother and my mother chaperoned our class for a day of computer learning at the community college. The other kids hated him because he was a mouthy nerd, and he carried a box of McDonaldland cookies he'd throw randomly at their heads, yelling, "Grimace," if he hit someone. His grandmother had no control over him, and she hadn't since he was left with her four years earlier. But I found him interesting. He was who he was and didn't care that he didn't fit in with a bunch of kids who stood in lines and stayed quiet because they were told to. I'd later discover that he knew things other kids didn't too, like how to cheat on *The Oregon Trail* and who Michael Dukakis was. We were the only two who cared about the presidential election in the sixth grade.

"What if I was your boyfriend?" he asked me once and then attempted to blow bubbles of strawberry Quik from his nose at the lunch table. It didn't work; he kept choking and half suffocating himself before it sprayed out all over creation.

"I think you just gave my answer," I said, and I rolled my eyes.

"What! You don't think I'm a catch? I'm going to be a millionaire. Bill Gates was like me, but I'm not a dick and I actually know things," he said. I snorted.

"I don't care about Bill Gates. I care about romance," I said.

My best friend, Sue, a tiny but fierce girl who would eventually become a black belt in karate, beat him up the last day of elementary school because he tried to kiss me. We were out past the dodgeball walls, under the eucalyptus trees whose leaves we had picked just the year prior to feed to silkworms, when he turned and gave me that look—the one that can either be love or something you ate.

"There hasn't been an afternoon as romantic as this," he stuttered.

"Yeah, there probably has," I said.

I knew it was coming when he cocked his head and his lips parted like he was about to suck a good flavor of Capri Sun out of that little straw. But I didn't know what to do.

I could run, but I found myself not going anywhere. My body was betraying me.

I wasn't supposed to want this, I was sure of that. This wasn't David Hasselhoff or some *Love in the Afternoon* soap opera hunk. This was just some kid I knew. I was supposed to wait for some dazzling moment where the birds were singing, and violin music was playing, and a man in a tuxedo would give me my happily ever after. But Daniel was a boy, and I was a girl who didn't quite feel like a girl anymore. And I wanted to feel like a real woman, if only for a few stolen moments on the grass.

But what would happen if everyone found out? What would they say if they knew what I had desired and, worse, saw that I had enjoyed it? They would talk about me, and then I'd be a girl who was talked about, and I would surely never make it up in the Rapture then.

A rush of fear came over me, and I let out some version of a scream as I physically pushed Daniel away. That's when my friend ran in and took him out hard and fast by the knees.

His grandmother thought he couldn't handle such a hostile environment for middle school, so she found a smaller arrangement. I didn't see him again until ninth grade. Somehow he forgave me for that assault on the schoolyard, and we talked in secret on the phone every night.

"I got some *Penthouse* letters," Daniel said, and I adjusted my pink princess phone receiver to my ear. I didn't know what that meant except that *Penthouse* magazine was the one that was too dirty for my dad's underwear drawer. "They're kinda weird," he said and then laughed as he proceeded to read the raunchiest, nastiest letter, with the most descriptive sexual vocabulary I had ever heard. Fucking and sucking and so much coming. The words were going over his visually aroused teenage male brain, but they were absolutely penetrating mine. My vagina felt warm and started to pulsate. And there was this soppy wet mess in my shorts. My hand was drawn down below, as I needed to rub this throbbing. I finally knew what Alison meant about that good funny feeling. And it all happened in regular cotton underwear.

"It kinda sucks just to read about things," he said.

Panting, I laid back on my pillow and agreed.

The first boy who kissed me gave me the chicken pox. It wasn't a real kiss, though. We were the leads in a production of *Bye Bye Birdie* at the local dance company that they called *Bye-Bye Long Beach*, but it felt so real to me that I threw up my lunch in the bathroom before it happened. I was twelve and Brian was thirteen, and the amount of hair gel he used made me think he might have expectations. Diane, our director, coached us right before showtime. "Really give it your all out there," she told us. We did, and the little red itchy bumps arrived over the weekend—doubling down on the belief my grandmother had instilled in me that any form of sexual interaction, recreational or professional, brings disease.

I felt all-around cheated in the first kiss department. The one that I kind-of-maybe-wanted but pushed away, and the one I had that was okay because it wasn't real left me susceptible to shingles for the rest of my life.

In my grandmother's mind, sex was a trap by the devil, and any pleasure experienced was just the devil's way of stealing a woman's body and all her dreams. "Once you do it, you're stuck, and then all you'll ever have is babies," she'd say, and this was possibly the most honest she'd ever be about the realities of her youth. She would never admit it, but if you do the math, she was probably pregnant on her wedding day.

My mother, who had been promiscuous in her youth, wasn't fire and brimstone like my grandmother. She was religious, but she didn't fear God for me as much as she feared her own mistakes would be repeated. She left her Texas Bible college barefoot and with only the clothes on her back to escape an abusive father and to marry a movie star's kid. She met Ricardo Montalbán's son when he was in the military stationed near where she lived. They danced at a party, and soon she was living at the Montalbán home in Beverly Hills. "One day I was in Texas, and the next I was having dinner across the table from Loretta Young," she said with the wistfulness of rose-colored memory. She lost a baby, and the marriage didn't last. And there were a lot of wild years in an effort to distract her from her losses, and from Texas, and from all the scars her father had left. It was as if she was always running, even well after she ran away. "Boys need it more than girls do," she said. "You'd be surprised at what they can convince you to do when hormones are raging."

I know that some boys kept her from realizing who she was, from pursuing her own dreams. Then she became a wife and a mother.

Between both of them, my grandma and my mother, sex became a game of outrunning the enemy—namely, boys. I knew what to look for and how to escape. But what left me awake and guilty and praying to a little gold-rimmed photo of Jesus every night were the hormones that were raging inside me.

How could I outrun myself?

I got my period the summer I was twelve, quite by surprise and in the middle of the night. I'm not sure why I was surprised. I was an appropriate age, and Alison and I constantly talked about it. She said she already had it, but she never produced any evidence, except for one wrapped tampon at the bottom of her clear-pink jelly purse. I guess the end of childhood just surprised me. I thought I'd have one more Christmas or Halloween. I sat there shaking on the toilet, lit only by an ocean breeze–scented seashell plugged into the wall, staring at the spots of blood on the toilet paper.

"This is a very grown-up thing for you," my mother said later, as she pulled out her box of maxi pads and proceeded to show me how to stick them onto my underwear. I thought that when I became a woman, I'd get tampons, not diapers. At least that's what Alison had said.

To her credit, my mom didn't act weird or anything, and she gave me all the information I needed for hygiene and personal care.

"You've got a lot of responsibility now," she said as she kissed my head and tucked me in.

The whole thing left me with the feeling that being a woman would be an injury I'd always have to nurse.

I called Alison the next morning and told her.

"What did your mom say?" she asked. I relayed what happened, and she laughed and said, "Well, at least it's not like my mom. She sent a welcome card to my new visitor and told her to make sure she comes back *every single* month."

When I was sixteen years old, I made the decision to lose my virginity in the fastest and least messy way possible when I saw my friend's oldest sister crying after she returned from an all-inclusive honeymoon in Acapulco. Holly Hill had taken a purity vow in high school, and she stuck to it all through city college until she met her husband at the budget hair salon where she took appointments. She and her father had made a big deal of it when they attended one of those purity dances at the church—the ones where the daughters dress in white and the fathers give them rings to promise they won't bone anyone until the father makes the decision that it's time for the daughter to be boned for the rest of her life by an upstanding church boy. Well, she had now boned in Acapulco, and she was crying.

"I have no purpose now that I've done it," she said, sniffling at the family breakfast nook. She was just back from her honeymoon, and this is what she was talking about? "They don't tell you you're nothing special once what you've been saving is spent." She wailed into the tissue. "And they don't tell you it bleeds!"

I had gone to that wedding. It was the kind of wedding I wanted, with pink flowers and Disney ice sculptures, and where the bride wears a dress with tiers like cake layers. They even brought her there in a carriage that sort of looked like Cinderella's, if Cinderella rode in more of an SUV-type pumpkin arrangement. Everyone thought she was an angel. The ideal daughter. My dad wasn't weird enough to do a purity dance, but wouldn't he still want to see his daughter honest in white when she danced with him?

Or at least give off the appearance of honesty.

The truth is, I couldn't think of any worse way to lose your virginity than on your wedding night. I could never admit this to anyone—not my mother, not the church girls, and definitely not my grandmother, although she'd probably just tell me to become a nun as long as I was still a Baptist. Why would I want to worry about bleeding all over my new husband? Or wonder the whole way through the ceremony if my vagina might split open later? And how embarrassing to think that everyone at my reception would know the precise date and time that it all happened.

I figured if they only thought they did, that would be good enough.

If I could get it out of the way and get a little practice, maybe I wouldn't embarrass myself—and I might even impress my new husband because he'd think I was a natural. Gymnasts don't earn tens their first try, but none of us, when watching them win gold, need to see the first time they missed the bars.

I selected Daniel as the one who would help out with this task.

"Do you like that?" Daniel breathed heavily into my ear, his hand up my skirt and rubbing what he thought was my clit as we lay back on his bed. "Umm . . . I think it's up higher," I said. I knew for sure it was, but I didn't want to tell him it was because Alison and I played a game of press the elevator button.

We had decided that Friday would be the night. Not because we planned to make this some huge, romantic weekend thing, but because his grandmother was picking up his brother from work at the JCPenney and taking him to see *Coneheads*.

We had the house to ourselves.

"If I let you do it one time, really fast, do you promise not to say anything to anyone ever?" I had asked him on the phone a few nights prior. The line was silent for a moment, and then he said, "How fast?" I rolled my eyes and flipped onto my stomach on my bed. "Like regular speed but before I change my mind."

He immediately pulled up the calendar on his Apple 2GS and we settled on the date.

"Can I at least tell my brother I'm not a virgin after?" he asked.

"No!" I said. Then I thought about how his brother called him "the pink one" because he said his dick was like a baby mouse. "I don't know. If you have to, tell him you saved up for a hooker or something."

"I don't think he'll believe I picked up a hooker on my bike."

"Listen," I said. "Just so you know, this isn't something all special and gushy." I cringed as soon as I said "gushy." "I mean, I just want to experience something for the first time, so I'll never have to experience it for the first time again."

"That's weird," he said.

"Do you want to get fucked or not?"

He shut up.

I showered twice before I left for his house that night, just to make sure I was all shaved and clean, and then I locked the door to my room and tried on every single pair of underwear in my drawer. I tried them on once, then twice, sometimes three times, and then back to pair one again, before landing on a sensible cotton blue set. I looked at myself in the mirror. I didn't feel sexy or especially beautiful, but I was anticipating what I would look like later. And I wanted to memorize my face and my body just before my new journey into womanhood.

Daniel and I sipped the classy cocktails he made us—Midori sours to calm our nerves—with the stuff he had bought at the liquor store where they didn't check IDs. I had bled pretty good some days earlier when we tried fingering, so tensions were high. But I was glad that I probably wouldn't bleed tonight.

"Suck it a little," he said, as he lay back on his bed and unzipped his pants. I had done this a few times before for him, and each time there seemed to be more hair. I wrapped a hand around it and started to lick it like Alison told me was the way to do it—like an ice cream cone you don't want to let drip.

"Hey, part of the deal was tits," he said to me, motioning for me to take off my shirt. I lifted it away and then nodded permission for him to take off the bra. I felt myself shaking as he watched me sitting there, tits out and bare to him. He had only squeezed them under my shirt before, and he had never stared. His eyeballs were glued to them now. "Those are some nice ones," he said. After I determined he had enough to remember them by, I made him turn out the lights.

The smell of his Drakkar toilet water was heavy as I lay back and parted my legs. He kept stroking himself and rubbing that same place he thought was my clit.

"What's taking so long?" I asked.

"I'm doing foreplay," he said. Then after fumbling with a condom and a few attempts to find my hole in the dark, he pushed himself partially and then all the way inside me. I gasped and then threw a hand over my mouth and started to giggle. I had feared it would hurt and had been warned by my teenage girl magazines that not all of it would fit at first, but there I was with a whole dick inside me.

"Stop fucking laughing," he said, and he stopped moving.

"I'm sorry," I said, gathering myself, but some snorts escaped even as I bit my lip to stop them. He was now losing concentration and confidence. I knew I had to instill within him some masculinity again.

"It was just shocking for a second," I told him.

That seemed to please him because, like all men, he thought it was because his dick was so big it had overwhelmed me.

I adjusted myself on his pillow and made sure I tossed out my hair. Even in the almost dark, even in secret, I wanted to be beautiful the first time a boy made love to me. He began to move back and forth, once slowly, then twice. I marveled at the fact I was actually being fucked and how great my hair looked as it was happening. Just before a third thrust, there was pounding at the door.

"Get out here, you shithead!" his brother yelled. "*Coneheads* was sold out. We got pizza."

Daniel was so startled, he pulled out and then immediately came into the condom. I threw my head back onto the pillow, deflated. I thought the boy was supposed to be better at these things, and I didn't know a girl could be so sexually frustrated about it.

Maybe that's the true reason that Holly Hill was crying. She was promised hallelujahs and rainbows, and it was really because the dick just wasn't any good and now she was married to it.

"They knew what we were up to," Daniel said, pacing his room, as I just lay there with my nice hair and no follow-through.

"Why do you think that?" I asked.

"Because where the fuck does *Coneheads* sell out?"

When I apologized to my picture of Jesus that night, I told him how sorry I was for giving in to my lust, but then I paused and said to Jesus, "But at least no one knows about it but us."

When I looked in the mirror, I was surprised that I didn't look any different. Same nose, same eyes, same lanky, unsure frame. I'd expected a dick to transform me, but I was still just me. It felt somewhat disappointing.

I reached a deal with Jesus that night: he would keep my sin a secret from everyone, and I'd keep our PR game strong.

CHAPTER 2

I SPENT THE SUMMER OF 1990 waiting for Jack and Jennifer to do it. They had been on a cruise, stuck together in a cabin since school got out, and *Days of Our Lives* had been teasing us with constant sexual tension and close-ups of her diaphragm. Finally, there was an explosion, they were shipwrecked, almost dead, and stuck in a cave. This was the moment Jennifer would become a woman! A public service announcement aired right afterward, with the actress who played Jennifer—who was twenty-three at the time—warning girls what a big step sex was and how they should be well informed and prepared.

I wondered why they never gave boys these kinds of warnings. Why, when a guy scored on TV, they didn't break away with a special message, with the scene's star cautioning young men that once you fuck, you'll never be the same. Why weren't boys warned of the apocalyptic pitfalls of enjoying their dicks or told that they better have a plan because if it goes wrong the first time, they can never take it back? Why did a girl's first time have to be perfect and a guy's just a buddy's high five? In no uncertain terms, Jennifer spelled out to me that summer that if you're a woman and you choose to have sex, you're giving some part of yourself away.

I didn't feel that I had given anything away to Daniel, but I knew that I was supposed to feel some degree of guilt, and since I didn't feel bad, then there was something wrong with me. I was flawed—like one of those sociopaths that relaxes and eats a bucket of chicken after hacksawing a family of four. I looked up to Jennifer and to Brenda and Kelly on *90210* and to all the girls on TV and movies who warned me that if my first time wasn't planned out and special, then I'd be an emotional basket case who could never respect myself. I trusted them, so how could I trust myself that I was really *okay?*

I started taking acting classes when I was ten so I could pretend to be someone else. A place in our neighborhood offered lessons—taught by a real actress who was a real extra once in *Staying Alive*—and I asked my mother to sign me up when a flyer was stuffed in our door. "She's so creative," she told my father, and while this was true, these classes were more than an artistic outlet; they were therapy for a girl who was shy and quiet but who also desperately wanted to scream and be heard.

I was never comfortable showing my emotions to anyone, so showing them through another character, in another place and time, was a relief. As an only child, I was, intentionally or not, under a microscope and held to standards that normally multiple siblings fulfill. My parents were always proud of me; they told me I was the best and the smartest and the prettiest and the best, Best, BEST, but that's a lot of pressure to always be at the top of every game. Sometimes I just wanted to be emotional and fussy and even sad. Sometimes it felt good to lose and to get lost in the emotion of that. And I could do all of that onstage. I didn't have to keep up the appearance of my perfection when I was applauded for playing imperfection so well.

"You rarely see a girl so young act when she's not speaking," the teacher told my mother. "It's like she says more in between the sentences than most of the kids say with the words." My mother thought this made me brilliant. I think it was just me feeling my way through the pauses and showing bursts of who I really was deep down inside in the beats and breaths.

Even at an early age, I knew there was something I had to say to the world that wouldn't be accepted by general society, and it was easier to do it beneath the veil of a character's words. If I wanted to fly high and away from the world, I could be Amelia Earhart; if I wanted to question the church and ideas of God, I could triumphantly play Joan of Arc; if I wanted people to see a brilliant woman with duct tape around the edges of her doorways and her head in an oven, I would read aloud the works of Sylvia Plath. Though these events were dramatic and mostly metaphoric, I wanted to be all these things at one time.

I was a drama kid in high school—not really a nerd but also not popular. I was clean-cut and tried to be preppy because it made me seem together and smart and my family liked me this way. Anyone who wore short skirts or rock band T-shirts wasn't taking school seriously and probably smoked.

I hid my body at all costs behind a towel in the locker room after gym class. I had such long legs, and my ass was dimpled against the elastic of my underwear. My crush on the drum major never went anywhere because I was too embarrassed to demonstrate to him that I was alive. While I wasn't hot enough to be a cheerleader or rebellious enough to be a punk, being in drama did get me noticed and gave me accolades. If I didn't have that outlet, I might've locked myself in the bathroom stall every day at lunchtime, just hoping the time would pass so I could go home. In fact, I did that sometimes. I guess my ability to play others made people like me better and this gave me real purpose. This mirage gave me a name.

THEY TOOK AWAY MY first name when I decided to be a professional actress. It wasn't a decision really, more like a chance presented to me that I took. The primary reason I have been successful in life is that I have been willing to take chances that most others would be fearful of or overlook. I'd seen an ad for TVI, a flashy actors' studio, and my parents, who allowed me to pursue my dream once my braces came off and I was old enough for a place like Wienerschnitzel, the hot dog joint, to hire me legally, took me there to sign up. They got their clients agent meetings, helped make demo reels, and fully packaged aspiring actors for sale. The agent I was paired up with was retired from New York theater and still recovering from the Northridge earthquake a few months prior. She was a chorus line of memory and struggle.

"Ashleys have absolutely overrun Hollywood," she told me as we sat at her dining room table. The living room was roped off and partially collapsed. "Your middle name. That's the star maker."

I hadn't ever thought about my middle name before—Maitland— except that everyone thought it was Matilda and I rarely corrected them. I don't even remember agreeing to the change, but I suppose my parents did, because the name was soon printed at the bottom of my 8 × 10s. I was no longer Ashley. I was Maitland. The name pressed between my first and last. Part of me was angry that they took away my first name, and part of me was happy that I could reinvent myself as a real actress with a new one.

My first audition was for the sitcom *Saved by the Bell.* I played some girl that the nerdy character Screech had the hots for. I was shaking in the hallway, seated in the middle of a long line of chairs filled by other hopefuls. And all of them looked like a Gap ad. I was definitely more Express.

The casting director, Robin Lippin, gave me the once-over when I walked inside her office.

"There are a lot of flowers on that dress," she said, with a point of her pen.

"I figured Screech would like flowers," I replied and felt like I had just buried myself in fertilizer.

"He's a nerd; he's probably allergic."

I kicked myself after for missing such a key element to character development.

I waited three weeks until I accepted the fact that I wasn't getting a callback for the part. Robin did tell my agent that I had green talent that needed to be honed but that if I worked really hard, I had a future in this town. A future was something, I supposed, even if it was green.

I immediately threw out the dress with the flowers.

My parents had told me that if people liked me, they would give me things—especially when it came to jobs in acting. "Be your nice, beautiful self and people will fall all over you," my mother would say. She was proud when people told her how good and sweet and likable I was. I guess it was a reflection on her mothering or evidence that she produced something great in the world. And she meant it as a compliment. But I was left with the idea that being liked was my value.

That's a dangerous thing to instill in a young girl.

TVI ADVERTISED WORKSHOPS BY casting directors who could give you your big break. Christy Dooley, who cast for *The Bold and the Beautiful*, was teaching one so, being the soap fan I was, I signed up. I wore a purple silk button-up shirt tucked into my jeans and I curled my hair loose like Jennifer did just before the *Love in the Afternoon* ship explosion and fuck in the cave. I was expecting shirtless young guys to act out scenes with me, but the class primarily consisted of women in their thirties and forties who smoked on breaks.

At the end of the class, Christy called me aside, and I thought I was in trouble.

"I want you to audition for a new character on the show," Christy said. "It's for a summer storyline coming up. It would be a contract role."

I squeaked a *yes* past the heartbeat that raced to tackle it in my throat. It would be my second audition ever, and I marveled that I could really be a Jennifer. I left the class giddy and hopeful.

"She liked me!" I told my parents, and I felt accomplished.

"I'm going to CBS Studios to audition!" I screamed into the phone to Sue that night. "They say it'll be a screen test where they do your hair and makeup and everything." I flopped my long blond mane over and twisted it up in a scrunchie as I paced my room. "It's some summer romance thing."

"Oh my God, you're going to kiss a soap stud!" Sue said.

I stopped pacing. Oh shit.

I flipped through the pages Christy gave me. She was right. The script called for that. A big, sloppy, wet one at the end.

And it would be on film! I didn't know if I could do anything that intimate on camera.

"Just kiss me like you're the kind of guy who gets girls normally," I told Daniel as we practiced for my big audition in his room. He took offense to that. "No, I mean like you're someone with muscles who girls fight over." It wasn't getting any better.

"You know, there are girls who would appreciate these lips," he told me.

"Listen, if I do well enough to get this job you can put this on your résumé," I said, and I pulled him hard and fast.

We spent a few hours kissing and studying different techniques in the mirror. Tongue, no tongue, head tilt right, head tilt left. "You can't come at me straight on; we'll bust our noses," he said when we tried it that way.

At the end, I didn't feel any more prepared than I had at the start. I would have to just go into that audition, throw myself at whatever guy they gave me, and hope for a miracle.

But maybe the guy will be cute.

Dylan was sitting down, studying his lines across from me with a blond named Brittany Daniel, when my mother dropped me off in the waiting room for the screen test. There were four of us there—two guys and two girls to be paired up to read the scene. I was the only one young enough to require a mother. My partner's name was Josh. He had a hat on backward and basketball shorts and would later land a twenty-year career role with the sister soap, *The Young and the Restless*, when he lost out on this part. Dylan wore a jacket that was blue and pressed. His jaw was angular and his hair a deliberate mop he kept brushing back.

He was a Dead Poets Society and a future vampire love story hero all in one. I didn't know if he was genuinely flirting with Brittany, or if he was really just that good at what he did, but all of it made me sure she'd be better at kissing and get the role.

He was definitely cute.

And I couldn't help but notice that he kept looking at me.

"Have you ever done this before?" Josh asked me as we rehearsed. I didn't tell him about Daniel, or that every time I thought about kissing and doing it all on film, my knees started to shake.

"Sure," I said. "But I like to save my kissing for the real take." I thought I sounded like I was making a strong creative choice, but he smiled because he knew.

I had kissed boys before, but not anyone with defined arms and a legitimate need to remove facial hair. He smelled nice, and his lips were plump and moist from the miniature pot of balm he kept dipping into and applying. I wondered if this was the kind of thing that separated the men from the boys I knew—weight days and Vaseline.

"Good luck," Dylan said to me as Josh and I passed him in the hallway. I smiled and said the same. And as our eyes locked and then parted, my knees started to shake again.

"They want you to read with Dylan," the stage manager told me as I was sitting in the hall waiting for my turn. Dylan was behind the big stage door with the flashing red light, kissing Brittany.

"But my partner is Josh," I said. My heart was pounding.

"They think you and Dylan would look good together," she said, and I was ushered quickly through that same big door and onto the stage.

Holy shit.

I wasn't prepared for this. All afternoon I had planned on kissing Josh. We had rehearsed and prepared, and I really felt that I could trust him to get me through it. Dylan was too perfect. He just seemed like the kind of guy I would get all flustered with and lost in.

"This is my first kiss," he whispered before we started the scene. I was startled he was talking to me, as I had my face buried in my lines. Was he kidding? Or making fun of me? He had a sly smile.

"I've done this before," I said, trying to play it off like a joke, but my voice was shaking.

I took a breath like I was sucking up a moment before a really important one was about to happen. He was about to sweep me off my feet, and I think some part of me knew that it would be a long time before I touched the ground again.

When it was time for the kiss, he gave me that same smile, like an inside joke shared between us, and put fingertips to my chin. I exhaled as our eyes connected. The kiss was soft and unhurried, and I felt like I was floating afterward. He seemed a little scattered from it too.

"Put it in water," Dylan said, as he handed me a rose that he pulled from a vase they were discarding on set. "If I never see you again, at least you can remember me for a week."

I laughed as I clutched it to my heart.

I didn't want my parents to see, so I tucked it into my pocket before I got to the car and put it in a glass on my windowsill when I got home.

The flowers arrived with a congratulatory note from production before I got the call from my agent. I would be playing Jessica Forrester, niece to the core family, and Dylan would be playing Dylan, an apprentice at my family's international fashion house. They liked his name, so they kept it. They also liked that my résumé said I played the violin. I had exaggerated, though; I could play only one song, and only if there were assigned red sticker dots under the strings. After one episode, the story of Jessica's future with the symphony quite literally screeched to a halt. To this day, whenever I run into the executive producer, he jokes and asks how the violin lessons are coming along.

"Oh my God, you're going to be on *General Hospital*!" a cheerleader who I'd never spoken to before screamed as she ran up to me in my high school's quad. "*The Bold and the Beautiful*," I told her, but she didn't comprehend the difference.

News spread like wildfire. Reactions ranged from excitement to contempt to asking for my autograph because it might be worth something one day—and those were just the teachers.

"Nothing will change," I told Sue as I drove her to the mall in my little white car that used to belong to my aunt. "I just won't be at school all the time, that's all."

We shared an Awesome Blossom at Chili's, and when the check for the deep-fried onion arrived and included an extra piece of paper for me to place my signature to Tammy with love, we both knew life was about to never be the same.

I split my time between regular high school and the studio, which provided me with the best of both worlds. I got to experience everything a typical high schooler does but only two days a week while starring on a television show. My tutor, Hal, was a navy man who had retired from coaching high school football and become an on-set educator because he got tired of watching the grass grow. He was fun to talk to, and I learned more from him than from any teacher I had before. But his presence was always a glaring reminder of my age when we walked down the halls.

Brent, the actor who would rival Dylan for my on-screen affection, asked me the second we met, "How old do you think I look?" We were in his character's bikini bar, and the script called for him to seduce me in a hammock. He was named Sly for his cunningness and the fact that he looked like Sylvester Stallone. I was dressed in a floor-length checkered dress to indicate my character was straight from a farm in Iowa, and he had a vest on with no shirt to indicate his character was an asshole straight from Los Angeles. I didn't know how old he looked. To me everyone with chest hair looked thirty-five.

"I don't know . . . twenty-two," I said.

"Yes!" Brent said, standing up, doing a victory lap around his chair, and then plopping down on it again backward. "I mean no, of course not. I'm going to be twenty-nine next week, but at least I don't look *that* old."

We spent the next two hours in that hammock, propped up with great conviction and consternation by his right ass cheek. You know a lot about a guy when you can immediately trust that he won't flip you over by easing his flex. He'd later surmise that the reason we became such good friends was that I was mature for my age and he was immature for his, so we met in the middle.

"I'm twenty-four," Dylan said as we shared our first lunch together at the CBS commissary right after they fit us for wardrobe, took pictures for our identification badges, and we got to play with the *Price Is Right* Plinko board next door. "I'm just too old for you," he said, and I froze up. He noticed I was flustered, and he laughed. "I mean in the script. It's so weird that you're so young."

I sank into my seat with the feeling that I was too weird for even my salad.

"I have a girlfriend," he said abruptly, and as he sipped from a water bottle, his eyes were trained on me. I thought he was noticing more weirdness at the time, but I think he was gauging my reaction.

They shared a townhome with two kittens, and she was leaving for some months on an educational sabbatical to Japan.

"I have some boyfriends too," I said, but it wasn't so convincing.

"You should come by some time and meet the kittens," he said.

"DO YOU HATE YOUR father . . . secretly, I mean?" Isadora asked me, smoking a third cigarette, her body shrouded by smoke and the wood of her armchair. Isadora was an acting coach that production hired to help Dylan and me achieve a believable affair. Once a week we'd meet with her separately at her home and then together to work on the scenes for the coming week. Production had had great luck with her in the past. She brought soap superstar Hunter Tylo to tears without blowing menthol into her eyes first.

"Go ahead," she said. "Tell me your thoughts."

I wanted to tell her I thought it was weird she wore dark glasses inside and that her pillow cushions all had sharp, plastic corners, but I held my breath. I had to: the smoke was choking me.

"No, I love my dad," I said, and it was the truth.

"That's because you haven't fucked enough men to know you hate him yet," she said. "Once you discover dick, your acting will get good."

Isadora lasted only about a month. She demanded more money, and the scenes we rehearsed with her lacked lightness and a spirit of youth. Plus, she kept wanting to inject sexual tension into a storyline with my cousin.

"Jessica needs to have a metamorphosis!" one of the producers said after calling me into the office. I sat and listened to her in my long braid and socks that covered all the skin that could possibly show past the hem of my dress. She said that although the audience loved my homespun sweetness, they were used to seeing "eyeshadow and hair." Probably legs too. They wanted to make a big to-do about it, so they enlisted celebrity hairstylist José Éber.

José, for all the hustle and hype leading up to the scene, was really a nice guy. I was terrified he was going to cut off all my hair and I'd look like one of those models in Europe who they praised in the magazines for looking like they shot up heroin, but he just gave me highlights, a movie star fluffing, and a solid trim.

When I passed Dylan in the hall, he did a double take. I thought he was going to compliment me, but he looked down at my new high heels and then stood on his tiptoes, measuring my height against his. "You're so tall," he said. "Be careful. You'll make me look bad." After flashing a smile, he walked away.

I went upstairs and told wardrobe that the new shoes weren't comfortable, and they gave me something lower.

The next few months Dylan and I did everything together. We had the same publicist, and she had great success marketing us as a pair. We did charity bowling tournaments and radio interviews and scores of international photo shoots. At that time, *The Bold and the Beautiful* was the number two show in the world, next to *Baywatch*. Both were easy to translate and showed lots of tits and ass. I met Dylan's kittens and spent more and more time at his place. My parents were comfortable with him. He was always respectful and dropped me off on time—though they never demanded a strict curfew if I was with him. I was surprised at how much they trusted him. My parents rarely trusted anyone, especially boys, with their daughter.

"It's so nice how he looks after you when we can't be there," my mom told me. "We don't have to worry about you being up in Hollywood alone."

"Are you a virgin?" Dylan asked me one night at his house after a long conversation about Pedro on *The Real World* and sex and AIDS.

I didn't know what to say.

"I haven't done anything yet," I said, because that was the line I'd always say, and I knew that was the answer he wanted to hear. He'd always get so happy when we talked about the things I didn't know about yet and that he wanted to teach me. And I really wanted him to teach me about this.

"Wait until you meet someone you fall for," he said, and for the rest of the show we snuggled under a blanket.

"Are you telling me no boy's taken you on a motorcycle ride before?" he asked me after we got invited to participate in The Love Ride, Jay Leno's charity event that had celebrities and masses of bikers riding to raise money for causes like muscular dystrophy and organizations like Autism Speaks. Dylan and I had been asked to go as a pair.

"No," I said. I was in high school. The closest thing to a motorcycle was one guy who rode a scooter, but no one wanted to ride on the back of anything with him.

"Wow, I'm really racking up a list of your firsts," and as he said it, he grinned. "Don't make me responsible for all of them."

Hundreds of bikes lined up for the race as flashbulbs went off. Dylan helped me with my helmet and strapped me in once I hopped on the back of his ride. "It gets fast, so just hold on to me," he said, wrapping my arms around his waist before he revved up the engine. I pressed my cheek against the hot leather of his back, and we took off. It didn't get that fast because of all the attendees and congestion. We just scooted along the freeway for a few miles until we reached some tape and barbecue stations that marked the finish.

"That really sucked," he said, laughing, and I agreed. "Let me take you somewhere."

This time it was fast—and dangerous and exhilarating—as we wound our way up through the hills in Malibu to an overlook where he used to take the girls he wanted to impress. My stomach flipped at the thought that he was trying to impress me.

"This is one of the most romantic spots up here," he said and then moved some hair off my face that had gotten messed up from the helmet. He held me to him, and his lips kept brushing against my cheek and the corners of my mouth. It was building to perfect until his body tensed and his mood shifted. He pulled away from me. "You're going to get me in trouble with my girlfriend," he said, and he sounded kind of angry with me.

"I'm sorry," I said, because I always said sorry when I didn't know what else to say.

"You should get a boyfriend and bring him up here. Why don't you have a boyfriend yet, anyway?"

I didn't know, so I didn't answer. I just hopped on when he started up the bike again and we left.

Dylan took my on-screen virginity not long after, and it was something he talked about—no, more like bragged constantly about—and prided himself in.

"Big day," he said with a smile as I walked onto the set where it would happen—his college dorm room, after a party where we would both get caught up in something we weren't supposed to. He kept commenting to hair and makeup how I was too done up, and I didn't look sweet enough or innocent. "It's her first time; you don't want her to look like she gets around."

"Do you like what you look like?" the makeup artist asked me pointedly, as she pulled me aside.

I did like the way I looked. I looked pretty and maybe a little more womanly in a shade brighter lipstick and a cute short skirt, but I felt myself shaking my head *no* when I wanted to scream *yes*.

They changed me so I would be more comfortable, which made Dylan more comfortable instead.

"I think they wonder if we're a real couple," Dylan said to me as we blocked out the scene.

"Why do you say that?" I asked. The crew was straightening the comforter on the bed where, in just moments, I would give myself to him.

"Because they always see us together and how we act." I thought he was getting mad at me again, until he smiled and said, "We should keep it up. Let's keep them guessing."

This threw me for a loop. And it made me excited and feel more connected to him when we, as our characters, pretended to make love.

Dylan would visit me on the set even when he wasn't working that day. He'd massage my feet while I was in the makeup chair, or we'd hang out in my dressing room and have intimate talks about life. He told a production assistant that he spent so much time there that they could just combine our names on the room door. Of course, my tutor, Hal, said no to that. Once Dylan sat in on an interview that I had with one of the soap magazines. He helped me answer all the questions, which I thought was cute, but the journalist later said how uncomfortable he felt for me having to sit there under Dylan's watch while he gave what should've been my answers.

"It's like he thinks he controls your mind and your thoughts," the journalist said, and it rattled me how disturbed about it he was.

One afternoon, we fell asleep cuddled on my couch. When his name was called over the loudspeaker to come to set, he kissed my head and said in 1950s sitcom fashion, "Sorry honey, I'm late for work." To which I replied, "Have a good day at the office, dear."

I was giddy for a moment, but then the moment changed as this bolt of realization shot right through me. He was now responsible for my every move. Good or bad, they were his. And I gave that power to him so he would like me better. I lay back on the couch once he left and cried after I got myself off. We were always walking a line between fantasy and reality that I didn't have the tools to draw. And I really think he knew that.

ED McMAHON SANG "HAPPY Birthday" to my father at a dinner in Florida the night I judged *Star Search*—that early *American Idol*-style show that had celebrities judge up-and-coming talent. It was my first trip to Disney World, where they filmed, and I required a chaperone. Since it was my father's birthday that weekend, the trip was special for him. Ed's wife took a liking to me, and after the trip she told my publicist that she wanted to set me up with her son, Lex, who was studying law. I talked to him a few times on the phone, and he invited me to a Super Bowl party at their house.

"Oh, great, he wants to be a lawyer," Dylan said with a roll of his eyes. "There's someone you can trust." I liked the fact that Dylan was agitated, so I played it up.

The party was fun, and her son was nice. Ed was nice too, as I accidentally locked my keys in my car, and he used his Auto Club membership to help me out.

Dylan called that night after I got home.

"So, what happened?" Dylan asked, and his *so* was so long and slithering, it was a snake.

"He was nice; we made some plans," I said.

"What kind of plans?" "Plans" hit a nerve and I discovered I liked that.

"He wants to take me on a vacation somewhere, and I think I may go."

"You're in high school," he said, and I could imagine him pulling at his hair.

"Not for long," I said, and I made an excuse to hang up the phone.

LEX'S AND MY RELATIONSHIP flickered out after my eighteenth birthday because he just felt too old for me. He was a college guy who spent the night of my party drinking and playing pool while I danced the funky chicken with my friends. I broke it off with him in the worst, most passive-aggressive way possible. When he asked me out, I said I was busy. When he asked me to choose any time that was good for me, I said I was busy a lot. This brought great relief to Dylan, who laughed and said, "Oh, the sting!"

When Becky returned from Japan, Dylan left me alone. The calls and visits stopped, and our pretend relationship vanished. "How are the cats?" I'd ask and he'd reply, "They really missed Becky." Our conversations began to serve two purposes: to make me know how happy he was without me and to criticize my life.

He brought Becky to the Soap Opera Digest Awards, where I was nominated for the Outstanding Newcomer Award. There we sat in the grand ballroom of the Beverly Hilton, he with Becky and me with a boy from school named James.

"You're going to win," Dylan told me right before we all piled into a limousine together. He was so excited about it you'd think it was his nomination. "And when you're up there, you're going to think of me and know that I was right."

He wasn't right.

I didn't win. A woman from *As the World Turns* who had a big pain reliever commercial took it, proving the power of Big Ibuprofen.

Although I was disappointed, I was more ashamed that I didn't win for Dylan. He lit up so much at the possibility that once that light was gone, I felt small and in the dark. I looked over to him and he was crushed, dejected. "You should've won," he mouthed to me, and all I could do was shrug.

He proceeded to get really drunk that night, stumbling around and telling everyone who would listen that I was robbed. I felt he embarrassed himself and me.

When I went to the bathroom, he followed me and cornered me outside the door, leaning against it so I had to hear his words before I could pass. His breath was thick and his frame around me overpowering.

"You're not going to think I'm your good luck charm now," he said before being distracted again by his drink.

"He's going to try and sleep with you at prom," Dylan said after I told him I was taking James. Months earlier, before Becky returned, we had joked about him taking me—though I don't think either of us was especially joking.

We definitely weren't laughing now.

I got ready for the prom at the studio. Hair and makeup and wardrobe took great care in making sure I was dazzling for my special night. Hal put me in the limo, and there was a tear in his eye when he waved his prized pupil off. Of course, my date didn't try to spike my punch that night and coerce me into some illicit rendezvous at the Holiday Inn. In fact, he didn't even try to kiss me, which years later I told *Teen People* was one of my most humiliating moments. My date read the piece and left a note of apology with my mother.

When Dylan asked me how it went, I remembered Jennifer's public service announcement and how every misogynistic male thought a girl's deflowering had to go in order for her not to be fucked up for the rest of her life. I beamed as I looked up at him and said, "It was perfect."

He wouldn't talk to me for a week.

CHAPTER 3

M Y MOTHER HAD SEX with my boyfriend just after I had turned eighteen while I was in a diabetic coma and being cared for by Larry from *Three's Company*—on the soap, that is. A lot began to happen to me after Dylan absconded with my cherry and barely missed imprisonment for statutory rape. My aunt had brought him to trial. He of course got off due to his boyish good looks and charm and my tearful plea on the stand. Aside from the diabetes and the affair and Larry teaching me how to give insulin shots using an orange, I would be almost roofied and tricked into getting pregnant for my family's fortune, tortured and raped in an alleyway, and then nearly set on fire simply because I lived to tell it all. I would discover that once you play out your role as virgin, the role of victim comes next.

"How do you poke holes in the condoms without anyone noticing?" Brent asked as we rehearsed the upcoming script in his room. "I mean, I don't mean to brag, but how am I fooling anyone with a hole that my dick just pops through?" I shrugged and agreed with this assessment.

While Dylan was carrying on behind my back with my mother, Brent and I were put together in what production called "a romance that would eventually meet its tragic fate in a dark alley." In other words, he was going to rape me. I was told that rape scenes were what won you Emmys and that I should be more excited about it.

"This is fucked up," Brent said, seemingly the only other one who understood how we were both sacrificial lambs. "Last summer all I did was party with girls in bikinis. This summer I'm Jack the Ripper."

"It's not looking good," Jack Tripper's former-used-car-salesman-best friend–turned–my doctor told my family, who were all gathered around my hospital bed, where I was fully made-up and tragic. I had just collapsed at my cousin Thorne's wedding, just before Dylan could tell me that he had boned my mother and wanted to continue boning her in the guesthouse with my blessing. I didn't hit the floorboards, though, on the way down from my dramatic fall from my virginal pedestal: Dylan caught me. And with his Herculean strength, he carried me to the hospital and to Dr. Larry.

"It's diabetes," Dr. Larry said. "Type 2. She's fallen into a coma." There were dramatic gasps and tears and guilty looks between Dylan and my mother. There were so many theatrics that by the end of it all, I half expected Dr. Larry to pull out his old *Three's Company* brochures and sell us a used car.

Instead, he said, "Only the love of one man can save her," and all eyes focused on Dylan.

"You've been spending a lot of time with Brent," Dylan said to me between takes, while I lay in my hospital bed and a real nurse told the crew how they should arrange things.

"He's my friend," I said. "We have fun." I couldn't talk or move too much, or the wires would fall off and everyone would know it was a sham.

Dylan smugly laughed. "I think his idea of fun might be different from yours."

The more time I spent with Brent, the more I saw what a normal working friendship should be. I didn't have to be on guard or worry that my conversations with him would later fall under judgment or the microscope. He didn't hate the boys I knew and grill me on their intentions. We mostly just discussed things like his tanning regimen and whether we should grab sushi. And every day at noon we'd sneak off to his dressing room to watch *Little House on the Prairie*.

"YOU DON'T HAVE TO say anything," Dylan said on a late-night phone call I didn't expect. I thought it was Daniel calling for phone sex. *The Commish* was over, so I just figured. "Just know that whatever he's been doing with you, I'm going to handle it." There was a pause.

"Handle what?" I asked.

Handle who?

Did he know about me giving jerk-off instructions to my nerdy friend?

"Brent," he said, with a spit of vitriol. "You've had more intimate scenes. And you've been going to his room."

I was stunned.

"I'm just going to let him know he better stay a gentleman with you. Don't worry about it, okay?" In an almost hypnotic state, I mirrored his *okay* back and he wished me a good night before deciding it was time we hung up.

"I wish I didn't have to ask this," the producer said after pulling me from set the next day. "Has Brent made you feel . . . uncomfortable in any way?" She looked at me with eyes that conveyed kindness but also fear of potential lawsuit.

"No! Brent is my friend," I said. I was shocked. Was Dylan really capable of bringing it this far? I imagined some more chivalrous end to this matter. Like a sword fight or a duel. But really, I thought he'd just pull Brent aside and tell him to behave himself. A part of me deep down and twisted up in him liked the idea of Dylan carrying a sword for me and riding in on a horse. But this was different. It felt like he was playing his own game of divide and conquer now. If he won, we'd be placed in positions he was comfortable with: me as his pawn and Brent the rook he kicks off the board. "I figured as much," she said. "I think there's just some rivalry there."

...

MY GRANDMOTHER BELIEVED THAT the two places most likely to lead an impressionable young woman down the road to hell were Hollywood and a sorority house. A close third was Spencer Gifts at the mall.

I attended college while working on the show to further my education and to go to parties. Mainly the latter. Studio life, and constantly being under the watch of Dylan, was stifling to me. I needed somewhere I could let loose and find freedom. I thought college would be a place where I could reinvent myself without being under a microscope, but I quickly discovered that I was wrong.

"You're the girl on TV," a guy said, after he pulled away from our make-out session and started examining me like a piece of toast whose burned parts resemble a holy character. We were at a Hawaiian-themed fraternity rush party where someone at the front would put paper flowers around your neck and say, "You've been *lei-ed*!" the moment you arrived.

I didn't drink that night, or ever in those days, so I just sipped from a glass of water that I hoped people might mistake for vodka. He kissed me, and it was nice to be wanted—until he figured out who I was, stood up fast, and asked if I needed another drink. I showed him my full glass of water and said that I was good. He never returned, but when I gulped the whole glass back, a guy sat down next to me, seemingly impressed, and asked if I was an accomplished alcoholic.

Some Bible study girls followed me to Long Beach State. Well, not me in particular. It was a good school in our hometown, so a bunch of them ended up there like hometown girls often do. A few even chose Greek life and rushed with me for my sorority, and it became their aim to make sure everyone knew I was one of them. "She's a virgin," they said to a frat boy at a party and word spread. "She doesn't drink," another said, so I couldn't pretend anymore with my water glass. "It's so cool that you stand up for what you believe in, in a place like Hollywood," they'd say. But the truth was, I was never standing up for anything. I was sitting down on my hands with a gag in my mouth while they spread their version of my truth. But I reasoned that it was better than the alternative. If I was no longer seen as good, then I was just another girl ruined by Hollywood.

"Are you on birth control?" the wardrobe girl asked me during a fitting, and she seemed concerned.

"No," I said, my cheeks hot with flush. I panicked that there were rumors being spread about me. I figured it was Dylan spreading them about me and Brent.

"Oh," she said, and she was quiet for a moment as she continued with her tape and measurements. "You've gotten a little fuller." She squeezed her tape around my chest and then around my ass. "I thought maybe your body was adjusting." She scrunched up her nose. "Just try and work out a little."

I thanked her in my state of humiliation, as if her notifying me of my fatness was a gift to me, and rushed to my dressing room. I took off all my clothes and stared into a long mirror and then I pinched the little roll around my waist, whose offered apology to my fingertips was bruising.

YOU KNEW YOU'D MADE it as a celebrity when you got an unsolicited discount at the MAC store on Robertson Boulevard. MAC offered big deals to actors and makeup artists and anyone who could spread the word of the brand. If the salesperson saw you when you walked in and said, "Don't worry, we'll take care of you," you knew you were MAC famous. I first heard these words from Estella—Stella for short, when I desired the matte, liver-hued shades of lip color that the girls wore on *90210*.

"You should go with red," she said, as I rummaged through pinks and various shades of brown. "Oh, I don't know if I can pull it off," I said, to which she replied, "Here, I can help you," and put a tissue-covered finger to my lips to take off what I was wearing.

"Some of the girls from your show come in here," she said and she overlined my top lip in a shade of blood. I nodded. "That's how I knew about this place." Stella was twenty-four, and she wanted to be an actress, or write poetry, or something. She had so many varied aspirations I got lost in them—and in her. She had eyes that now I'd describe as brandy colored but then I could only equate with a warm, flat A&W root beer. A sweet, deep brown, sans the enthusiasm of bubbles. After she finished and my total with discount was paid, she said, "Call me if you need anything more," and then wrote her number in blue ink on a card. I went to my car and flipped down the mirror. My lips looked fuller and softer and somehow more dangerous. They made me want to walk around the Beverly Center so that everyone could see them in this retail and social destination.

Stella had a studio apartment not far from CBS, and I went over one afternoon after work for her to show me some tricks with makeup. I had called her and left a message on her machine, telling her I needed products for some event I had coming up. It was an excuse really, because I just wanted to see her again. I assumed we would meet at the store, but she insisted on her place.

"You need to take more risks," she said as she finished my eyes, and I wasn't sure if she was talking about makeup or something else. She had offered me a drink before I sat down in her chair, and this time the vodka wasn't water. I didn't want it to be.

"You look so fucking sexy!" she said as she jumped back to take me in. I noticed she wasn't wearing a bra. She handed me a mirror and told me to look at myself. The eyeliner and black shadow were like smoke.

"I like this risk," I said, and when I looked up, she passed me my drink.

We sat on her sofa and sipped our cocktails and just talked. I mostly just swirled my vodka around the glass, listening to her speak of books I'd never read and art house films I'd never heard of. The clinking ice made me feel grown-up. I set mine aside at some point because I knew in a few hours I'd have to drive to my parents' house.

"You're a lot of fun to be with," she said, and her voice was lower now, more a sultry whisper. "I like that you came over. I didn't think you would."

I smiled, a mix of nerves and excitement and hard liquor that churned my belly.

"I wanted to come," I said.

Her eyes were glassy, and she took me in with a cocked head.

"I can see that now," she said, and then she leaned in to kiss me.

I froze and could feel myself shake. She pulled back. "Is this okay?" Her breath was warm on my lips—my new red ones. I inhaled her, giving myself a moment to think but also to take it all in.

"Yes," I said, and I lay back on the couch beneath her and she made love to me there.

I was obsessed with fucking Stella. All I thought about was having her mouth on me and her fingers inside me. I would sneak away to her apartment whenever I could. I liked to listen to her stories and that she didn't really know any of my friends. One night, after she showed me the literal ins and outs of a dildo, she told me rather abruptly that she had a boyfriend.

"So we can't do this anymore?" I asked.

She laughed and reached over to smoke some of her joint. She offered me a drag, but I refused it.

"No, not at all," she said, and she snuggled into me. "He wants to meet you . . . I mean, if you want to meet him." She ran a finger down my breast. "With me there." And the way she looked at me, I knew it wouldn't be for dinner and Monopoly. I gulped and said I'd let her know my schedule before I said a faster good-bye than I had wanted to.

THERE WAS A GREAT scandal when a group of the more rebellious sorority girls decided to attend a BDSM club and extended me an invitation.

"What does that mean?" I asked. I didn't know the term. I was young and naive and this was well before *Fifty Shades of Grey*.

"Bondage stuff," the girl spearheading the event said and then explained a little more. She was matter-of-fact about it. Telling me about power play and dominance and submission. Hearing about it kind of scared me, but even scarier was that it intrigued me too.

I told her I had to think about it, but once word got back to the Bible study girls, all heaven broke loose.

"That's where they beat people and do Satan worship," one of the Bible study girls told me. "They're trying to lure you and chain you up to have a threesome. They want to make God not love you anymore."

God not loving me weighed on my mind for some nights—not so much about the BDSM club but about Stella and her proposal. How did my love for God get tied up—no pun intended—with my desires to have sex with another woman and a man? This would be what the Bible girls dreaded the most—a threesome. The lines were drawn in no uncertain terms that I was no longer a good girl if any of this happened.

I brought six condoms in my purse the evening I arrived at Stella's apartment. I was only planning on using one, but my anxiety needed to account for five potential disasters and be prepared, and I didn't trust a guy to bring his own. I told my parents I was staying over with a nice friend from sorority, so we had the whole night together. Stella opened the door wearing a long black kimono, and I could smell the joint being smoked inside. "I'm so excited you made it," she said, and she gave me a hard kiss against the door once she had shut it.

Jeff was sitting there on the sofa and stood up the moment I came in—I'm sure to seem like a gentleman and also to brush the ashes from the joint off his lap. He was moderately tall, with a nice build and sandy brown hair. Nothing to go wild about, but I could see why she thought he was cute. He put the joint in the ashtray and then held out his hand. "You're sexier than she told me," he said, and I was glad I'd worn the red lipstick.

Stella got us all drinks and we sat around and talked—and talked, and talked, and talked. She had ordered Chinese food, and I fumbled with chopsticks. I tried to eat the noodles seductively, but I ended up feeling like one end of *Lady and the Tramp*. I wasn't sure what the protocol was in these things. Is there a point where we stop talking about movies and our cookie fortunes and someone stands up to say, "Let's all fuck!"?

"Why don't you kiss Jeff," Stella finally said as she situated herself across from us on an ottoman. I nervously laughed, at what I don't know, and then turned to look at him. He motioned for me to get closer and then leaned in and started to kiss me, and I was surprised it felt really good. "You okay?" he asked as he pulled back and I nodded, and he leaned in again for more.

I could see Stella out of the corner of my eye touching herself between drags of her joint and sips from her glass. She had pulled the robe apart and her fingers were on herself, then inside.

"Stand in front of Jeff and take your clothes off," Stella said. I was scared, but I did what she told me. Jeff undressed himself as he watched me. I worried he'd see the fat around my waist, but he was just staring at my tits as he jerked himself.

Stella kept shooting out commands, and I wondered if Jeff had actually wanted to meet me or if it was Stella who had initiated him being there. Either way, he was happy when I was on my knees, sandwiched between his thighs, and sucking him off. "Put him down your throat," Stella shouted, and I gagged on him so hard, I was worried I would lose my noodles all over his balls. While I wasn't smoking the joint, I was inhaling it, and I wondered if that, along with the strength of the drink, was making me feel more uncontained.

"Fuck him," Stella said. She sounded turned on but a little angry too.

"I think she means to ride me," Jeff said, and he helped me up to straddle him. I had never been on top with a man before. It had only ever been missionary with a nerd. He tried to push inside me, but I quickly pulled away to grab my purse. "She's a prepared Girl Scout," Jeff said as I handed him a condom.

After a few tries and different angles, I sank down onto him. I was so pleased with myself that I forgot I had to move. Jeff slapped my butt for encouragement, and I wondered if I was in the middle of this thing that they called BDSM. While I felt like a siren riding a sexual wave, it was a lot of work, and I couldn't find good leverage, so I flopped backward at some point and let him finish with the hard labor. "I love fucking this tight young pussy," he screamed out, to which I quite happily replied, "Thank you!"

We used another condom that night and one more in the morning before Stella woke up. He moved slow behind me, and told me to be quiet, but I knew she was awake and listening. Before he left, he told me to save the rest for next time, and my sore pussy winced but also fluttered as he drove away.

"Why didn't you join in last night?" I asked Stella.

"Next time," she said as her teakettle whistled.

It was strange to me that they never told me how long they had been together or where they met. And he didn't say good-bye to her like a boyfriend would before he left. The next week when I called and asked her when we could all do it again, she told me she had broken up with Jeff. She had met someone new, and as it happened, he wanted to meet me too.

Stella and I soured quickly after that. She wanted me to help her get a role on *The Bold and the Beautiful*. I told her I couldn't promise that, and she went into a rage.

"You've always thought you were better than me," she said.

"WE'RE GOING TO SEND Jessica away to England for a while," a producer told me as I spoke to him on my thirty-minutes-a-month brick phone, in my car, so as he was firing me, it was costing me too. "She's got a lot to deal with and we think she can better deal with it off-screen. People like you so much, they don't want to see you recovering from all this pain. You can see that, right?" I actually squeaked out a *yes* as I choked back some tears.

I can't say it was unexpected. I felt a shift toward me after the rape. Something uncomfortable that nobody wanted to talk about. I thought of that rose Dylan gave me the night of our screen test and how I'd put it on my windowsill. It was beautiful. But then the sunlight frayed the edges and, as with all cut flowers, it eventually died. I tried to keep the petals in a book, but it was impossible not to lose them.

Also, I know they thought I was fat. I should've seen the firing coming when a piece of cake was physically pulled away from me at the last anniversary celebration. And when Dylan lifted me during rehearsal when I passed out from my diabetic coma and commented aloud how days at the gym hadn't prepared him for this. I threw up in my dressing room on break, hoping that when he had to lift me again when we actually taped the scene he'd comment out loud that I was lighter.

My last big scene was at Sly's bikini bar. After all the torment I had endured, when I finally gained the courage to turn him in as my rapist, he kidnapped me, tied me up, and poured gasoline on me before he set the whole place on fire. Brent apologized for what they were making him do, and we laughed about what a disaster it had all become. We also made plans for lunch the next week. And we would remain good friends.

Sly ended up dying in the flames, and I was saved by Dylan running in and rescuing me just one more time. Dylan and I hadn't really spoken for months, but that day, we stood off to the side and he talked about a book he was reading and how he needed to get out there on the audition circuit again—and he didn't look at me when he told me he was going to marry Becky. At the end of it, we just said casual good-byes. I actually would've preferred for Jessica to die in that fire. At least there would be some conclusion, some end, and Dylan couldn't play the hero for saving me again.

And I never did get that Emmy.

CHAPTER 4

HERE'S A LITTLE-KNOWN FACT: black hair dye becomes red when you aggressively try to bleach it out after you've decided goth is not really your color and you have to go on a European press tour. Or maybe everyone knew that but me.

"You mean like a dark brown?" the woman at the salon asked me, hoping I didn't mean the swatch that matched shoe polish I was holding.

"No, I want it as black as possible," I said, and she reluctantly proceeded to do her job.

I got the idea to go darker while filming a part in *Killing Mr. Griffin*, a made-for-TV movie starring Jay Thomas, Mario Lopez, and a young Michelle Williams. The casting director, Robin Lippin, who said I had been green back on my first audition for *Saved by the Bell*, got me the part. The plot saw a group of teens accidentally killing their teacher and hiding the body in some mountainous area. I was a nerd at the school, so they wanted my hair a shade to match my mouse. Although it wasn't beautiful, I liked how a new color brought me some anonymity and separation from Jessica Forrester. It felt like a shift, but I needed it to be a more dramatic one, like an ice bath or a scalding shower. Something to wake you, clean away what came before and that shocks you with its honesty.

"She's joined a cult," my grandmother said at my hair's big unveiling.

"It's not a cult, Gladys," my mom said. "It's the style."

"The style of what?" she asked. "The devil?"

My friends began to look at me differently too. Like they were trying to figure out if I was stupid or rebellious, or maybe I was dying, and it was really a wig. I was trying to figure that out myself. I had wanted to break away and prove that I was more than a prop for Dylan's heroics, but I couldn't look at my long blond hair and tearstained eyes in the mirror and envision myself beyond the girl who wasn't good enough to hold on to even that. It's hard to go from being on TV every day to being just a girl in the crowd, especially when the crowd is staring at you and gossiping. Jessica Forrester had become my life far more profoundly than I had realized until she was gone. The black hair draped around my face scared certain people away, including my own eyes from the mirror, and helped me hide.

"They even did your eyebrows, huh?" one of the Bible study girls asked.

"I asked them to," I said. "I think the darkness really brings out my eyes."

She concluded the conversation with an invitation to a circle of prayer.

"How do you expect to travel to Europe looking like that?" my publicist asked me as we dined at a café. I was going on that dreaded tour for the soap—the one that happens once you've been canned and all that's left for you to do is to be paraded around as some monument to your yesteryear, like Indira Gandhi before they burned her body on a pyre. Only Indira would be dead while this was going on. I had to wave and sign pictures. "They might like to see a different side of me," I said. "They want to see the girl on their television; they don't want to see the real you," he replied. They took away our plates, and he handed me the bill.

My agent took fewer of my calls once the checks weren't coming in. In fact, in the time I had been on top, I had barely heard a peep from her except when the checks were late. I decided to take matters into my own hands and look for a manager.

...

"YOU DON'T LOOK LIKE your picture," Rosalyn said with a low growl as I walked into her condominium for a meeting. She was a middle-aged woman who I think used to be an actress because the place was covered in black-and-white pictures of her with teased hair and dramatic charcoal-rimmed eyes. She still had that same hair. I guess hair was really important to her.

"I'm twenty now; I thought I needed a change," I said as I sat down on a chair across from her in her living room. "Do you think you can get roles looking like that?" she asked as her standard poodle, Shadow, barked at me funny. His vocal cords had been removed as an abused pup, so he always sounded like someone in a dream who wants to scream at the world but can't find his voice. I identified with Shadow.

"I think I might be able to go out for different kinds of roles now," I said.

She replied with a sarcastic laugh, "You think?"

I wasn't sure what roles I wanted, but I did know I wanted Jessica Forrester to be dead, even though I kept hoping they'd call me and tell me they made a mistake letting me go. I needed to be seen by everyone differently, including, or especially, me.

I ended up signing on with Rosalyn. She was intense and tough, but she left me with a belief that she'd work for me and that on some level, she gave a damn. And that wasn't nothing. She called me that night and said she had an audition for me, but she'd only tell me the information if I called her back from the hair salon.

The same woman who'd put the shoe polish black in spent the next eight hours taking it out.

"This shade really sticks," she said as she washed my hair for a sixth or seventh time; she and I had both lost count. It was nearly midnight by the time we finished, and the salon had been locked to the outside world long ago. She apologized that she couldn't get it all the way back to blond and that I'd have to come in again. If she did any more, she would collapse from exhaustion and all my hair would fall out.

"Can you live with this for a week or so?" she asked as she turned me in my chair to face her mirror.

I braced myself for the result.

"Wow," I said, examining myself. "It's not bad."

It definitely wasn't bad; in fact, it was good. It was red. The warm tone really did bring out my eyes, and I no longer looked like I sucked the blood out of small woodland creatures at midnight. It was bright and fresh—and unexpected. I decided to keep it.

And if I hadn't experienced that extreme state of black, I never would've found it.

EUROPE TURNED OUT TO be fabulous, even though I caught strep throat and had to stay in my hotel room for half of Holland, most of Belgium, and the first part of France. (Belgian doctors make house calls to hotel rooms in the middle of the night, FYI.) From the sickness to all the walking and travel, I ended up losing a few pounds, and by the time I landed in Paris, I felt like myself again and I could fit into my tightest jeans.

"Your red hair is like fire," one of guys—a model, I think, or an actor, or I can't remember or never really asked—told me as a group of us remained after a dinner. He was definitely European, though, maybe. European adjacent?

It was just me, him, and a few nice Scandinavian girls who were fans of the show and followed cast members from city to city, having drinks at a hotel bar. The girls ended up leaving to go to a club, and I was left alone with a little more alcohol and this man with the indeterminable career and passport.

"I have music in my room you should listen to." He smiled and brushed his fingers on my leg.

"What makes you think I'd fall for that?" I offered a coy smirk.

He leaned into me with his cute smile and dark eyes. "You wouldn't be falling, but you'd be on your back."

I wasn't on my back but rather my knees, and we never listened to any music. His dick was inside me as soon as we reached the bed and before I thought about the fact that we weren't using a condom. The way he thrust into me was so primal and so necessary. This was the best sex I'd had, out of the little sex I'd had, and I didn't want to stop it to search Parisian drugstores for rubbers. He was kind of rough with me and said things I had only read in those *Penthouse* letters.

"You act like some nice girl, but I knew you were such a whore who would open those legs," he said while knotting up my hair in his fist. I was surprised how much I liked all that—and I wondered if it was all about the red hair. It was transforming.

I panted for him to pull out before he came, but he accomplished this only partially. "You just feel too good," he said, panting, with his dick swinging around, making its victory lap to a bottle of water.

"I better go to sleep. I have to work tomorrow," he said, while I was still sprawled out half-naked with his semen in my vagina and on my thigh.

I got the hint that he wasn't into cuddling and probably didn't have any morning work, and that it was my cue to go.

I went back to my room and took a bath—lavishing my well-fucked body in French soaps and oils I discovered were made in New Jersey when I read the fine print on the back. I decided to keep imagining they were French as I masturbated in the warm water and suds, thinking about how hard I had been fucked by a maybe-European and how womanly it felt to hold a man's cum inside me.

The next morning and in the following weeks, it was less sexy to me and more a crippling fear. I believed I was pregnant, had an STD, and would die from AIDS—yes, all three at once. I reasoned on the plane ride home, a week or so later, that the antibiotics for my throat probably caught the STD, but the other two were still real possibilities. I visited the gynecologist shortly after. She checked me out and told me I was clean, and even though I assured her that I didn't intend to be the kind of girl to supply in-and-out privileges for random bare dicks, we discussed birth control options.

...

THE TIMELINE OF THE following year can be measured in the lengths of my hair. What started out as a healthy trim to rid myself of the damage all the dying and bleaching had caused became a progressive journey in ridding myself of Jessica Forrester. I began to get more roles during this time too—comedic ones, which was completely unexpected. I couldn't land another soap to save my life. Rosalyn tried. But *Home Improvement* hired me to play a goofy student, and I got praise on the set of *USA High*. A casting director told me I was a mix between Lucille Ball and a young Jane Fonda—two women who were complex and funny and had fearlessly paved their own ways. I can't say I believed I could really be like Lucy or Jane, but it was the first time I felt recognized as someone who had the possibility of playing a part she hadn't been formerly assigned.

The roles were also sexier as I was now turning twenty-one. I wasn't treated like a little girl anymore but more of a young woman—one who could have boyfriends and wear cute crop tops on dates. I had just gotten my hair cut really short in my last streak of rebellion and as a final blow to Jessica's long blond locks when I auditioned for a television pilot called *Zoe, Duncan, Jack and Jane*.

Michael Jacobs, the creator and executive producer of *Boy Meets World*, had created this new pilot. It was about a quirky, hyperobservant girl who was surviving the times and her world with biting sarcasm and a little help from her mishmash of friends. He was sitting with a group of writers and producers when I walked into the audition. He didn't smile like the rest of the group or make idle conversation; he just looked at me and waited for me to speak. I figured he was tired. It was the end of the day, and I was the last one to read.

"Why did you say it that way?" Michael asked me after I had read a line. I think I had only gotten out three. Zoe, the character, was supposed to be talking to some man, and all she could see and think about was his connected eyebrows. She became obsessed over them and fascinated.

"I don't know," I said. I really thought I did, but I also thought that if people saw me confident about something and it was wrong, they'd either send me out or they'd all laugh, so I played dumb.

"You have to know," he said, tapping the pad he'd scribble notes on against his knee. "Get into this girl's head and do it again," he said, and I did again, and then again.

More scribbles on his pad. More shaking of it against his knee.

This stop and start would go on, all up and down the three pages of sides I was reading from. I wondered if Guinness should be alerted, as this was becoming the longest audition in history. No one on *The Bold and the Beautiful* had ever directed me like this. By the end of it, I thought that everyone in the room, but especially Michael, absolutely hated me and everything I did. But when I stood up to say good-bye, he surprised me and said, "You're fantastic. We'll see you again next week."

I returned again right before St. Patrick's Day. I thought it was cute that I wore green, being that I was new to this whole redhead club, and I hoped that it would bring me luck.

The room felt different, less like an audition and more like a lecture in some school hall as Michael took whatever happened last time and doubled down on it. He proceeded to go over every line with precise direction, every joke and word. He threw a pen my way so I would take his notes and remember them.

"You'll test for the role next Tuesday," he said after what felt like an hour, which it probably was. "We'll call your manager with the details. Be ready."

I tried to act cool, but once I reached the door, I skipped out, bouncing all the way to my car. I just knew it was the green I was wearing, but Michael later told me it was the red hair that gave me good luck.

I worked day and night on the script with my mom, memorizing every part and every line precisely the way he'd told me. I took his direction as a challenge, and my anxiety concurred. He was the first person I had met in Hollywood who looked me straight in the eye, gave me something tangible to work on, and then expected me to return with results and no bullshit. While I was more stressed about this audition than any I ever had been in my life, including the soap, I discovered that I liked a challenge I was actively working for instead of waiting around to be idolized but ignored.

There were four of us sitting in the waiting room. A girl I thought I knew from the soaps was sitting across from me, and next to her was a blond in long socks and Doc Martens. My real competition, though, was Selma Blair. She was serious yet quizzical and had dark hair, kind of like the color of the dye I had bleached down the drain. She talked a lot and about everything, and everything sounded interesting coming from her mouth. She was quirky and mysterious and spoke of her excitement for the arrival of Cadbury Creme Eggs at the stores.

When I walked inside the audition room and addressed the group of suits, Michael gave me a nod of recognition and a smile—not a happy one, more like an Olympic coach who sends you up the ladder and off to your turn on the diving board. I took a breath before I jumped and hit the water. I don't mean to brag, or maybe I do, but I totally nailed it. It's the only audition in my history where I hit every mark and landed every line. There was no splash, and my form was straight when I cut through the water. At the end of it, while the group of them were thanking me for my time, Michael looked up and there was this moment where I knew that he recognized me as something formidable.

"That was perfect," he said, and I felt myself marching up to a podium to accept gold.

"YOU DIDN'T GET THE part," Rosalyn told me that night, and my heart absolutely sunk.

"Why not?" I asked. "I did everything he said. Everything was perfect. He told me so himself."

Rosalyn sighed. "Jacobs wanted you. Casting said he fought for you, but the rest of them said you were too green."

There was that fucking green comment again! Hadn't I graduated beyond being compared to a blade of grass?

"They wanted a girl who could play that she had experienced some life and knew it was all shit, but she had to laugh."

They chose Selma.

It was the quirkiness and the mystery and the oddball interest in the Cadbury Creme Eggs, I just knew it.

I cried into my pillow that night and the following day. And I even cursed a display of those eggs when I went to the store.

Rosalyn left six messages on my answering machine that fated Friday. Every single one said that it was urgent and to call immediately. She always had a gift for drama, so I thought it was an audition for two weeks from now that she needed me to start preparing for yesterday and for the rest of my life. But when I called her back, she could barely get anything out or catch her breath. For a moment I thought the receiver had been knocked off and I was talking to Shadow.

"Are you sitting down?" she asked, and I lied and said I was. "They want you. They've sent a holding deal over," she said.

"Who? What is that?" I asked, and this time I sat down.

"Disney and Jacobs. They want you for *Boy Meets World* next season and they don't want anyone to scoop you up in the meantime so they're paying you for three months just to sit there."

I stood up fast and screamed, then sat back down again, realizing that's what I was being paid for. After asking Rosalyn a million times if it was really true, she told me to drink some champagne and she hung up, probably to buy a good bottle and down it herself.

I hugged my mom and then my dad, who had heard all the ruckus when he was coming up the drive.

"I'm going to be on *Boy Meets World*!" I said with another scream. I then realized it was Friday night. So my parents and I turned on the TV and waited for the show to start.

CHAPTER 5

A WEEK BEFORE I REPORTED to the set, I moved into my own town-home in West Los Angeles and got a Chihuahua. I called him Léon and pronounced it French. It was my first apartment, my first time away on my own without my parents, and the first time I'd clean up dog poop by myself. Both of my parents cried when they saw me off, and my grandmother hugged me tight just before she rehashed the story of actress Rebecca Schaeffer's murder.

"Don't open your door to anyone," she said. "Nobody good ever knocks at your door in Hollywood."

And so I was frozen when I heard the buzzer.

"Hello! Is this the girl who plays Rachel?" a guy yelled through the loudspeaker on my security door intercom.

Rachel?

Why did he call me that?

I gasped as I thought about my grandma's story of the sitcom starlet murder. My Chihuahua was alarmed too but lost interest in my security when he found a stray Cheeto on the floor.

"Why don't you know my real name?" I asked, and I tried to sound tough, but I was so strained, it sounded like he caught me on the can and it wasn't going well.

"Listen, all it says is Rachel. It's some script."

Oh, right!

I forgot they'd mentioned they'd send one over for the table read.

"Sorry," I said as I stepped out to meet him. "I'm not used to opening front doors on my own."

Rachel, my character on *Boy Meets World*, was named after Michael Jacobs's daughter but also because Jennifer Aniston and her haircut were insanely popular on *Friends* that year. She was to be quirky and likable, the girl you know from math class but also the one who would quite literally take the shirt off her back to help you pass the test. So week after week, I was always walking the line between pleasing my father and having great tits and hair.

"We want Rachel to keep these boys on their toes," Michael said, as I sat across from him in his office. They had been thinking of adding a new character for some time, to give college roommates Jack and Eric, played by Matthew Lawrence and Will Friedle, something—and someone else—to play with other than themselves. They never drew up a character profile or put out a casting call; it was just out there in the wind. But he said, "When you walked in, and the network executives proved they were just a bunch of fuckups with no vision beyond the crawl space in their own assholes, we just knew."

It was the closest thing to "I love you" that ever left his lips.

Michael never sat down when he talked to you. Even at restaurants or weddings, he paced. He had a uniform of blue denim and sneakers, and every time he walked up to you, he delivered abrupt news—not like tragedies or disasters, mostly things like sports scores and what he thought of penny stocks. Even something as innocuous as "Summer is coming" would make me tense and question my preparedness for its arrival. While he had been instrumental in making hits of shows like *Charles in Charge* and *My Two Dads*, *Boy*, as we all called it, was his baby. And anyone he cast on the show, for better or worse, was treated as one of his own.

I was told that Will was funny and Matt was extraordinarily shy, so if he doesn't speak not to take it personally. "Ben, Rider, all the boys will love you," Michael said. "But Danielle Fishel will absolutely hate you."

When I asked him, panicked, as to why the star of the show, Topanga, would have it out for me, he laughed and said, "Because you have red hair and legs."

"Oh my God!" Danielle said, spinning around in the chair where she was getting her hair trimmed when I walked into the makeup trailer later that week. I was there for a style assessment from the team, but I feared an assassination attempt first.

I startled when she launched from the chair and stood next to me in her short shorts and flip-flops.

Was this a showdown?!

"I only come up to your boobs," she said, and she fell back, giggling into the chair. As she kicked her feet, I noticed little daffodils painted on her toes.

She was bubbly and talked a lot about rap music and all the boys she dated over the summer, who basically all circulated within the Disney teen star universe, but she definitely didn't seem to hate me. In fact, we connected over things you wouldn't expect, like our love of Chihuahuas and pet rats. Still, no matter how well we got along, there would always be a part of me that distrusted her and her motives toward me, and it all stemmed from Michael's first warnings.

I wonder now if anyone gave her the same warnings about me.

Trina McGee-Davis actually was grown-up. In her late twenties, she was cast as a high school student—and part of a groundbreaking biracial pairing with core cast member Rider Strong—who missed his own calling in porn with that name. His character, Shawn, fell in love with hers their senior year, all while Trina was pregnant in real life with her third child. She tried to hide it for awhile, but I heard that Michael caught on to the large sweatshirts and props in front of her belly and asked her point-blank, so she admitted the truth. Michael, the consummate family man, completely supported her impending motherhood, but I'm sure the pacing sneakers and blue denim were pissed they weren't told about it first.

I felt sandwiched generationally between the two women on this show yet separated from them as well. We had roles aside from our characters, ones we didn't realize we were playing, and maybe no one consciously did. Maybe. I was the provocative one, Danielle was the golden child, and Trina was the grown-up: points of a triangle separated by the lines.

Had it been intentional from the start to separate us from each other? To plant seeds in our minds that made us see the others as something other than ourselves? The boys were the boys, and they were encouraged to play in a large group, as boys are. But the girls were very much the girls, cherished and solo. Michael loved for us each to come to him and trust him—a sage father who gives his daughters guidance and advice, and it all seemed helpful. But the question is, if we all played together, would we really need him that much?

Just a question. And it's one that I don't think I'll ever answer to my satisfaction.

I met Matt Lawrence's mother, Donna, before I met him, as I heard was often the case. "Matt's looking so forward to working with you," she said and then she wrapped me in a hug. "He just had some new leather jackets delivered from Italy; he should be down in a minute."

Donna was a manager to all three of her boys, Joey Lawrence being the most famous, but she spread her time around equally. She made all their calls, mended all their clothes, and was at every taping from the start to the end. The family moved from Philadelphia to LA when Joey hit it big with *Gimme a Break*, and everyone changed their last name to Joey's middle one. "Lawrence is a better name for a Hollywood family," she said. And I knew from experience that once you change your name for Hollywood, there's no going back, especially when it's a group deal.

When Matt finally came down, he smiled and gave me a hug wearing his carefully tailored jacket. He was adorably sweet and a little nervous around me, but I figured it was because his mom was standing there watching.

If the Lawrence family was tails on the Hollywood coin, the Savage family was heads. Like the Lawrences, the oldest Savage boy, Fred, found fame and success early on, making it big as Kevin Arnold on *The Wonder Years*. The Savages were highly successful in real estate and business and didn't rely on a penny of their kids' money. Joanne, the mom, was far more serious and reserved than the dad, Lew. He was a grown-up Ben, the life of any conversation and party who loved to joke and laugh. You always knew when he was in a room, especially when Joey Lawrence was visiting the set. "Hey, Joanne," he'd say to his wife, quite loud, and she'd try to shush him. "Have you ever seen a guy with shirts that small?"

Lew Savage was one of my favorite people and a champion of mine early on. He was worried when they said they were going to add another cast member; he thought that it might be someone who would take away from things or detract. "But you come in here like Geena Davis," he said, "but when she was on *Family Ties* as the housekeeper, not *The Fly*."

"Poke my belly," Will said, right after he introduced himself in the voice of Cartman from *South Park*. "Go ahead. Right there in the center where it's all squishy."

I did as he asked, and he laughed like the Pillsbury Doughboy. It was kind of fun, so I did it again. We would repeat this give-and-take almost daily during my run with the show.

"Sorry if I smell; I just took a smoke," he said, shrugging as he cursed the habit he picked up before middle school. "Blame it on Nickelodeon."

It was odd being on a set made up almost entirely of young adults who had only known life growing up on soundstages. Things I'd talk about that would be commonplace to almost any kid in America drew blanks. How strange to live the entirety of your growing years as a product of small studio classrooms and tutors and a system that raises you up even as it's keenly aware that it'll spit you out one day. I'd had some of that on the soap, but I had already been seasoned with years of an average adolescence. I had been afforded anonymity, and I realized that had been a gift. I think it made it harder for them to relate to the outside world. They had never known anything outside this bubble.

There was a lot of heartbreak at the beginning of that first season: Rider and Will's failed relationships and the unfortunate ghosting that Matt did to Danielle, or so the rumors went. Danielle, it was said, had gotten it into her head that she and Matt should be dating, and Matt wasn't so sure, so I guess he just didn't return her calls. We all watched and waited with our proverbial popcorn to see what would happen when they both arrived for that first rehearsal. There had been some smack talk from both camps, some *will she or won't he*, but like most pivotal moments of teenage angst, there were a few looks and a couple of targeted hellos, and then we all went on with our lives.

"Love broke my heart," Will told me as we rehearsed the scene where Rachel breaks up with her boyfriend in the hallway of the apartment building and ends up living with Eric and Jack instead.

"That's so poetic," I said. "It was *love* that broke your heart instead of a stupid girl." I gave him a supportive pat on the back.

"No, it was actually Love," he said. "Jennifer Love Hewitt dumped me for Carson Daly, and it sucks."

Ben Savage, as it turned out, was the one most affected by the red hair and legs. He got the idea that I was a seductress and lived a scandalous life off the soundstage. I'm not sure how he reached this conclusion, except that I was tall, kind of quiet, and brand-new and he took any mystery and height as evidence that I probably tied up men in some dungeon and tortured their balls.

"Like what happens on a date with you?" he asked, but not in a way that would make me uncomfortable. It was more like a little brother who found out his sibling was having sex and had to know all the details, but it just so happened that the sibling was a hot sister who wasn't blood related to him.

"I make him buy me dinner, then I turn off all the lights . . ." I said. His jaw slacked. "And then I plug him into the electrical sockets, and we have a time."

He looked wildly and thrillingly confused as he gulped, and I think I saw a chubby.

I used to tell him exaggerated stories of all of my trysts in great detail and tape up Polaroids of myself in various stages of undress over the Vanilla Ice poster outside his dressing room door.

"Why do you give me these blue balls?!" he'd yell across the hall.

Ice, ice baby, it was.

And to think, Ben Savage literally has my first Onlyfans-level selfies.

I teased Will like this too. One time we played a game of *who could shock each other the most with a dirty line.*

"You're too sweet to win this," he said, though looking back, he probably just wanted to rile me up with extra incentive so he could hear me talk about his cock. And I wanted to do the same. We went back and forth a few times, but it was all "tug on my dick" and "squeeze my tits," and it would serve only to make a nun blush.

"You're weak!" he said. "None of this is shocking."

I took that as an insult, but also a supreme challenge. The inner porn star, which I didn't know was there yet, thought up the dirtiest possible thing and I whispered it into his ear, "My wet, throbbing pussy is going to milk your balls, and once I'm done, I'm going to sit on your face for you to swallow it all up."

Needless to say, I won—or, actually, we both did.

Bill Daniels would arrive earlier than everyone every day, regardless of when anyone got there. I could plan to be there at dawn, just past the sun, or even before, and there was his Jaguar parked there in the first space. Bill was the ultimate professional and someone we all admired, yet at the same time, we were intimidated by him. Much like Mr. Feeny on *Boy,* he wanted to help us kids "do good" and succeed, but he would rather it be from behind his own fence and next door. As is understandable.

Bill's career spanned decades before any of us were even alive, so the thing we were impressed with most (especially me) was that he was the voice of KITT on *Knight Rider*.

"Say it again!" Ben begged during a production meeting. We always had them sitting in the student union set. Ben used to bounce up and down from the chairs to the sofa cushions, because he could never contain any of his excitement about anything. "Please, Bill!" He fell to his knees, folding his hands in prayer.

Bill, with an amused roll of the eyes, looked over to Jacobs and said, "Michael," just like he did to David Hasselhoff. And we all fell over in hysterics.

I never did tell him how when I was a girl, I fantasized about him officiating when David Hasselhoff and I got married, but in that moment some childhood dream was realized.

While Cory and Topanga spent their time planning a future with a white veil and a fumble beneath the marital sheets, my character was landing in more and more provocative situations with the boys in the apartment.

"You mean she's actually choking on a wiener while I'm thrusting her from behind?" Matt asked the director while we were blocking out a scene that involved me retching on a hot dog and him performing the Heimlich maneuver.

"You're saving her life, Matt," the director said.

"But my hands are under her boobs and I'm bending her over a countertop and doing this." He motioned some version of hip thrusting but then he stopped because you could tell he was too embarrassed by it.

The director rolled his eyes. "Not everything is sexual, Lawrence."

But everything to do with my storyline was kind of sexual, and no one tried to hide it. There was always an undertone or innuendo—some joke that junior high boys might make as they compared dick size next to their lockers. I could just see the writers sitting up there in their room thinking about what off-color joke a sexy girl like Rachel could play out without ABC and Disney getting them in trouble. It was as if it was the first time that they had anyone fun and juicy—and scandalously daring—they could play with, and they were going to take advantage of it.

"Do you mind if I stick a toe in your mouth?" I asked Will during rehearsal for our famed food fight scene. The writers had made sure that my pretty feet were out and squishing around a lot in globs of marinara sauce. They even made a point to tell me I should really push it around on his face.

"No, not all," Will said, and he commented that my freshly vamp-painted toes looked nice as they tiptoed up his chest.

The crew packed the set with various food items we'd have to navigate, like salad and bread, but mostly the marinara sauce that was made to really stick. Rachel was teaching the boys that they shouldn't be on their best behavior simply because she was a woman. They should let their mess flags fly by getting all sticky and dripping with her and wrestling as a threesome over countertops and barstools and all over the floor. We could only do it once, so we had to get it right—whatever right means when your eyes are full of crushed tomatoes and you're beating your costar with a two-foot-long baguette. But, in the end, it felt like the high point in every dream you have as a kid at the dinner table and every fantasy you have as an adult with feet and wet food.

Someone up in the office really had a thing for tits, feet, and food play.

"Just throw him up there; he can take it," Michael said at a production rehearsal for the scene that Will and I played out in the laundry room. Again, Rachel was teaching a lesson about being yourself that involved domination, home economics, and pinning him down with her appendages. And she was this intense seductress who could manipulate men with her voice and other vibrations.

"You've got me so hot," I said as I locked the door and cornered Will's character at a machine set to *fluff*. He cried out, "Wee," as I threw him roughly onto the dryer, his ass vibrating against the metal. I pinned my arms on both sides of him, a dominating presence to the boy who would now obey me. Everything Ben thought I was to men on dates was playing out before everyone's eyes. When the scene was over, the room was quiet. So was Will. So was Michael. I think Ben may have fainted and fallen between the couch cushions. But no one had laughed once.

I was about to apologize for screwing up the scene when Michael said, "If you ever need anything, come to my office and do that."

A FEW MONTHS BEFORE I left *The Bold and the Beautiful,* I met the man who would be my husband. I was standing just off the set, waiting for Dylan to finish with his push-ups so he could feel muscle-pumped enough to start a scene. John, or rather Terry, which was his middle name and the family nickname he went by in those days because his dad was named John too, was visiting someone in production. He wore a checkered button-up shirt, and I noticed his eyes were blue when he asked me my name. We laughed at the fact that we both went by our middle names.

"I'm just in town for a break from college," he said to me. "If you want, I could call you. Maybe we can do something wild like have dinner on the beach without our shoes."

"I wait until the third date to get my toes naked," I said, laughing as I handed him my number.

I didn't think much of it after he waved good-bye and found the person he was meeting for lunch, but a makeup artist who saw the whole encounter told me, "You should find a nice boy like that to marry."

"My ex-girlfriend got pregnant by the fish guy at Ralph's," Terry said, right after I got into his car on our first date. I was annoyed; I hadn't even buckled up and he was talking about one of his exes and her grocery store fishmonger.

"How do you know this?" I asked as I smoothed the pleats of my skirt and adjusted my seat belt.

"She and the guy called me and asked for financial advice since I'm studying business."

After the fish talk and some pasta, he took me for a walk on the Santa Monica Pier. But we kept our shoes on.

"You can see the whole city up on the Ferris wheel," he said, and we took our seats in a swinging bucket. I'd like to say I had butterflies from love when we reached the top, but I was really just scared of heights.

We went to a club afterward—one that advertised on a local radio station and was pricey. It was supposed to be fun, but the place was packed and the house music sucked.

"Do you wanna get out of here and have some real fun?" he asked.

I looked up at him and nodded. I was touched at how he paid such attention to my mood and what I was feeling, and that he was willing to shift and change, no matter that it cost him something, just to make sure I was happy. And I was happy when we toasted with two ice cream sundaes at Jerry's Famous Deli at midnight.

"Can I ever see you again?" he asked, as we sat in my parents' driveway at the end of the date.

"No," I said, dead serious in my joke. I guess I was too good at acting it out because he fell for it.

"Okay," he said, staring into the steering wheel. "Well, thank you for tonight, and I wish you all the best."

I told him I was joking and to definitely call me again. I knew instantly that he was a good guy. First, he didn't tell me he was one. And second, when he thought I was breaking his heart, he didn't turn all fuckboy bitter on me. He politely thanked me for my time, wished me well, and then said that he would be on his way.

We first fucked the day Dylan married Becky. Well, it was actually the night before they married and completely by happenstance, but I woke in the hotel room we had booked to a friend frantically paging me to tell me the news. I didn't plan it this way, but I guess the universe really wanted to land a punch line to the big joke of my young life that was Dylan. I had to laugh, though, that Becky and I had something in common. We both got fucked that day, though I ended up with the better deal.

"You should marry him," Michael told me, not long after Terry finished school, moved back to LA, and Michael met him when he visited me on set. "Don't become one of these Hollywood girls who's dating all over. Settle down. Have a family. You'll be blessed."

Settling down and having a family was the last thing on my mind. In fact, I wanted quite the opposite. I was only twenty-one then, but it wouldn't change when I was forty-two. And this resistance to normalcy and tradition would mark the path of my relationship with Terry for the span of that time.

Love seemed a place higher and more fear inducing than a Ferris wheel.

MY HAIR BECAME A hot topic for debate at ABC and Disney about midway through the season. Apparently, my style and shade weren't having the intended societal impact. I wasn't Jennifer Aniston, so it all had to be changed.

"I want you to have a haircut nobody else has," Michael told me as I sat in his office.

"I don't know if many people have my haircut now," I said.

"Exactly! They don't want it. We need a new haircut nobody has so it can become a haircut everybody has because it's a haircut everybody knows."

Mona, who worked for the show but was also actress Marilu Henner's personal stylist, was assigned the task.

Michael gave detailed and specific instructions before leaving us to go wait for the results in his office. But when he returned, he was disappointed.

"My mother got a cut like that in Florida!" he said. I guess this offended Mona greatly, because what happened next was probably the most traumatizing event in my young career. She dyed my hair bright pink, took the scissors to it, and left only a half inch of uneven sprouts.

"They've drugged her," my grandma said as I sat on the sofa dressed as an M&M. It was Halloween so I wasn't crazy, and Terry was there dressed as an M&M too.

"Oh, Gladys," my mother said. "It's the style." But even she didn't sound so convinced when she said it this time.

I kept feeding myself M&M's from the candy bowl and then realized I was just cannibalizing myself.

Mona was fired immediately, and someone else was assigned to clean up the damage. The pink was easily reversed but the length was not. Although Michael had been furious, the reaction from the audience was shockingly positive, and production was happy with it. "You really have a look nobody has!" he said. But I'm not sure anyone ever wanted it.

"You're going to have sex with Jack," Michael told Matt and me one day in the makeup trailer, and we both spit some coffee.

"You mean like on the show?" I asked. Matt was too dumbstruck to speak. I think he feared it was happening right then and there.

"Eric's going to catch you two, and it's going to break his heart, and then you two will hook up and live together," Michael said. It sounded shocking.

"You mean, the viewers are going to know this is happening?" Matt asked.

Michael nodded with a smile.

"This show is all grown-up now!" he said.

Disney would let the show grow up only so far. While the storyline forged ahead, with Eric catching us making out on the sofa and us breaking his heart, the word *sex* was like Voldemort: he who shall not be named. Jack and Rachel lived alone in the apartment, made out all over the furniture, and gave grown-up dinner parties, but Disney made sure it could still be assumed that at the end of the day, we slept in separate bedrooms—like when your parents come to visit and your live-in boyfriend sleeps on the couch.

I related to this mirage.

CHAPTER 6

I WAS ASKED TO TRY on lingerie for the producers in the office. This happened more than once, as Rachel was the only character to consistently take off her clothes. An assistant would gather me from my dressing room and take me upstairs where I'd be provided with a series of options, some playful and girlish, some so provocative I knew that Disney would never approve them, but still I would try them on. There I'd strip down behind a curtain so thin I'm sure they could see the silhouette of my naked form. As I changed, I could hear the group of them—mostly men—making small talk and laughing as an audience would before a show. When I stepped out, I was directed to stand in the center of their half-moon circle of folding chairs while they'd make their judgments on style and color and whether it showed too much or not nearly enough to get the boys excited.

"You're like a daughter to me," Michael said, shaking his head, with a laugh of embarrassment.

And then I'd be directed to try on something else.

Michael specifically picked out the famed purple number for the episode where Rachel danced around washing the dishes to teach Cory and Shawn, as well as their girlfriends, a lesson. "It's not too much but just enough; those guys will go crazy," he said. During the final season, Rachel moved in with the girls after separating from Jack. They said it would expand my storylines, but really it just felt like it allowed for another set of boys to ogle me—this time, the girls' boyfriends.

When it came to Rachel, the writers portrayed Cory and Shawn like fuckboys. Somehow, they were these great guys to the women they loved, but when Rachel came around, they got sexually overcharged, which seemed to morph into something dismissive and edged with hostility. When Rachel didn't perform the way they liked or expected, they got angry. Unlike Eric and Jack, who tripped all over themselves to earn Rachel's affections, these two thought it would be fun to sneak around while she was in the shower and rummage through her diary pages and panties. When she caught them, clad only in a towel, she was livid, demanding they respect her privacy. They wrote her off as being sensitive and not any fun, and even their girlfriends agreed with them.

Rachel decided that the way to teach these boys a lesson was to get down to her undergarments, because how else could you teach men not to invade your privacy other than dancing around in some version of your underwear? Of course, dancing around on your own in this way would not be acceptable; it would mean you were morally questionable and probably crazy. This became Rachel's mode of operation: if you can't nag them to death, hypnotize them while half-naked into doing what you want. This reminded me of my grandmother's view of sex and bargaining.

I can't say I didn't like the attention it gave me. The audience hooted and whistled when I came onstage and started to dance. There was something exhilarating about eyeballs fixed on my scantily clad frame, even though I wasn't all that comfortable with my body yet. The degree of my nudity wasn't the problem I had with the whole thing. In fact, if they had come to me and asked my thoughts on the matter or how I wanted it to all play out, I would have had a lot of fun with it. What bothered me was that I could never get past the feeling that the writers were having fun at my expense and devaluing me in some way—like I was a punch line to a joke I would never be privy to.

Wearing no clothes on your own terms is a lot different from being naked for someone else.

"Can't we find out more about Rachel and who she is?" I asked Michael as we rehearsed for Cory and Topanga's wedding. While the year prior there seemed like there was some plan for her, this season she seemed like a prop—a failed experiment but one that still provided thrills.

"Rachel is great. Everyone loves her," he said. I knew this couldn't be true. She had only three personality traits: nag, tease, or complete ditz. And she seemed to navigate all three without any real rhyme or reason. Whatever dart the writers wanted to throw at women that day, that's who Rachel was.

"I have a few ideas," I said, though not loudly enough to prevent him talking over me.

"We have to do this big wedding. We'll get to it," he said, and then his Nikes scuffed down the hall.

"You should play dumb more." This came from Jerry Levine during rehearsal. Jerry became known playing Stiles from *Teen Wolf* and was also one of our directors and Michael's longtime friend. Rachel was bubbly and happy as the girls got ready for Topanga's big day, and somehow, he felt the need to highlight this ditzy performance. "You're more likable that way; sometimes you come off as a lot." And the way he said it, I felt like he was taking a personal shot.

Of course, I didn't have the nerve to speak up. I just got quiet and started to question myself and how I was perceived. Was I asking too much for Rachel to have more value? Was I causing waves because I didn't just read my lines and shut my mouth? I danced for them without complaint, and even when I was cold and felt fat, I smiled as I stood there in that room and tried on all those outfits. Wasn't all that enough? Was I being punished now?

I wore a crop top one week, and Michael called me aside. "What are you doing?" he asked me as he pointed to my bare belly. It wasn't an especially sexy top. It had Oompa Loompas on it. Will and I had just laughed about that, and he teased that he wanted to borrow it.

"I just thought it was cute," I said.

"Put on a sweater for rehearsal. You don't want everyone thinking you're desperate."

I didn't feel desperate, and I certainly wasn't trying to portray anything like that. Jenna Elfman wore tops like this on *Dharma and Greg* and people thought she looked cute.

"You have talent. You should take yourself seriously," he said. I didn't understand how showing my belly button had anything to do with the depth of my talent or character, or why it was okay to show myself like this on the show but not on my own time. But I put on the sweater.

THERE WAS A BEAR on set the day I took the dirty photos that would later be used to humiliate Rachel. Everyone was buzzing around, wondering how we were going to manage wrangling this great beast, while I had a fan blowing at my sheet-draped body at the corner of the stage by the craft service table. It's an icky thing to have to act sexy while hairy-backed crewmen schmear their bagels.

"Sorry you have to stand out here like that," the director said as we took photo after photo. I exhaled with a great deal of relief and out of nowhere started to tear up, not because it all made me sad but because there was someone who recognized that I could have feelings on the matter.

"The War," even with the issues I was having backstage, was actually one of my favorite episodes, mainly because everyone in the cast got to work together and Rachel was showcased as more than just someone to plug for kicks. Though the nag and the tease elements of her were front and center, what fascinated me was that it also offered one of the most psychological insights as to how production viewed the characters—and its real-life cast. It was a game of pranks and retaliation taken way too far that divided everyone—old cast members versus the new. If fans pay attention, it's really a commentary on how the show was mapped out and run.

At the start, Cory and Shawn park in Rachel's spot, another fuckboy move. Rachel had earned the spot by taking a special job at the school, and they completely dismissed and devalued anything she had earned because they simply didn't want to have to walk so far. Rachel, of course, becomes enraged and calls them out. The war begins with the boys parking her car in her dorm room. Rachel and her roommate now, Angela, awake to the alarm blaring and the flashing of headlights. Rachel screams in rage and when they hear it echo throughout the campus, the boys toast with coffee mugs in the student union. Mr. Feeny is sent to talk to them, since he has always offered them guidance and sage wisdom, but this time all he does is laugh and pats them on the back for a joke well done.

Rachel then obtains a bear. A real bear. We never see Rachel get this bear, so I'm not sure if she danced half-naked for an animal wrangler or nagged him to death, but all of a sudden it appears in the classroom doorway ready to strike—at which point, Cory, Shawn, and Topanga discover that Rachel has superglued them to their seats as honey pours down onto their heads, leading the bear to do one of those Hollywood standing growls. They end up surviving, of course. In response, the boys steal private sexy pictures Rachel took for Jack—how they knew where to find them, I don't know—and proceed to put up multiple life-sized posters of one in the student union.

Revenge porn before anyone knew it was a thing.

Rachel is demoralized and breaks down into tears. Everyone turns to Cory and Shawn, absolutely shocked at how they could do such a terrible thing. And while this was finally a moment that the boys got called out in a major way, it also served to me as a strange message Disney and Jacobs wanted to send: it's far worse to be seen publicly in the nude than to attempt to kill your friends with a grizzly bear.

As I stood there taking those photos, the fan blowing little pieces of boa feathers up in my face and the smell of lox and crewmen sweat permeating the air, I started to feel out of control. I needed to be compliant when they wanted to use my body as a story point but guilty when I wanted to express anything with it on my own. Even if I really let loose and started to enjoy taking these pictures, I would be held back from that. Michael would come down and give me a talk about how wildly desperate I was being perceived and that I needed to mind myself and handle this professionally and without a smile. It felt like they liked seeing me in a state of undress but only if I was a little uncomfortable with it. After all, girls should always feel that way. I was tired of everyone else having a question or a comment about my body and how it was to be used.

Just then Will approached.

"Are you on your period?" he asked.

That did it!

I rolled my eyes and looked at him and said, "No!"

I couldn't believe that even considerate and fun-loving Will would feel comfortable enough to ask about the affairs of my vagina and be so nonchalant about it.

"Well, good," he said. "I'm asking everyone because there's a bear on set and if he smells blood, then we could all be goners."

I SPENT THE ENTIRE summer break between seasons 6 and 7 in bed with pneumonia. I tried to lose a few pounds since I was scrutinized being on television, but I also lost iron and vitamins and wore my body down. Terry took time off to take care of me. It was the first time I was sick and not cared for by my mother and the first time I'd ever let a boy see me in such a miserable state. As I looked at the ceiling one night, clutching my chest when I coughed, thinking somehow the pull of flesh from bone might lessen the pain, I heard him snoring next to me, in harmony with my Chihuahua, and I thought to myself, "Oh, fuck me, I'm really an adult."

By the end of the summer, my bond with Terry had strengthened, like soldiers who'd battled and won some war. But also like in wartime, I began to wonder, *When it's over, what's left for me?* The better I got, the more I feared us turning into an old shoe. How could he see me as sexy anymore now that he'd cleaned up my wet tissues and we'd watched reruns of *Match Game* every night?

"Just turn over if he tries to start anything," my grandmother said on the phone after I was well on the mend. My family was fine with him being around, but only if I could barely breathe.

"Grandma, I'm still hacking up my lungs," I said, and I forced a cough as if I'd have to offer proof.

"Listen, sometimes men late at night don't even mind. Be aware."

But what about *me*? What if *I* didn't mind? What was to stop me, this dangerous sexual creature, from waking up, pitching a leg over the top of him, and commanding him to fuck my throbbing vagina? Why couldn't he be the one to roll over and tell me to go back to sleep? Women weren't allowed the luxury of lying in the dark at night cursing their blue balls.

I didn't relay these thoughts to my grandmother. She would've been shocked I knew the color of unsatisfied testicles and even more so that I knew the feeling of them. I just told her he'd be back sleeping at his place the next week. I knew that's what she wanted. And maybe that's what I wanted now too. To be alone, living in some corner of Los Angeles that was my own, where I didn't have to make any commitments or take any vows, a place that was free from the talk of eventual china patterns.

THE OLSEN TWINS HELPED us kick off a big party for TGIF—the name of the family lineup for Friday nights on ABC. They were returning with a new show, so ABC decided to broadcast the live event for the whole TGIF lineup during the commercial breaks. They were quiet and only really ever spoke to each other unless they were speaking to their mother. It's often the case with child stars, I've found—until they rebel and never really speak to their mothers again.

The boy band NSYNC was introduced to the world and to Danielle that night. I remember a buzz surrounding them as they started to perform. She spent the majority of the evening hanging out with them next to the stage. "She's just throwing herself at those boys; it's embarrassing for her," Donna Lawrence said about it. I don't think she meant any ill will. She was just being a Disney stage mom. But why is it the job of the Disney stage moms to judge a girl who wants to go up and talk to boys?

"Would you look at how desperate this is?" one of the stage moms on set said, referencing Jessica Biel on her shocking cover of *Gear* magazine—the one where she covered her breasts with a hand bra. The issue had been circling since word got out that the *7th Heaven* girl almost showed her tits. Jessica was a girl who ran in the same family-friendly television circles, which meant she was a girl people felt comfortable tying to a stake.

The vitriol thrown at a girl just hitting womanhood was shocking to me even then. "She was a sweet girl," someone said, as if any kindness in her personality had to end the second that she removed her top.

I thought she looked hot, and I was envious that she was confident and brave enough to do it. I wished I would have the nerve to be on a cover like that. Jessica later apologized, and I was sad when I read that. I had hoped no one made her feel she had to. To apologize for something that you wanted to do just because people had judgment on it is an awful feeling.

The turn of the millennium was a hard time for young actresses. We were expected to exude sexuality and erotic appeal, but also to remain a virgin until we were married. This was around the time Britney Spears was coming onto the scene as a Catholic schoolgirl and just before Jessica Simpson portrayed a ditzy housewife on the MTV show *Newlyweds*. America fell in love with the fact that she could barely read tuna can labels and saved her hymen for her husband. Stupidity and hypersexual-ized virginity became valued commodities. Women's desire or sexuality became solely focused on what a man on the other side got out of it, whether it be a spouse, or a father, or just a guy in the audience. Britney could be this desirable creature for the masses, but if anyone thought that she, in the privacy of her own home and own bed, was enjoying a sexual relationship, she was viciously ripped apart.

For all my issues with Michael controlling my sexuality and the expression of it, I think that Danielle had it worse. He had raised her character from a tender age, writing storylines and plot points that would present her to the world as the daughter, the girlfriend, and eventually the wife that every man wanted. In no universe could Michael have seen Topanga lose her virginity before her wedding night. In no universe could he have written that she left Cory to attend Yale. That would be her leaving him behind. Sometimes I just wanted to scream out, "Topanga, go to that Ivy League school; don't get married when you're twenty and scrimp and save to buy a house you'll live in for the rest of your life that you'll eventually resent. You're beautiful! You need to have lots of boyfriends and become the wild success you were meant to be!"

But I wasn't writing the story. And neither was she.

Danielle came back that last year with a little white Maltese and a smoking habit, both of which she'd make a big deal of showing off. "My mother hates it when she catches me," she'd say between puffs with an air of victory. A part of me was repulsed by the cloud of smoke that suddenly and constantly surrounded her and her dog. But another part was envious and wished I could light one up for the world like she did—if only just to see their eyes widen in disbelief.

We were told we weren't coming back the next year. The ratings had fallen off, and the cast was less connected and looking out separate windows and in new directions. Michael, who had always been so sure as he paced, was scrambling in this new place of uncertainty. "Hollywood is changing," he said. "None of what we have here will ever happen again."

He was right. Everything would change after that. We would all be shocked by how much. Overall, *Boy Meets World* was a great environment to work in, with funny people who really cared for each other in spite of any differences. Even with the issues I had, and would yet to have with Michael, there was and will always be a love there. It's complicated, though; he was like a father to me and to us all, and sometimes relationships with fathers and children are hard, especially when the father stops writing the outcomes.

Michael called me into his office shortly before the last day of taping. He called everyone up there separately to give us advice on how to navigate life beyond this nest. It was important to him to feel that he had a stake in our lives. He had a picture of Halle Berry hanging behind his desk, signed and in a slightly tarnished frame. She looked like a baby, so you knew it was from an early project that they worked on. He pointed to it and said to me, "You know, I was the only one on that gig who knew she'd be a star." He smiled as he looked at me sitting there in front of him. "One day I'll put your photo up there too."

And I still believe him. I just wonder what photo he has up there of me now.

CHAPTER 7

I WANTED TO BUY A rabbit—not a furry animal but the kind of vibrator that I had heard girls talking about—the ones who fully identified with episodes of *Sex and the City* and didn't have to research anything they talked about afterward. I had never bought an actual vibrator before. Masturbation in my family was a taboo worse than sex. It was assumed you'd have to open your legs one day for your husband, but childbirth would be the penance for any enjoyment.

It was Terry's fault—or maybe mine. I was horny and he was now gone, and my fingers were no longer enough.

We had decided to take a break after he almost knocked my tooth out. Well, *that* wasn't his fault really. We were having rough sex and I was riding him, telling him, "Fuck me like you want to get it to my throat." Then his forehead accidentally slammed into my mouth, and my front tooth was left hanging in a limbo equal to the state of our relationship.

"We were cooking, and a pan hit my mouth," I said to the ER doctor as he put the tooth back into place. "Well, be careful when you're watching that *Food Network*. They do things that aren't always reasonable and achievable between real-life couples," he said. I was glad I had an excuse to cover my face with a bag of frozen grocery store vegetables.

"You always have to take care of me," I said to Terry as I held a trio of frozen carrots, corn, and green beans against my mouth later that night. "I don't mind," he said, and he kissed my head.

This set me off.

"Why are you so nice?" I asked him, and he looked confused.

"What? I'm not supposed to be nice?" he asked.

"No!" I stood up fast. "You're young and you're supposed to be out there fucking and not held back by a tooth!" I winced from the force of my words pounding against the bloody swell of my gumline.

"But your tooth got knocked out from us fucking," he said.

I threw the vegetable medley down.

"Well, maybe if we were fucking different people, we wouldn't have been fucking each other so hard and my tooth wouldn't have tried to leave my face!"

It devolved from there.

I cried all night long, clutching a thawing Jolly Green Giant bag and my dog, who kept trying to pick up the loose carrots falling out. It was awful to be there without Terry, but I was sick of people asking us when we were going to get married and then have babies, and then, and then, and then . . . Eventually you run out of those questions, and I guess you just wither up and die looking out at the big world from a house and an old swing on worn boards. I wasn't ready to have a front porch yet, but I felt ready to have a vibrator. For me, the step was of equal terror and value.

"Can I help you?" a sales guy at the sex store asked me, startling me away from a wall of dog masks and collars and chains.

"I take it I didn't take a wrong turn into Petco?" I laughed. He didn't.

We moved on, walking past the whips and chains and heavy bondage equipment. There was a woman who looked like she might do taxes just casually shopping for a strap-on like she was examining heads of lettuce for a wedge salad. There were cages and handcuffs, even little cock trappers with keys, and everything about this walk felt like descending into something. I wanted to look away but just couldn't. There was something desirable about this sort of spiraling.

"Dildos and vibes," he said, and he motioned to a wall so colorful, it looked like Skittles started selling schlongs. "These are what you want," he said as he directed me more specifically to the ones with beads in the center and little pincher ears.

He handed me a long purple one and flicked the switch for me. I jumped from the pulse and electricity but also because I was actually holding a dick with beads and ears that revolved and buzzed in all directions. This had the possibility to bring me great pleasure, but also looked like something satanic my grandmother might warn me about.

"Has anyone ever been electrocuted?" I asked.

"Only on aisle seven," he said.

Before I lost my courage, I headed to the counter to pay.

"Here," the salesguy said, handing me a flyer with my bag. "I saw you looking at all the BDSM stuff back there. I thought you might like to learn more."

I looked down at the paper. They were giving a class on the basics. Basics?

For what—beating people?

I'd heard all about that club back in college, and I wasn't interested, *was I*? But I know I kind of was. I folded the paper up and threw it into my bag, and I was afraid I lost it when I went digging for it the next morning, right after my rabbit lit up my entire life.

THE ROOM WASN'T FULL when I walked in—only four or five people spread out among a dozen chairs. Nobody looked like they wore those dog faces or liked to have their balls tortured, though I didn't know what that kind of person looked like with their pants on, but I figured it might constitute a grimace or crossed legs.

Devon was sitting alone, in the second row, when I sat next to him and introduced myself. He was about my age, with dark tanned skin, and he was the only one in the group who didn't look to be expecting anything more than information. He knew where he was and who he was, and he was just living to soak it all up.

"I haven't seen you before," he said to me as I settled on a folding chair.

"Are there regulars at these things?" I asked, and he smiled.

"No, just people like me who really want to learn things."

And I have to say his smile and his smoky voice had me damp.

I thought we were being shut down when an old lady waving a cane entered the room.

"Respect for your partner and for your implements is the foundation," she said, and I guessed she was the teacher. The entire lecture felt like she might suddenly burst out into Slavic wartime poetry if someone brought out a pot of good-strength coffee. There was a book we were required to purchase that she authored. It had spiral rings connecting regular typed pages, so she obviously put it together herself. "Chapter 3," she said, clearing her throat and reading the opening paragraph: "There is dominance and subservience in all relationships, sexual or not. There is pleasure and freedom in the most extreme roles."

I had always been told to practice moderation in all things. That was the mantra of my father, and it always seemed a sound one. The ends of any spectrum are too far away from what is safe, what is acceptable, and it leaves you in danger of drowning in some deep end. Though my father never lived life on the edge or took any chances, he was always comfortable and safe, and he kept the family from choppy waters. But was I really afraid of the water?

For the first time, someone was talking of the merits of extremes, and I was listening.

"Do you want to grab a drink?" Devon asked me after we were dismissed from class. It was only about ten and there was a bar just down the street. Plus, he was cute. "Sure," I said.

He was an actor too, of course, but he didn't seem like a guy who just wanted to get laid but rather someone who wanted it to be an experience. "I've taken a lot of these classes," he said as he sipped a whiskey that he ordered neat. I didn't know what "neat" was, so I thought he was just instructing the bartender to do it exceptionally cool. "Not just BDSM," he went on. "I take everything." He leaned in and took a slow sip of his drink. "One of my favorites was cunnilingus." The way he licked the drop of whiskey off his lip with his tongue made me want to try it.

A week later I was laid out over his desk, floral peasant skirt around my waist, with his mouth on my vagina. I was absolutely right about that whiskey tongue, and it was obvious he had been a really good student. I ripped open his pants with both hands, so ready to have him in my mouth and inside me. "I want to choke on you," I said, until I saw what was in his pants and realized it might not reach my molars.

I would find over the coming weeks that sex was a production for him. We would never do it on a bed or a couch; even a kitchen counter was too ordinary for him. Sex had to be something of wild expectation, with extreme elements or someplace we could possibly get caught. He liked bathroom stalls and department store dressing rooms, and he loved anything in nature.

"Let's drive somewhere to fuck in the rain," he whispered in my ear as we sat at a booth in a restaurant one evening.

We decided to drive out to Laguna Beach, up on the cliffs. It wasn't raining, and it was pretty dark, but it felt dangerous having sex on the hood of his car. "Look at all those people watching in that house," he said between aggressive thrusts, nodding up to a large home that overlooked the car. "They're watching you get fucked."

I startled and looked up at the windows. I couldn't see anyone watching, and I'm sure this was him just fantasizing, but lights were on, so there was a possibility. As he was pounding me, or attempting to with what he had regarding equipment, I imagined a particular window opening and one or two people watching. First, I saw them angry, and then I envisioned them excited—a man and a woman who would touch each other as they watched us. I came so hard imagining their eyeballs on me.

I found out from another actress friend of ours that Devon had taken a new girl to a bar.

"Every time he takes a new class, he tries someone out," she told me. "What a big dick."

"Yeah, not really," I said.

I was so mad that I broke things off with him right before the blow job weekend we had signed up for started. "I really want to focus on choking on something in this class," I said, and I walked away.

"How are you doing?" I asked Terry when I called him on the phone that night after I used my rabbit. The toy was nice, but I was lonely. I missed him. "Good," he said. We were silent for a moment. I didn't ask him what he was doing—or with whom because I didn't want to know.

"People are asking how we are," he said. We hadn't made any official announcement of our separation, especially to our families. We had both agreed to keep quiet until we knew for sure what we both wanted. "I know," I said, and we didn't say any more.

"*Match Game* is on," I said, and we both turned on our little bedroom TVs, in our separate little lives, in our little corners of Los Angeles and watched it together.

And it was nice.

"OH, RIGHT, *BOY MEETS Girl*," a casting director said, trying to identify me as I stood in front of him at an audition.

"No, *Boy Meets World*," I said as I straightened the jacket of my pantsuit I just nabbed at the Ross Dress for Less store. This particular role called for a detective who tackles oceanfront crime but also nabs hearts, so I went for a professional but cheap polyester. I figured no one walks around the beach looking for murder weapons in exceptional wool.

"Yeah," he said, "I know," and he just smiled and nodded. "The one with Fred Savage."

I bit my tongue and decided to just begin the reading.

After a performance full of intrigue and drama and a mystery about a woman's bikini strap being tangled up in an international fishing net and channeling the best of Mariska Hargitay, the guy started to laugh before he stated my fate.

"I'm sorry. I'd love to hire you, but I just keep seeing you acting up there with Fred."

This became a constant theme: casting directors who had never watched the show or knew anything about it would become hung up on the fact I had ever been on the thing they never watched. I wondered how you could typecast someone you barely recognized.

"When people grow up with you, they have this idea," one woman in casting told me, the way a nursery schoolteacher explains the reasons you cut your leg open running on the playground.

"Well, they didn't exactly grow up with me," I said. "I was past twenty at the time."

She sat there for a moment, and I thought my statement had really reached her, until she said, "Oh, I didn't realize you were *that* old."

It's a soul-wrenching thing to be aware that you must hide your age before the age of twenty-five.

The Hollywood graveyard of family sitcom stars is vast, and the headstones are rarely etched with an epitaph. You are a name in their credits and then you disappear, only to live on in their reruns. But there was no way I was going to let them dig my grave.

I had to become unrecognizable again.

"Higher," I said, as I stood in a pair of designer heels at a boutique Hollywood girls would go to. I was there to replace my entire wardrobe with something sleeker and polished, so I could play roles made for grown women. If I could shock casting directors off their seats, maybe they'd take notice. Looking in the mirror, I liked the way I was shocking myself already. The salesperson brought out a selection, and I picked the black-pointed-toe classics and kicked away the kitten heels. I liked the stiletto because it was sharp.

I took headshots with a photographer who had done work for

Playboy and Guess and prepared monologues from dramatic, more introspective works and recorded them for my reel. It seemed to work because a short time later, I got an audition for a film that would require smoking, espionage, and stilettos. I felt ready when I walked into the casting office wearing a bustier with a pencil skirt and a deep black cat eye. But the reading didn't go well. The casting director said my voice was too high and I wasn't believable when I smoked.

"I'll be better when I actually get to light it," I said, showing him the dead cigarette that I was using as a prop. I had been told there would be no smoking in the office.

After an awkward brush-off, I walked out in heels that were now causing a blister and daggering holes in the grass. But I promised myself that if I ever had a cigarette in my mouth again, no matter the warnings, I would light it.

I met the producer Rob Cohen while attending the premiere of his film *The Fast and the Furious*, and we got along right away; I found him funny and welcoming, especially since I was some girl who had been on TGIF, and this was his big premiere. "You're a beautiful girl. You're going to do so much," he said, and later I got his number.

We talked casually, mostly back and forth about my career and where I wanted to go with it. Eventually he got the idea that we should work on something together. He was going to start filming *Triple X* with Vin Diesel and wanted me to play a part. It was too early in my timeline to see the serendipitous humor in a film with a title like that.

But as more time passed, I thought that the part was never going to happen unless I made physical payment to him. It was like he kept throwing out the bait to see if I would bite, telling me how my character was going to jump off the screen and make me a star. Something in the pit of my gut was warning me, though, that I was playing with fire. He seemed kind and wonderful, but like my grandmother always said, "Wolves wear the wool of sheep right after they skin them."

He eventually left a message on my voicemail telling me they'd gone with someone else. Someone who fit the role better. I was heartbroken at the time, but I heard later what a monster people thought he was on that set. And looking back, I think I really dodged a bullet.

"Do you nauseate easily?" I was asked by my agent after casting from *Boston Public* called offering me a job. "I don't think particularly so," I said. "Good," she said. "You won't gag eating your own hair."

I didn't gag, but I was asked to throw up in my mouth, or at least hold similar contents in there, playing a student at the high school who suffered from trichotillomania—the disease of pulling out and then consuming pieces of one's own hair. Like a cat, hairballs have to come up sometime. They'd pour a special mixture of soup and pudding and mashed peas into my mouth each take, and I had to heave and wretch until they cued me, and then I would let it all splash out onto the linoleum. It was quite the dramatic scene as the classroom watched me expel this projectile hairball. I can't tell you how disgusting the whole thing was, but I was happy to do it if I could be taken more seriously.

There are worse things than holding vomit in your mouth in this industry.

That was the only serious role I got, though. Everything, including pilots and episodic work, really started to dry up after that. They didn't like me as Rachel Maguire, but they liked me even less as someone new. My disappearing act wasn't enough. It brought me back to my childhood bedroom, where I tried to train my bones to shrink and crush my height. I started doing versions of that during auditions, trying to please people constantly and make them like me. I'd laugh at every joke, agree with anything they said, and have the cheeriest smile on my face even as they showed me the door, so maybe I could fit into the space they would allow me under their drawn line. But even that wasn't happening.

I was beginning to think I'd never work again and starting to grapple with what that meant for a future I didn't have another plan for, when my agent called about a new Wayans brothers movie that was looking for girls over 5'9" who were sort of athletic looking. He thought I'd be perfect for it.

The film was *White Chicks*, and Shawn and Marlon Wayans would portray, with makeup and heavy prosthetics, girls modeled after the Hilton sisters. In fact, they were originally called the Wilton sisters, which was changed to Wilson. The sisters had to be of a comparable height and frame to the guys so they could get away with the ruse.

The length of my limbs and the fact that I could read complete sentences that the models called in for the role couldn't got me called back the next week to meet Keenen Ivory Wayans and producers. I thought it would be more of a closed audition, but every girl in town with legs was there.

"Are you from the Tip-Toppers club?" an old guy in a derby asked as he passed. That's a club where tall people gather to both celebrate and commiserate the fact that they've got long legs to stretch but also nowhere comfortable to do it. One of the girls shouted out, "No, we're from a small island in the Amazon and a company is harvesting our eggs." He nodded, smiled, and then walked away.

"I hope I don't have to bleach my hair 'til it falls out if I get this," a girl sitting on the floor next to me said. I hadn't noticed her before. She was long and lean but also had the ability to disappear into a ball.

"I'm ready for a change," I said as I brushed my strawberry locks off my shoulder.

Would I go blond again?

When I walked into the room, I saw Keenen right away, sitting in the middle of the table of producers. He was quieter than I expected and dressed in a simple gray sweater and jeans. I got kind of nervous and spit out that I loved Homey D. Clown, his character from *In Living Color*, only that wasn't his character. "I'll tell Damon you're a fan," he said with a laugh.

I finished my audition and stood there for a few moments waiting for a reaction. Keenen just kept eyeing me and then looked back and forth to a list in front of him.

"Let's bring in the other girl," he said, and someone scurried outside to get her. I stood there frozen. Had I been that bad that they needed to recast me before I had even been cast, right there in the room? Was he that offended by the Homey D. thing? I wanted to curl up in a ball and roll away and die in my vomit on *Boston Public*, when Annie walked in. The little ball from the hall.

"Thank you for your time," I said and started to leave.

"No, you girls read together," Keenen said. "As sisters."

Oh, that's right!

I noticed right off that we had chemistry. We could bounce the lines back and forth with good timing. We got some good laughs too, which is exhilarating when Keenen Ivory Wayans is the one laughing at your jokes. By the end of it, I really thought we might have a shot.

"You're really funny," Annie said as we walked out, and I thanked her, returning the compliment.

"Maybe I'll see you in Canada," I said, and she shrugged before we parted ways.

The next time I saw Annie, we were getting plaster poured onto our faces in the valley. We had the jobs, and now our faces had to be molded and copied to be fitted to Shawn's and Marlon's.

"Lift a hand if you can't breathe," a guy told us as a team cleared our nostrils of the wet white goop. He had proudly just shown us various characters from famous movies with bloody gashes and outward-reaching guts that he had constructed. I wasn't sure if by the end of this, I'd end up suffocated or a big star, which is always a chance you take in Hollywood.

"Be careful. It's a big city," my grandmother told me as I packed my things for the trip to Vancouver. This would be my first time living away for any length of time on my own, and my grandmother thought that meant being sex trafficked and murdered.

"Grandma, I live in Los Angeles," I said.

"But this is a foreign country with foreign rules," she said, and I rolled my eyes.

"It's Canada!"

CHAPTER 8

IF YOU WANT TO see celebrities, don't go to Los Angeles. Go to the Sutton Place Hotel bar in Vancouver. That's where we were staying. Everyone, from all the big films and projects, stays there in the little apartments they have on one side of the hotel. Funny, Jessica Biel was right down the hall from me while filming *Blade: Trinity*, though it felt like it would be wildly inappropriate to knock on her door just to tell her that I supported her taking off her top on the cover of that magazine.

A whole group of girls cast in the film gathered in the hotel lobby, including Jamie King, Jennifer Carpenter, and my old friend from my soap opera audition, Brittany Daniel. She was going to play one of the rival sisters, who were the Wilson sisters' fierce nemeses.

"The last time I saw you, you stole my job," she said, and we laughed as she gave me a hug.

It all felt liberating, like I had arrived at summer camp or at a sorority house on rush day and my parents had given me cash for snacks and magazines. But this wasn't like the college experience I had; it was the one I always wanted. Nobody really knew me here. I was finally away, on my own, and I could decide who I wanted to be.

I had met Busy Philipps and Jessica Cauffiel on the plane ride out. "You have a fucking iPod!" Busy said, looking at the new white dial contraption Jessica was holding. "Yeah, you can store all your music on it. I was up all night loading my CDs," Jessica said, and I was awed by it. They were both outgoing and talkative and you could tell they would relish being friends.

And everyone had iPods by the end of the shoot.

I did go back to blond again. Embracing the change, which was actually my origin, was odd but also a thrill. I was so different the last time I had light locks. So much had happened. Though I didn't need to make the change, since they informed us that we were now going to wear wigs for the entirety of the movie to help with continuity, it still felt good to revisit my roots.

And it felt separate from Rachel Maguire.

"Shut up! You were on *Boy Meets World*!" Rochelle, another cast member, said during a group dinner when she suddenly recognized me—proof that separating myself was going to take a little more than a bottle of bleach. "I used to watch that show all the time."

The whole table turned, sushi stilled on chopsticks, and all eyes were on me, like I was this newly discovered archaeological specimen. Some relic from some lost city.

We all had a lot of time on our hands while Marlon and Shawn spent hours and days and weeks testing makeup and prosthetics to get ready for the shoot. A good month passed before we ever shot a thing.

Jessica, Jennifer, and Busy spent the most time together, lunching, getting facials, and cleaning out the trendy Aritzia store on Robson, which was really the place to be.

Brittany and I worked out together a lot, finding spin classes at the local YMCA or just going on the treadmills at the hotel gym. Even though it was just one audition way back when, we had a history, so that made us sort of friends.

"I really hope to settle down," she said as the thump of her soles punished a treadmill. "It's hard to trust guys in Hollywood."

I agreed, though there was a guy back in Hollywood whom I did trust. That made me miss Terry. Though I didn't want to settle down. I wanted to take some chances.

Annie and I became inseparable playing sisters. We'd hang out in our trailers and have little parties that featured the frosted pink grocery store cookies from craft service and trail mix with M&M's. We called ourselves Skittles and Couscous for reasons I can't remember now. She even tried to help me smoke a more believable cigarette for auditions. "You have to learn to inhale it. I'll plug your nose while you suck it in," she said. It was a good trick.

Fridays and Saturdays were club nights for the cast. They'd rope off an area at some hot spot, and there the whole group of us would drink and dance and just let loose. Annie would join us only occasionally, always saying she was tired or needed time to think. Whenever she did show up, she wore a sweater and jeans and then made an excuse to cut out early. "My man is in Tanzania, and he's calling me after a global presentation he's making," was something she would say.

Most of the time the group of us girls would dance, and the more progressively drunk we got, the more we'd be all over one another.

"Hey, now, there's a show happening here," Marlon said, laughing at Brittany, Rochelle, and me getting down and dirty on the dance floor. I liked when the guys watched us. You could tell they were turned on when we touched each other and there was an excitement in that for me.

I met two guys, one tall one and one short, on one of these club nights. They were in town filming a movie and I guess someone in production met them at the hotel gym and invited them along. They were actors but weren't known for anything yet. They just hung around the periphery hoping to seem like they were a part of it all.

After a few drinks, we began to dance, one at my front and one at my back. They grinded me on both ends, which was something I had never experienced before.

"You like us doing this?" the smaller one asked me as he rubbed his dick into me from behind, and I nodded. The alcohol and pounding of the music and the strobe lights had me unraveling. The taller guy leaned in and started to kiss me, and I could feel the one from behind holding my hips firm as he made thrusting motions into my ass.

"If you're curious, we're having a party in my room later," the tall one said and then took a pen off the bar and wrote his room number on the palm of my hand.

I went back to the hotel and raced upstairs to change my panties before I knocked on their door. I didn't want anything cotton and ridiculous getting in the way.

Annie saw me walking to the elevator. "Where are you going at this hour?" she asked.

It was after 1:00 a.m.

"The gym," I said, and she laughed and wished me a good time pounding the treadmill.

There was no party going on when I got there, just some music and a few joints in a tray. Nobody else was there but those two guys.

"We thought you'd wuss out," the tall one said, laughing as he inhaled some weed and then passed the joint to me. I never really smoked anything, but I pinched my nose like Annie taught me and took a quick drag. I coughed a bit and they laughed. "Lightweight," the short one said.

My head definitely felt a little lighter.

We didn't do anything for a while. We watched some skateboarding competition, and they kept passing the joint over me and to each other as I sat between them on the couch. I'm not sure how the fire alarm didn't go off, except they had all the windows open—so much so I was nearly freezing.

"You getting cold?" the small one asked as he flicked at my nipple through the fabric of my shirt. It was definitely hard.

Thankfully they put out the joints and closed the windows.

The tall one began to kiss me as the little guy unbuttoned my shirt. He popped one of my boobs out of my bra and started sucking a nipple. "Pepperonis," he said, and then the big guy was undoing my pants.

We eventually all got one another naked and lay down on the bed.

"We're both gonna take our time with that pussy," the big guy said as I sucked him off. What a wonderfully weird feeling to have a dick in your mouth while another one slides into you. I loved it—even as a little voice inside my head was telling me I was going to hell.

They took turns with me, and we had sex in every position possible. They were synchronized and really knew how to pleasure a woman in the most unexpected ways. "Do you guys practice?" I asked in the middle of it, and they laughed. I went to sleep with them, thoroughly fucked and satisfied.

I woke up the next morning to the sound of moaning. I thought it was in my dreams until I opened my eyes and saw the big guy getting sucked off by the little guy. "Fuck, you do me so good," the big guy whispered as he pushed down the little guy's head all the way to his ball sack.

I immediately jumped up and wrapped the sheet around me. "What the fuck is going on here?!" I yelled, rushing to get my clothes.

"What, you didn't think we fucked each other too?" the small guy asked, and they had the nerve to laugh at me.

"I don't want to be a part of this," I said, and once I was half-dressed, I ran out the door and back to my room.

I CRIED FOR AN hour and then sat there numb, trying to figure out why I was so upset. So they were with each other? I was supportive of anyone being gay or bi. What was it to me? Was it the lying? But they didn't lie to me; they just didn't tell me right up front, but why did they have to?

I realized that I wasn't mad about their experiencing each other. I was shocked and scared at what I had done. I had just experienced living at the end of one of those extremes the lady from the class was talking about—and I loved the whole thing.

So that's why I hated it.

It wasn't the act that was so upsetting to me, or anything to do with the way they chose to express their sexuality. The truth of the matter is, I hated it all because I enjoyed it so much.

And I wanted to do it all again.

A rumor had started circulating that Brittany was fucking Marlon. "We just like to dance and have fun," she told a group of us as we grabbed a drink after workout class. "It's nothing serious." The way she stirred her drink, looking down into the clattering ice, made me feel she wasn't being totally honest, but who was I to care or judge?

But I wasn't the one out there passing whispered judgment.

Some of the girls began to suspect she was trying to curry special favor, and there was a growing animosity toward her because of this. It got even worse when she started to focus her attention on Keenen.

It was interesting how no one blamed the guys in any of this. They were just doing what guys do when seduced: they fuck. Brittany, though, was being judged for some supposed diabolical plan she had hatched. By using sex, they thought she was going to get in with them by getting them in her, and I'm not sure why it all mattered in the end, except that she did get cast as the hot girl in *Little Man* shortly after this. Plus, Keenen and Brittany eventually came out as being in a long-term relationship.

"What are you looking at?" Terry Crews said to some guys trying to approach us girls outside our hotel. They weren't bad guys; they were just horny little wimps, and they proved it by launching themselves across the street as soon as his towering presence raised a voice. "Did you see that? Those guys were running like their pants were on fire!" And he clapped and laughed at this victory.

TERRY CREWS IS A complicated thing for me.

If you had asked me at the time, I'd tell you that Terry Crews was one of the nicest guys who ever lived. He was talkative and funny, and he made everyone happy on set. "He really watched out for us girls," I would say. And that was something he felt that God had ordained his strong, masculine frame to do—to protect the slighter of the sexes. But as is often the case with men who view themselves as strong, it gets wound up and twisted in an oath of protecting a woman's virtue so she isn't ruined and soiled. This was so clear to me when he came out as a sex addict—and more specifically an addict of porn. He didn't seem to view women—namely, women in the adult industry—as beings with lives and bodies who he had no business to control, but rather vehicles that served him when he was obsessively getting off. They were vodka to an alcoholic, cigarettes to cancered lungs. They were objects to obsess over, and if you couldn't control your obsession with them, they must be destroyed.

I can never see him in the same way again, after he came out and called for an end to porn, with no regard of the livelihoods of women who are supporting themselves and their families with these jobs. Or even the women who just want to do it for a reason that's none of his business. He is not a protector of women; he is a protector of their virtue. And what are they if they aren't either usable or virtuous to him?

Little girls need to stop being told that big, strong men who chase away boys and give teddy bear hugs are there to protect them.

ANNIE AND I WERE nearly kidnapped and held for ransom our last night in Vancouver. We had decided to go to the bar downstairs for a glass of wine when a guy sitting across the way sent a bottle of nice champagne to our table. It wasn't the best, but it offered the impression that he had disposable income. We rolled our eyes but still made small talk with him, pretending to be like our characters but never divulging who we really were.

"Our father sent us to school here because we got kicked out everywhere in the United States," Annie said, and I bit my lip to stop a laugh.

"Yeah, he's very wealthy. He's in Africa picking out animals for our zoo," I said.

At some point, the bartender came over and Jägermeister shots were passed around. I'd never had Jägermeister, and I didn't know its strength. Suddenly I was extraordinarily drunk.

During the course of all this, the man had called a bizarre middle-aged woman in a long gold gown to join us. Her breasts were saggy and nearly falling out of her dress. She arrived all frazzled, like she had been rushing to get there. Rushing to see us? It was never explained who she was, or maybe we were too drunk to realize it, but I do remember her staring at the two of us all night. I was really out of it and excused myself to the bathroom, where she slipped away from the table and followed me.

"You're very pretty," she said as she smeared coral lipstick on, barely looking in the mirror. "We have a car here. You and your sister will come with us. You'll like it. Does your father have a phone number?"

Just then, Annie burst through the door and grabbed my arm.

"Our father is calling from his safari, and we must go," she said, and we ran out of there fast.

Since we had already been drinking and needed security from our stalkers, we rounded up a few guys on the crew to go out clubbing.

"You have to protect us," we told them, and we ended up dancing on the bar, sharing a joint, and then going back to Annie's room to watch porn. To this day, I wonder if anyone in the film we chose to watch is my friend now.

One of the guys from production walked me back to my room. He did it to protect me in case the woman in the gold dress was there with chloroform and rope. I was seriously afraid of this. By the time we got there we started making out against my door.

"It would be an honor to fuck you," he said.

"You sound like King Arthur. Just shut up and fuck me," I said.

I think the sex was okay; I don't remember much. But he told me I pushed him down onto the cushions and ordered him to keep watch on the couch after I was done with him, as that's where I found him curled into a ball the next morning.

I was impressed that I became a Dominatrix overnight and upset I only remembered half of it.

I never really saw Annie again. She didn't go to the premiere, which was the most massive thing I had ever been a part of. Each of the actors was assigned a handler to walk down the carpet, and fans were screaming out our names. At the after-party, Brett Ratner told me I was the most beautiful woman he had ever seen and handed me his number. I wasn't falling for the same lines I had with Rob, so I never called.

This was my first real taste of starring in a Hollywood blockbuster and would be my last for an indefinite number of years. You don't know that at the time. When the flashbulbs are going off and your name and your film are up there in lights, it seems that it will go on forever.

That's the trick Hollywood pulls on you because at any minute, it can all be gone.

And you're not supposed to do a thing about it.

CHAPTER 9

DANNY DEVITO OGLED MY ass while I pointed out strange foreign cities on a weather map. It garnered a laugh and applause when the little miniskirt I wore rode up when I reached to point to downtown Qeqertarsuaq, a city of about eight hundred in Greenland. Michael Jacobs had called me to work on a pilot the two of them were producing for FOX. I would act opposite Wayne Knight and Valerie Bertinelli, who played a news anchor losing her career to the hot new ticket at the weather board. "I told you she was good," Michael said to DeVito about my performance. "Oh, she's the best," DeVito said as my stick pointed up so far that a kiss of my ass cheek was showing.

The cast was amazing. Wayne Knight and I spoke daily about all the carrots and apples he fed to his dog. "My dog is fat and depressed since my split. I had to do something." Valerie, an absolute delight of a human being, introduced her son to me. "Wolfie, here's someone taller than you," she said, and he got a kick out of that. The network loved the cast too, but they still shut down production. I think Michael's reputation as a family TV guy hurt it, even though it was good, and I know that was a sucker punch to him. They wanted something daring and new, but I don't think they believed any ties to *Boy Meets World* or TGIF were going to do that. Even though I was still the butt (quite literally) of the sexual jokes, I was deflated because I was comedically really good in this and it could've been a huge break.

"You were the star of that show," Michael said on the phone when he had to break the news to me. "I told you it's a different world out there."

It was a vastly different world for him too.

I was cast in another pilot that focused on three men figuring out their lives. Most shows at that time did. The director picked me out because I had chemistry with one of the leads—Eric Lively, Blake Lively's brother. He was tall and funny, and I would get to play his free-spirited girlfriend, who was a brainiac in a bikini top on roller skates.

While Eric was charming and chatty at first, hanging out in my dressing room and rigorously and even flirtatiously going over lines, he barely talked or looked at me as the week rolled on. I knew something was up.

"You're really funny," he said to me, right before a run-through for producers, but he wasn't smiling. He seemed to be having trouble with the material, and the director kept giving him notes. He obviously didn't like it and was getting frazzled, and then he blamed it on me. "She's not giving me a performance I can react like this to," he said.

I shouldn't have been surprised when I was fired and replaced before tape night, but I was.

"You didn't elevate his performance," they told me. As if it was my job as an actress to prop him up. And, in the end, that was all the explanation I was given.

TO BE EXPENDABLE IS to be a woman in Hollywood. And you're not worth anything to anyone if you can't prop your man up. Unfortunately, that's true for women in all walks of life, not just on soundstages. I would say I longed for certain more complicated, intriguing roles, and I did, but in those starved days, in that time, there weren't many for women. All of us were just scavenging for the best scraps.

I had been on a soap opera, a sitcom, and in a big movie, and none of that moved the needle for me. I thought *White Chicks* would, but I was even getting typecast for that now too.

I would appear on only a couple more TV shows in guest spots before Hollywood closed the door on me: *Out of Practice* and *Rules of Engagement*.

Everything stopped after that. The scripts, the auditions, the phone calls. My manager at the time didn't even bother to tell me my agent dropped me. I had to find out from a casting director at one of my last meetings, who asked me if I had new representation.

"No. I'm still at the same place," I said.

"Well, they just told me they don't work with you anymore, and to stop calling, so I'd check on that."

Without any time to process, I had to read my lines. I kept stuttering and losing my place on the page, my voice breaking as the casting director kept watching me. Like I was a circus leaving town. I walked outside after it was over and gasped for air. My palms scraped against the messy brick wall behind me, and I leaned back, even as it cut me, and cried.

For a week I stayed inside, mostly in bed, mostly curled up into a fetal ball. I knew I needed to confront someone about this, but I didn't feel brave. I actually worried that if I called my old agency or my manager and raised my voice, they would list all the ways I had failed them. I couldn't face that, so I left my manager a message on her voicemail late one night, firing her, when I knew there wouldn't be any chance that she'd answer the phone.

I ran into Terry at the Bristol Farms in Westwood—the one where we used to buy expensive produce and foreign wines to pretend we were grown-up. I wasn't sure if I should approach him or just act like I didn't see him and run, but I was frozen watching him there in the aisle. He was buying pasta and fixings for salad and also a bottle of wine. It looked expensive and French, and I wondered if he was picking out bottles with someone else.

He looked up and saw me standing there.

"Big night?" I asked, not sure if I wanted to hear the answer.

"It could be," he said and the way he smiled at me still had me weak. "How about you?"

He looked into my basket, which was primarily filled with junk food to numb me.

"Yeah, potential *huge* night," I said. "They had mac and cheese at the food bar."

We both laughed.

We made small talk. He asked about my parents and my dog. When he asked how I was doing, I had to bite my lip to stop its quivering. It was the first time anyone had asked about my well-being in a long time. I told him I was good even though I wasn't, and I think he knew that.

His phone was buzzing repeatedly. I held my breath when he moved to answer it.

You know what I like so much about macaroni and cheese?" he asked as he turned it off. I shook my head. "I like that it can be so simple but also complicated. It can be this majorly impressive gourmet thing, or you can just eat it out of a mug straight out of the microwave when you want some comfort. But no matter how you make it, when it's there right in front of you, it's always good."

"Do you want to share?" I asked.

And so we had macaroni and cheese that night. A lot of it, a lot of different ways. And all of it was good.

"Who have you slept with? I want to know," I said after trying to tickle-torture him in bed under the covers.

"I'm not going to be one of those guys who kisses and tells," he said, holding my wrists to prevent my next attack.

I gave him a big old raspberry and flopped on my back.

He turned over and propped himself on an elbow beside me, "I can't get you off my mind," he said, and I smiled.

"I know," I said.

He got the *Star Wars* reference, and we had sex again.

My school friends started to get married, and I was invited to all their weddings. I didn't want to go alone, so I constantly asked Terry because I trusted him to help me through the miserable day and he was fun to dance with. "When are you two going to walk down the aisle?" some mother or aunt at the table we were stuck at would inevitably ask. The pressure of settling down is the last thing I wanted. It's amazing that even the most independent ones were all peeling off, tying matrimonial knots and landing in this suburban vortex, where they would immediately start having babies and live the rest of their lives in their thirty-year boxes.

"I don't ever want to get married," I told Terry one night after a wedding and after sex. Since we had started seeing each other exclusively again, I wanted to make my intentions known. If he wanted that white picket dream, he'd have to leave because that wasn't ever going to be me.

"Okay," he said as he sat up and propped himself against the headboard. "But why not?"

I sat up and wrapped the sheet around me.

"Because it's the biggest day in your life and I don't want a 'biggest day' where I know every day after that is going to be worse." I sighed. "I just want the possibility that there might be something bigger after that. Somewhere. And even if there isn't, I don't want to know that going in."

He adjusted on his side and stroked my hair.

"Why does it have to be the biggest day of your life? Why can't it be a great day that's just the start of more great days?" he asked. "You're too hooked up in conformity."

He was right. I couldn't think outside the box when it came to marriage, so I didn't want the box at all, but did that mean I was missing out? Had I been too focused on running away from the norm that I didn't stop to challenge it?

After weeks of thought, I cornered him in my kitchen all of a sudden, holding a knife. We were cutting vegetables; I wasn't trying to murder him.

"I want you to know that I'd be a terrible wife," I said as I brought the knife down on an onion. "I won't keep house or cook your dinners." I realized I was actively cooking dinner, but I just kept chopping. "I don't want a house full of kids, or maybe any kids at all. I want adventure and chaos and possibility. And I'm sorry, but the last thing I want is to die with you on a porch swing locked away behind some white picket fence." Whether it was the emotion of the moment or the onions, I was sobbing.

He took the knife from me and set it down.

"Then you'll marry me?" he asked, and through my tears I said yes.

We got married on a sunny day in October. Our families were beaming, which floored the little girl in me who thought they would never want to give me away. Maybe that had really been a hang-up of mine, not theirs. I was the classic bride, in a Monique Lhuillier gown, walking down an aisle of rose petals just as the sun was setting. I know I said I didn't want to conform, but I relished this fanciful day. As I held the arm of my father, just before he walked me down the aisle, he turned to me and smiled at his princess. "I'm so proud of you," he said, and his eyes got weepy. "I love you, Dad," I said, and he marched with me, letting go of me so I could find my future.

Then I remember the flower girl screaming and being dragged from the aisle.

My soap opera family, minus Dylan, was there. The Savage parents and Michael Jacobs and his wife and kids sat together at a table in the center. Danielle came, and we shared an emotional hug, and she wished me all the best. It really felt like she had grown up, and so had I. Maybe our bond from the show was real, and maybe we could continue with the friendship that never really took off in our youth but might now as adults.

But we didn't know yet about *Girl Meets World.*

"You would've been a star if that pilot had taken off," Michael said to me as we did a sweet father-daughter-type dance on the floor.

"I guess, if it had been meant to be," I said. He was proud to see me married. "Babies are next," he said just before he walked away.

I had had a dream to live in New York City ever since I saw *Annie* as a small child at a playhouse in San Diego. My mom told me all about Broadway and the big city, even though she had never been there herself. I was dazzled with dreams of lights and tall buildings and the fact there would be seasons beyond summer and Christmas vacation. But any time I now shared this dream, I was told I should stay where I was. "Hollywood is where all the studios are," agents and managers and everyone would say. "New York is too far away."

"We should just move there," my new husband said after I was particularly frustrated that no one anywhere was responding to the new headshots I sent out. I don't know why I was surprised, but my need for approval from this town was habitual and self punishing.

"I can't just up and leave for New York," I said, holding on to a mug of coffee that was only serving to agitate me even more.

"Why not?" he asked. "We're starting a new life together. Why not start it somewhere you've always wanted to be?"

"Because I have a career here," I said. Then I stopped myself to take a sip of scalding morning roast and grasp the realization that I didn't.

"Well, maybe," I said. "I could do theater there."

THE DAY WE ARRIVED in New York, I sliced my toe open and nearly fainted next to the toilet in a pool of my own blood. The little piggy that cries wee, wee, wee got caught under the door at the entrance of a Brazilian restaurant—the kind where the waiter comes to your table and slices the meat right off the bone and onto your plate. The door just so happened to do the same thing to my little toe.

"I think I may have cut myself," I told my husband and excused myself to the bathroom downstairs. On the way down, it got progressively worse, and I was leaving a trail of blood behind me. I locked myself into a stall and tried to wind toilet paper around the wound to make it stop, but I couldn't. I finally recognized that I was bleeding beyond my control, and so I called out for help.

I wound up in the hospital to get stitches and after the doctor patched me up, he held his hands out and said, "Welcome to New York."

Something about my injury had jarred me into experiencing this moment, and this city, fully. That's what New York does. It confronts you. And it's up to you to decide how you'll respond to it.

While LA felt like it was yawning at my existence, New York was like morning. Nobody knew me here. I could really start fresh. Sure, people would recognize me now and again, but for the most part, the city buzzed around me and left me alone. I could walk the streets in anonymity, and I would walk for hours—through the park, up the avenues, and to destinations unknown. I'd find myself in the library or art museums or coffeehouses just watching the weather outside change in the sky. I'd walk in the rain a lot. I liked how the city was already making me feel things I wasn't comfortable with.

I took theater classes in the hopes of realizing that long-held dream of becoming a Broadway star, but I couldn't sing. I could act, though, something I had started to doubt before I came here. I found myself performing in workshops and the tiniest theaters. There was absolutely no star treatment or outside recognition attached to this, but that didn't matter to me. I was finally able to do meaningful work, and the work I did was good. I liked that the theater audience clapped only in the present and in real time.

At an after-party for one of my workshop showcases, Terry and I met a girl who wanted to be a dental hygienist and was paying her way through school by way of lap dances.

This girl was pretty, with mocha skin and dark, clear eyes. I could see how she made money with her body. It was stunning and natural, and she was intoxicating when she danced.

"It's my birthday," she said as the clock struck midnight. "You guys should come and help me celebrate!"

We ended up celebrating at a club in Brooklyn. Some friends of hers got a table and everyone was drinking. "Wanna take a body shot?"

she asked me as she placed the lime in her mouth and poured tequila into a shot glass cradled between her breasts.

I looked over to Terry. He smiled and encouraged me to go ahead.

"Okay," I said, and she sprinkled salt on her chest. I didn't know how exactly to do it but I leaned in and licked the salt off, tentatively at first, but as I tasted her and felt the swell of her breasts beneath my tongue, I really started to enjoy it and I kind of lost control. She squealed, and I felt glee in the power I was having over her. A crowd had gathered and was now cheering us on. I liked that they were watching us; something about the eyes on us made me more daring. Urged on by the crowd, I nibbled her nipple through her shirt and that elicited a big reaction. After I took the shot from her tits, I reached for the lime in her mouth with my tongue and there was a riot of applause as we French-kissed.

"You should come to my place," she whispered as our bodies gyrated on the dance floor. "He can watch." She giggled, pointing to Terry, who now was watching us from the bar.

A few more tequilas and I was begging her to let me come as she flicked her tongue perfectly on my clit. This fast tongue probably got her into a lot of trouble and probably out of some too. The night was hazy, and I only remember the cab ride to her apartment, this moment, and seeing my husband watching this from the corner of the bed. "Are you okay?" I asked him, but then I came so violently I forgot the question.

I woke the next morning back home in our bed in a panic. I had a headache, and my hair was wild over the mascara-smeared pillowcase. I could hear Terry in the kitchen making coffee. The grinder was loud. I sat up and clutched my stomach. It was tight and guilty and nauseous from tequila shots. How did I let last night happen? I was with a woman right in front of him—my new husband! And I had never told him I liked women.

Well, he sure knows now!

"I told you I'd be a terrible wife," I said, wound up in the sheet as I stood in the doorway that separated our night from morning.

"Why?" he asked, leaning against the countertop. He was calm. Was this a trick?

"Why did I do it?" I asked. "I don't know." I took a deep confessional breath. "Actually, I do. I should've told you something about me. . . . I . . . guess after last night, you know . . . that I like girls. Don't get me wrong, I love men—I love you!" I wrapped my arms around my waist to keep the sheet up but also to hold myself together. "I thought being married would end any desire for that. But I just got caught up in the moment. I'm so sorry." I felt like I was back in my room again, begging for mercy from the gold-framed Jesus.

He moved to me and wrapped me in a hug, and I started to cry.

"Forgive you for what?" he asked, wiping my eyes as he pulled back to look at me. "Last night was fun. I loved seeing you enjoy yourself like that. I don't think I've ever seen you that . . . free."

"You mean you're not mad at me?" I asked, stunned.

"Mad? Are you serious?" he asked. "I'd be mad if you kept hiding from me." He kissed me on the forehead and then he laughed. "And I have to say, seeing you with a girl like that was hot! The way you moved when everyone was watching you. Wow."

We talked about my feelings and my desires over breakfast, and my long-suppressed need for feminine connection. "It doesn't take anything away from us," I said. "I love you."

"I know," he said, and he smiled, throwing that *Star Wars* reference back at me.

On my walk that day, I thought about how many years I had been hiding. Since I could remember, anything I enjoyed I had to be able to deny later. No matter how far I grew up and away, I'd always have to return to that altar in my room. If my knees weren't bruised from begging for mercy, who was I? But my husband wasn't mad; he was happy for me. And he was encouraging me to use this time in a new city to really find who I was now.

"Do you think I'm bisexual?" I asked him as we readied for bed one night.

"Yeah, I guess. I mean, you like girls," he said and then he kissed me before spooning me underneath the comforter. "And me."

He was right. I am bisexual. I had never thought of myself in terms of labels before, but that was because I never gave that part of myself any validity. But now I was owning it, and that was empowering. But it was also terrifying. What was next for me?

On one of my walks, I found an erotic bookstore—not a sex store but one that sold literature and informational books. Most of the books were older, some second- or thirdhand, as the spines were taking their last breaths on the haphazardly placed wooden planks that were shelves.

"Are you looking for something?" an older woman stacking paperbacks on one of the planks asked me.

"I don't know," I said. "I just happened in here."

"No one just happens into a place like this," she said with a knowing smile.

I quickly got lost inside there, pulling out books on all kinds of subjects that had to do with sex. There were books about sexual orientation and gender fluidity and more information about BDSM and kinks and fetishes than I could count. Anything I was interested in someone had written a book about, and that was comforting. I wasn't alone in the world.

I found myself lingering on a shelf of women who had all, in their own way, challenged something of their time. Their voices were not perfect but were honest and rare and braver than I ever thought I could be.

"*Monsieur Vénus* is one of my favorites," the old woman said as she pulled out a copy from a stack and handed it to me. "And to think it was written before the turn of last century."

I peeled through the copy later that night. I marveled that Rachilde was able to write something so provocative and challenging—in her time or any other. What might it be like to share such a naked expression of yourself even as you risk peril because of it? I liked that it was all deviant and shocking, but it also made me think.

"You should write," the old woman, who I now knew as Dot, told me after I had been coming in for a while. She had been right. No one just happens into a place like this. "I had so much stirring up inside me when I was young, I would've burst open if I hadn't put it down on paper."

I took her advice and purchased a laptop.

I started writing erotic and detailed stories and masturbating to them after I read them back. Writing down your fantasies is, in fact, the greatest turn-on. These stories became a twisted and dark fascination for me, and also an extension of who I was becoming. I loved that I could control the narrative and imagine for myself different outcomes and futures. During my career, words had been put in my mouth, but now I was putting my own words down onto the page, and that was liberating.

I would sit on a bench in Central Park and write as horses and cyclists and a whole world clueless to my filthy mind passed by. I liked dressing in prim dresses and closed-toe shoes and having people think I was such a good girl when underneath my skirt, my panties were soaked from my wickedness.

My only issue was how I could live all these fantasies out in real life.

MY GRANDMOTHER BROUGHT US back to Los Angeles the next year. At the ripe old age of ninety-one, her health was failing. On her deathbed, she no longer spoke of conspiracies or cowered under the fear of God. She looked me straight in the eye that last time and said, "Just spend your life happy."

And that was all.

CHAPTER 10

M Y MIND RACED AS I lay on a slightly warm, wood-plank table in
a yurt, waiting for a North Hollywood priestess to come in and
massage my yoni—Sanskrit for vagina. Terry and I had been back in
LA for a little while now, yet I had no focus, and neither did my vagina.
We had both seen things and done things since we'd been away, and we
were ready for a fresh start, but something was stopping us. It is said
that when your yoni is blocked, then all the parts of your life suffer. It
was time for my vagina to find release and purpose and inspiration, so I
could find the same. I whispered to my good girl as I took off my towel
and got under the blanket, "We're in this together."

"What's a lingam?" my husband asked as he lay on the table next to
me. I had dragged him along for emotional support, and also a group rate,
making him believe it was just a new kind of energy-healing massage
and not a spiritual hand job.

"It's your penis," I said, and he sat up.

"You mean this girl is going to give me a happy ending?"

"No," I said, and he lay down again. "This is yoga. There are no
happy endings. Just the journey."

The door cracked open, and our therapists came in.

"Well, me and my lingam are going to enjoy the vacation," he said,
and I threw a lavender sachet at him while the women were warming
our genital oils.

It was a long process, though remarkably less of one for him, as they massaged our entire bodies and then the pressure points of our genitalia. "Let go and breathe upward," the priestess told me as her fingers vibrated my inner vaginal walls. The way she pressed was less sexual and more confrontational. Like every stress and strain trapped up there, every fuck whose energy was bad and never cleared, was under interrogation from her fingertips. I almost expected her to blurt out to it, "Where were you on the night of January 4, 1997?" and for my vagina to answer back that she didn't remember.

"What are you holding on to?" she asked as I lay there petrified and frozen. I didn't know, but something was holding me back from experiencing everything I wanted to. I mumbled out, "I think it's just tight 'cause of Kegels."

She stopped what she was doing, and she got so serious and quiet I thought she might be casting a spell.

"It isn't tight; it's trapped," she said.

My husband snorted a laugh and muttered, "I could've told you that."

After I told him he better enjoy it because it's his last all week, I settled back again, took some deep, therapeutic breaths, and then really allowed her fingers to penetrate me. She started this vibrational thing all the way around inside until landing at my G-spot, where she really took energetic hold.

"Release!" she commanded, while shaking me there. It was intense and unyielding. I wanted to come, but with this demand on me, it seemed impossible. "Breathe it out! Breathe it all out!" She was shouting now, playing my vagina like a sound bowl. The very moment I thought for sure that nothing was ever going to happen was when I let go. All at once, I lost myself in my breath, and I felt a warm, tingly sensation travel up to my chest and then to my nipples and up to the top of my head. Some sound emanated from my throat that I didn't recognize. It was full of emotion and satisfaction, and it all felt like I woke from the depths of some dream.

"Your yoni is free now," she said. I agreed that it was.

Running around town with a free yoni, you do things you might not normally do. On a whim, I decided to study to be a yoga teacher. Though I would never really try and teach anyone other than my husband or my mom, I wanted to strengthen my practice and find myself, especially in tantric healing. The priestess said you find yoga at a crossroads. There I was at a fork in some road with my vagina spread and at the middle of it. I wanted to study the relationship between sex, the body, and how it serves your spirit. Sex, at its core, is governed by energy. I wanted to know how I could harness that. It felt like power to me.

While pushing my body to the extremes, I also challenged my intellect by enrolling in a screenwriting program at UCLA. Michael Weiss, who was known for writing films like *Journey to the Center of the Earth*, was my first teacher and the best I would ever have. Willie Ebersol, the son of Dick Ebersol and Susan Saint James, was also in my program. He wore things like American flag suits with fluorescent suspenders and bowling shoes and then got irritated when people stared or made even casual commentary.

"You want to write a story about a suicidal sex columnist who starts selling magic mushrooms for the Amish mafia?" Michael asked, and I nodded. "And it's a romantic comedy?" I nodded again. I knew it wasn't your garden-variety idea—well, technically it was a garden-variety idea but not like the gardens most people frequent in—but I felt there was a calling for this kind of thing. Who wouldn't like drugs, sex, and crime from people who don't use electricity?

"Well, okay," he said, and it was the most liberating shrug of the shoulders any teacher could have given me. If he had dismissed my ideas, I may never have continued, and I would've been too scared to ever think too far outside the box again.

After a few read-throughs of my scenes, he called me aside after class and said, "You know, I doubted a suicidal Amish drug comedy would work, but I was wrong."

All my scripts seemed to fall back on the same theme: a woman who was wronged and loses it all and has to fight tooth and nail for redemption, all the while using her brazen sexuality as a force for this change. And I couldn't admit yet that these characters were all me.

Although most of my classmates were champions of mine and supportive, there were those who had a hard time with this concept. While everyone stood behind a woman trying to reinvent herself and take her power back, sex was the part a lot of people couldn't get past.

"She's trying to legitimately redeem herself by having sex with everyone?" one of my classmates asked. The older woman had obviously never had her yoni rubbed out before.

"She's taking full power in her sexuality, which gives her back control of her life," I said.

Willie, in a shirt with bathtub ducks on it, immediately landed what he thought was the bomb of the night: "But why would we root for a girl who just fucks everything that moves?"

All eyes turned to me.

I sat there, and while Michael changed the topic, I thought about that for a while. Why would a woman's value and redeemability be diminished just because she's sexual? And why can't her liberation be marked by her very need to harness that sexual energy pent up inside her and break out? Why do we, as an audience and as a society, feel better about rebuilding the life of a woman we feel is chaste, or at least apologetic and making amends for past promiscuity?

Why is sex a story saved for a road of apology and not one for liberation?

Just before Michael dismissed us from class, I said to everyone: "Because she is who she wants to be. And that's her power."

I realized that to get anyone to see my scripts or hear me out, I needed representation again. I contacted Marty, a manager I knew during my soap days. Why? Because no one else would return my calls. Although he wasn't a power broker or on the line daily to the big studios, I knew people who worked with him, and they'd done well. I was just looking for a foot in the door again, and at least he had a toe in.

"You're writing movies now?" he asked as he labored with the condiments on his corned beef sandwich at our lunch meeting.

"I have three ideas I'm pretty confident about," I said.

"The only thing I'm confident about is that this meat wasn't cooked, and you need a new acting gig for any of that to matter."

He was right. At this point, most of the town probably thought I was dead—or at least Hollywood dead, which offered less sympathy to my corpse.

"Do you know Robin Lippin?" he asked when we got to his office after the meal, to which I immediately replied, "Oh yes! She loves me!" His mood lifted with my exuberance, and he dialed her up on his old speakerphone. "She's a great friend of mine," he said while it was ringing. "I'll see if she can get you in on that new pilot she's working on. I think Tony Danza is involved. Or maybe it's Willie Aames."

Robin was the one who cast me in *Killing Mr. Griffin* all those years ago and the one who told my agent I was good on that *Saved by the Bell* audition, even though I was green. She had called me in for a lot of roles over the years and was one of the few casting directors to encourage me and offer support. What luck that he was calling someone who I would always list as a casting reference.

"Oh God, she tried to hit me up for advice too," Robin said, not knowing I was listening to every word. "She messaged me on Facebook a little while back and asked what I thought she should do. I wanted to tell her to quit." She laughed out loud, and I could see his face drop as he stared at me sitting at the little chair that seemed to grow littler by the second, in front of his desk. "She's always showing her body. It's really sad what's become of her."

She ended the call by advising him to ignore all of mine.

I sat there absolutely crushed, though I refused to show it. I don't even remember how I got out of there, but it was fast and I offered some apology I didn't owe. I could feel my footsteps slosh in muddy puddles, but I couldn't see anything but my car that was parked down the steep hill. It was raining, but I had no umbrella and was wearing a dress with no sleeves. I was wet and filthy as I opened the car door and locked myself inside so I could cry.

I went back on my Facebook and reread the letter I had written to her. I had fallen on my sword and asked in a heartfelt way for her advice as a decent human being and as someone I considered in my corner—or at the very least, someone who wouldn't actively try to derail me. She had written back and told me to take some acting classes to get back into the swing of things and then wished me luck. I was naive enough the first time I read it to think that she was just busy, and she was offering her best help. But she was clearly writing me off, and the luck she wished me was a lie. I was about to reply to her and tell her that I heard everything and that I hated her, but I stopped myself. She'd laugh at that too. I vowed to one day show her, and everyone else who thought this about me, instead.

But that seemed a far-off dream.

Around the time I had given up on ever having a career in acting again, *Girl Meets World* was announced—the new spin-off of *Boy Meets World* that Michael Jacobs was heading up. Cory and Topanga would now have a daughter, who would discover the world much like her father did, only it was on the Disney Channel now and everything in the world had changed.

I was invited to the pilot taping but had already planned not to go. "I don't want to live in the past," I told my husband that afternoon when he brought up the subject. I had been trying to reinvent myself, so why would I want to go to a place so far back in time? I was in my sweats and ready for a night in when Lew Savage called from the set.

"Michael's yelling at everyone!" he said. "You and Terry have to get down here. It's like 1999 again!" And I could hear Ben screaming for us to join the party in the background.

My decision to stay away from it all crumbled when I heard everyone's voices. They were familiar and made me laugh. A thirst for nostalgia and a coming home again won out.

Will and Rider were the first ones we saw when we got to the set. They tackled me with hugs and introduced me to their partners, who would soon become their wives. As we watched a new generation acting in a familiar classroom, we didn't talk about when and where any of us would make an appearance on this show, but we were all wondering about it.

Ben was definitely Cory again, and he was relishing being back in front of the camera.

"You're wearing that perfume that drives me crazy!" Ben yelled to me.

"It's because I'm trying to seduce you," I yelled back, and he mimicked a dagger going through his heart.

He was Mr. Feeny now, teaching these children in a classroom and giving them sage advice. Everything about the world had come full circle.

"It's exactly like old times," Michael said as he cut his eyes between the kids rehearsing onstage and Rider, Will, and me catching up next to him. He had all his family together again in his world, and this was Michael at his most content. I believe he thought he could get everything back. But he had forgotten the words he told us when *Boy* ended: "None of what we have here will ever happen again."

Danielle didn't speak to me at all, which I thought was odd. She barely acknowledged that I was even there. I hadn't seen her since my wedding, but we hadn't had any ill feelings or bad blood. I had thought we'd made progress in our relationship since we grew up and away from Michael's hovering umbrella. But there we were under that umbrella again, separated by those same lines with many added years between. I don't know if this is true, but there were whispers she didn't want any of the past female cast members to share the screen with her. That's why her character would never interact with Trina's when Trina made an appearance on the show, and that's why she didn't like me popping up on the set.

Bill Daniels was back as Mr. Feeny again, which was exciting for cast and crew and everyone involved. It's remarkable how he stepped back into the role so seamlessly, and it was clear how much it meant to him that a generation saw him as their beloved grandpa. I took a photo with him and posted it on my Instagram, which was new and something mostly for my family and friends. I only had a few thousand followers. I nearly fell over the next day when that picture was on every major blog, news site, and entertainment show: "Rachel and Feeny on the set of *Girl Meets World!*"

That's when the wildfire started.

Everyone who ever knew me in the town asked me, "Are you going to be on *Girl Meets World*?" Out of the woodwork they crawled. People who had left me for dead now wanted studio audience tickets and information, though they still wouldn't offer me a worthwhile job. "I haven't thought about it," I said, but the truth was, that's all I was thinking about. And it was freaking me out.

It's like when an ex who once meant everything to you suddenly comes back into your life. You know it's been over for a long time and it could never work again, but there you are being late-night drunk texted.

It was scary how easy and comfortable it felt to sit back in the cushioned seat of my former role, even one I had worked so hard to grow away from. All the attention I was getting was hypnotizing, though it wasn't doing anything for me personally at all. Still, it left me with a sense of relevance again, and when you've been starved for that, that starts feeling enough. And it's why so many child stars of yesteryear go to the Hallmark Channel.

I could imagine no worse fate than a Hallmark Christmas movie.

I saw myself playing something adventurous now, like Lara Croft, or something hilarious like Kristen Wiig's character in *Bridesmaids*, or maybe some controversial woman of history that would really have people talking. I had an urge to rattle people. I knew I didn't want to be trapped in the hell of my own Christmas story, where the eventuality is getting an engagement ring in the hometown skating rink. Why do we curl up with comfort to movies that tell us that women who have high-powered careers are nothing without men and children? That they can't be happy unless they return to a place where they were once small and become small again. There's nothing wrong with having a family, but there is something wrong with the ending always having to be the same. I decided to imagine a film that would shock Hallmark—one that would have me crack the heel of my skate blade into the ice and watch all the pieces travel and separate. One that would see me floating away to some far-off place on my own little island of ice. There, I could be anything I wanted. I hadn't figured it all out just yet, though.

But because there was so much interest and attention now, I needed to figure out a way to use this spotlight so people could see who I was now. Nobody would give me a platform before, but now I had a microphone and a stage, and I quickly embraced the opportunities that this stage was giving me.

I hired a publicist.

"Photographers should be capturing you doing real-life things that we set up," said Glenn, the new publicist, said as we ate sushi and talked strategy. He had worked with some of the other *Boy* actors in the old days, and I had met him on set, so I agreed to dinner when he reached out to me about working together now. "If you're squeezing melons at the supermarket, we should capture that," he said and he threw an edamame shell into the bowl.

I was squeezing my own melons into a triangle bikini top that next week. I was told to buy a Hula-Hoop, wear something playful, and then show up at the beach. There we were met by a photographer who would take photos of me playing around in the sand with this Hula-Hoop, and then she would release them to the press as if paparazzi had found me playing with a Hula-Hoop entirely by accident.

Around this same time, Danielle posed for the cover of *Maxim* and the fallout came hard from Michael Jacobs and Disney.

"Did you see what a disaster that was?" Glenn asked me, but I couldn't see what he was talking about. She was dressed in pretty modest lingerie doing housework, which didn't seem like a big deal, though during the interview, she revealed that Bob Saget once offered her cocaine, so there was that. But the underage drug talk was way less shocking to the powers that be than the fact her tits were popping out while she was vacuuming. This felt like Jessica Biel all over again, though Danielle was now in her thirties, and it was no one's business. I think it was her last gasp of being able to be out there and show her sexuality in any way before she was trapped in the role of Topanga as a mom for the rest of her life.

Glenn advised me to dress seriously at the next events we were attending. He was obsessed with pleasing Disney and Michael Jacobs.

"Bows at the neck are cute and look smart for business," he said. I didn't know why we cared about what kind of clothes I'd wear to the office and no one, except for Disney, wanted to see me with little bows around my neck. I had seen the reaction with the Hula-Hoop, and I had liked how I appeared so free. I wanted to continue with the narrative of my freedom.

"What are you doing in that dress?" Glenn asked me as photos from a red carpet event the night prior were blasted out on the blogs.

"It's my style," I said.

"Naked is your style?!"

I laughed to myself. Maybe it kind of was.

The entire cast of *Boy* was invited to attend the ATX Television Festival in Austin, Texas. It would be the first time we'd all be together again and the first group appearance since the new show was announced.

"People are lined up outside the block to see you guys," Michael said right before we filmed a segment for *Good Morning America*. "I always said, *Boy* was this generation's *Happy Days*."

We all posed as a group as the crowds screamed and cheered down below, and I again posted the photos to my Instagram. And again they went everywhere.

It was a good weekend for everyone. The only castmates who didn't attend were Will and Danielle. We all had authentic barbecue one night in the heart of downtown. We broke bread as a family on wooden benches with ribs and brisket. Michael gave a speech before we ate, saying how everyone in the room was special to him, that we were all family. Family, no matter the miles and years, always remains close.

This weekend was everything for him. He was lauded as the legendary creator of a show that made a generational impact, and he was our father again.

There was a panel discussion where the cast took questions. The audience was on their feet and cheering at the top of their lungs when we all took our spots on the stage. Michael promised the crowd in no uncertain terms that every cast member would return to the new show.

I would be the only one who eventually didn't.

We nearly missed our flight back because Ben was singing in the shower and doing his hair.

"Why did you take so long?" Matt asked Ben as he threw his stuff in the car.

"Because I care about making a good impression."

Ben, Matt, Terry, and I were in a car racing to get to the airport when, of course, we got stuck in massive traffic.

"Great impression, Ben," Matt said.

When the car pulled up and the doors opened, we raced for the terminal. People were screaming and waving as we ran by.

"I'm sorry, your seats have been relinquished," the girl at the terminal said, and we all cursed our disappointment. When we were told there were no more flights that night, Ben pleaded with her for help. "These guys will kill me if we don't get out of here," Ben said. "I don't want to be murdered for making my hair look nice."

They made an announcement on the plane, asking if anyone would give up their seats for the cast of *Boy Meets World*, and we immediately got takers. They got a good deal out of it: the airline gave them free ticket vouchers, we gave them all autographs and took photos, and there was a good story to tell.

"You are all wonderful people," Ben said as he group-hugged them.

As I sat back in my seat, the weekend played back in my mind. I watched Austin disappear and the clouds take its place. I knew I had a decision to make, and it wasn't one anyone would advise me to at that moment, after that weekend. We were all one big happy family again.

I knew I had to break away.

I WAS DRESSED AS Batman's sidekick, Robin, when a reporter on the red carpet of the *Playboy/Kick-Ass 2* party at San Diego Comic-Con stopped to ask me who my favorite porn star was. I gave it some thought. I wasn't someone who watched a ton of porn, but I had favorites, so I threw out a few names.

Glenn immediately jumped in to stop me.

"She's not speaking on the matter," Glenn said to the reporter as he pulled me away. "Never admit you watch porn to anyone, especially a journalist," he said.

I shut my mouth fast, but I wasn't sure why.

This was my first Comic-Con and the first time I wore cosplay—costume play, where you dress up as your favorite characters from comic books and entertainment—that anyone noticed. Glenn thought it would be a good way to get me to meet Hollywood insiders, but I was more interested in meeting fans and dressing up.

"Pose like a superhero," a photographer yelled out, and I fanned open my cape and readied my stance. I was a complete geek and obsessed with anything comic book or *Star Wars*, so I loved this. To be asked to do this was like a kid being asked to eat all the Halloween candy. It was fun and a rush. I wasn't privy to professional costume designers yet and did not make anything for myself. Still, my store-bought costume elicited a reaction in myself and in others.

There was a huge bungee jump thing in the center of the party, and

I wanted to try it. Glenn stood in line with me, and we talked about all the buzz and attention my photos and red carpet appearances had been getting.

"I've never seen photographers get so excited about someone," he said. "And if we're smart, we could be on the verge of something big."

As I was being strapped in, I agreed with him, but then I got sucked up on the ride, and I was flying all alone.

I WORE A SKINTIGHT, bright green Mark Wong Nark dress that hugged all my curves on the final night of Comic-Con to the *Bates Motel* party. I had never worn something this tight, with this much cleavage and a color so bright before, but I was in the mood to shock the world.

And again, the world was shocked when they saw the Internet on Monday morning.

Tom Mark, the designer behind Mark Wong Nark, contacted me for a meeting at his West Hollywood store.

"You are my beautiful movie star," he said, with an air of his wonderfully dramatic signature flamboyance as I walked into his showroom on Sunset Boulevard later that day. He was gracious and offered up any of his designs for all the red carpets and photo shoots I'd be doing. "You must only be seen in the designs of an artist," he told me.

Tom began making custom pieces for me, and all of them were tight and showed everything off. "Your tatas were made for the world to see," he said of a new red creation that graced the carpet at the stage production launch of *The Wizard of Oz* in Hollywood. Each new party or premiere, I'd show up on the carpet with a tighter and more 3D—for my 3Ds—dress that would have the blogs online salivating. Glenn began to get nervous about this because he felt they were giving off the wrong impression. But there wasn't anything wrong about it except it was an impression he didn't like.

"Disney is not going to think well of this," he said as I walked the line of flashing bulbs at the *Sharknado* premiere.

I didn't care about Disney. I liked being seen this way in the flashing lights.

Glenn set me up for a meeting with a new agent, one who handled a lot of former and current Disney-type stars. "We see you as an original," the agent said, and the two female assistants in the room nodded in agreement. "A one-of-a-kind who would make a great mom as a series regular. Disney is always looking for new moms!"

I was waiting for him to mention the Hallmark Channel. I didn't have to wait long. "You'd be excellent in those Christmas movies with your red hair."

I called Glenn and said I needed to meet with someone else. Glenn was struggling to tell me something, and I told him to just spit it out.

"He's the only one who will take you right now," Glenn said. "But that'll change when you guest-star on *Girl Meets World*."

So my whole career now relied on whether I'd relive a character I'd been trying to grow away from? What's the point of passing Go anyway when you're always kicked back to jail?

I was depressed about it but decided that maybe if I was more vocal and more insistent on how and where I wanted to take my career, they would listen. So I asked my new agent if I could be seen for roles a little more provocative and daring. "I really love writing erotica. Are there any films like that out there?" I asked.

He laughed.

"Are you kidding? You were on *Boy Meets World*!"

After a spin class, the teacher, Aaron, who was also a good friend, showed me an app he thought I should be using.

"You just take pics and videos, and they just disappear afterward," he said as he told me to download the little yellow box with the white ghost.

"Why would anyone want a picture that would disappear?" I asked.

"I guess they want to be in the moment with you," he said with a muscled shrug. "The here and now."

I took a video of myself, all sweaty at the gym, and posted it. I didn't have anyone watching at first, but then word got out and eventually thousands and thousands joined. And almost overnight I became what *MEL*—the popular men's online culture and lifestyle magazine—coined me: the resident sex symbol of Snapchat.

This was how I began my here and now.

CHAPTER 11

I DIDN'T WEAR ANY UNDERWEAR on the night that would change the course of my life, and I wanted everyone to know it. I had it all planned out. I was invited to the premiere of the Wayans brothers' new film, *A Haunted House 2*, so I picked out an eye-popping sheer black mesh dress with only a studded cross covering my most intimate parts. It was Easter that weekend, though I wasn't planning for sacrilege; I was planning to be noticed. But many consider everything I do the same thing.

When I saw the dress hanging in a designer's loft, I was immediately drawn to it. It felt daring and beautiful and the way the mesh hugged to my curves, sheer to the flesh beneath, felt like a dress that was made for me. When I stepped out of the dressing room, my husband's jaw dropped to the floor. The designer wasn't sure I could get away with wearing it—or should—at a high-end, big-budget event. "The whole world is going to see you like that," the designer said. And I just smiled as I turned around, taking myself in in the mirror. "Then let them see me," I said.

I knew it was a good choice as my husband and I fucked in the elevator that led to the designer's loft before driving home.

My husband and I knew the drill, and we came to the event prepared with a trench coat, slippers, and a fast run. No one but the stars of the film would be invited to have their picture taken on the red carpet; this was standard protocol, but that had never stopped us before, and it certainly wasn't going to stop me in that dress, on that night. We had been going to events like this for some months, mostly whispered to me speakeasy style by the red carpet photographers, who would sneak me out and shoot me before anyone but the photo editors at news desks the next day would be the wiser. They shot me because they knew my photos were always daring and original, and I would sell. I'm sure studio executives looked at these photos from events and wondered how the hell some girl from TGIF's past ever got there. The truth is all the big publicity I'd ever gotten was from being in places I was told I didn't belong. But at no other event where I'd stolen my place under the spotlight had I worn a dress like this.

We planned to get there early. I'd come wearing my Inspector Gadget trench, which would hide me from any suspicious studio flack on the way in and could also be quickly removed when the time was right. I would throw the coat to my husband, dart out onto the carpet, and meet the sea of flashing lights. My husband would document the whole thing on my social media to create a real stir and fanfare. Then I'd throw on the coat again and be on my way.

This carpet was tricky, though. It was longer than the other ones I'd been to and packed solid with press and, more troubling, security. Everything about the environment made me more apprehensive, yet at the same time gave me more incentive to accomplish my mission. Fear is never a reason to back away; it just makes you take different steps.

"Just go out there now," a gray-haired bespectacled photographer named Dave said to me as I assessed how and when I'd make my entrance. "Security is dealing with Floyd Mayweather's entourage. Now is the time."

He was right. The coast was clear.

I hurriedly walked down the line, and it wasn't two feet before I tripped in my heels and hit the red carpet with my knees. The shoes had been too big, and I had stuffed toilet paper in the toes.

For most people, scraped knees and humiliation would probably bring their charade to an end, but I picked myself up and kept walking. I knew I had arrived when the blinding lights met me there.

"You and your lady garden are going to be extra famous tomorrow," one of the photographers said to me as he shot the side of my bare ass. If my garden was to be infamous, it felt wildly appropriate that a lucky shamrock tattoo was growing in it—the one I got on St. Patrick's Day some years before to denote that I was lucky, Irish, and mildly intoxicated.

As I turned back, my vision still obscured by the onslaught of flashbulbs, I felt my body slam against something solid, covered in sweaty cotton, and made of flesh and towering bone.

I was caught.

"I was just walking . . ." I said with a squeak as I looked up at a man who appeared to be the progeny of a rock wall and a side of beef. I wondered for a moment if the studios were now employing assassins for security.

"Wait a minute. You were in *White Chicks!*" he said, his rocks crumbling as he made this discovery. "Hey, Floyd, it's the Bitch Fit girl!" Floyd Mayweather Jr. turned around, offered me his hand, and smiled. After he introduced his bodyguard and we had casual conversation, he looked me in the eye and said, "I wish you nothing but a lifetime of success and happiness. Big things are coming for you."

I had been blessed by the champ.

"HEY, AREN'T YOU A *Star Wars* fan?" Dave, the photographer, asked me as I buttoned up my trench. He wore a flannel shirt with a Sid and Marty Krofft—those famed puppeteers who created colorful children's television shows in the seventies and eighties—commemorative tee underneath, and when I complimented him on it, he bragged that it was signed by the lady who played Witchipoo on *H.R. Pufnstuf* and Charles Nelson Reilly. Nothing about his presence was threatening unless you were an In-N-Out burger. "May the Fourth Be with You is coming up. If you want to shoot something, give me a call," he said and handed me his card. "I have an authentic Slave Princess Leia costume the press would go wild for."

"Did you think being naked, with a cross covering your tits and practically none of your ass, was a good idea on Easter weekend?" my agent asked the next morning, and then he proceeded to list all the news sites that had plastered me and my dress across the Internet. The madder he got about it, the more I felt I had accomplished something. I was pushing buttons. His need to punish me made me want to act out more. I mean, what had he done but promise me he'd try to get me in to read for a guest part on *Modern Family*? And that never happened. I was tired of trying and trying and waiting and hoping. I was ready to do.

"Everyone is talking today. My fans love it," I said, and I could hear him scoff like a cat with a complicated relationship with a furball.

"Well, maybe you should ask those fans of yours to pay your bills because your career is going down in flames."

I could think of worse things than going down in fire—namely, dying slowly, like a cold, wet pizza box left on the side of the road, the rain pounding down its rejection until it starts to disintegrate, and all the tattered pieces of the name it bore once just slide down the drain. At least fire causes a disturbance and leaves no scraps of you on the way out.

My husband and I met Dave at a comic book shop on Sunset Boulevard the next week. Meltdown Comics would serve as the backdrop for our *Star Wars* celebration for May the Fourth Be with You. Dave had to fit me in the costume, which had elaborate wiring and pieces like a collar and cuffs and multiple chains. I immediately felt comfortable with Dave, even though I was completely naked with him in the back room of that comic bookstore. I felt he really got who I was and what I wanted to do out there, and he wanted to help me get somewhere. This was the first time he would dress me but certainly not the last.

"Now remember, you're posing as your favorite character, on your favorite holiday, so act excited," Dave said, though he's so curmudgeonly that even his excitement sounds depressing. I guess I took his direction to heart because what started out as some traditionally simple poses around the shop ended up with me pushing a Jawa head to my crotch. "Somehow I knew you'd be good at this," he said.

The store workers all stood around with slack jaws, watching as my boobs bounced and my skirt twirled around the setups and statues of *Star Wars* legends. The skirt wasn't actually a skirt but more like peekaboo curtains—one for the front and one for the back. I was wearing only a tiny thong underneath, which was a step up from the premiere, but if I turned fast or the wind blew, you could see pretty much everything. It was fun watching their reactions, along with the customers' faces who just happened upon this shoot. The place started to get busier, and I wondered if word hadn't spread somehow. That was exciting to me. Something about everyone shocked and watching me made me want to act out more.

"Too bad we don't have Jabba," Dave said with real planning and thought. "We could really do some things with his tail."

If the cross dress got headlines, the Slave Leia costume was its direct rival. This accidental encounter with a photographer on a carpet had launched me legitimately into another realm. I wasn't just shocking with sheer nudity; I was establishing myself as a professional cosplayer—and being offered money for it. This had always been something that I loved, but I never knew there was a possibility that I could make a substantial branch of my career out of it.

"I told you people would eat this up," Dave said, and with this immense success, we planned to shoot more with the variety of authentic costumes he had in his arsenal.

"Where are Leia's buns?" my agent cried into the phone, again listing off headline after headline I had embarrassed and enraged him with. When I told him that she didn't wear buns in *Return of the Jedi*, he called me a liar. "She was being held by Jabba the Hutt at this point," I said. "Well, leave it to you to turn intergalactic sex slavery into a promotional event," he answered.

While I knew how to wow and dare the press in my photos, Dave knew the ins and outs of the publicity game like the back of his hand. More important, he knew how to get these photos out to the various press agencies and for the photos to be noticed.

"It doesn't matter what you're doing as long as there's either a theme, a shock, or some degree of so-called accidental or totally purposeful nudity. The press will eat it up," he said. After decades of paying huge money to publicists who did nothing for me, Dave was getting me seen and out there and wasn't charging me anything. He would make money if my photos sold, which made me a hotter commodity and a bigger star.

Comic-Cons around the country were inviting me to attend, as interest in my cosplay was booming, and we would use these events to build interest on my social media and in the press. Dave had costumes ranging from Aeon Flux to Barbarella to Star Trek that were at my disposal to choose from. I wanted to play them all—so I did.

Dave sewed me into a Red Sonja costume at the Comic-Con in my hometown. There was a write-up on my attendance in the *Long Beach Press Telegram* and a line was waiting for me at my table on the main floor. But they didn't have real dressing rooms or facilities to change there, except packed bathrooms where Dave and I couldn't enter together. So Dave and I stood in the most glamorous of places, the hall where all the workers schlep the food back and forth, as he held a metal bikini against my breasts, using fishing wire to secure it. My husband took some funny shots of the whole thing that wound up all over the Internet and created a sort of fan following for Dave. #HeIsLegend, someone wrote underneath a photo of him lifting my tit to secure the piece under my arm. The title stuck. And the online legend of Dave was born.

"You're wearing bandages now," my agent said as he saw photo after photo me as Leeloo from *The Fifth Element*. "That's fitting. You look like you went to the hospital and lost your decency."

I gauged my success by his calls. If he didn't constantly sound like he was on the verge of an aneurysm, I'd think I was doing something wrong.

"Those aren't bandages; it's the costume," I said.

"It's disgusting and not what an actress with credits should be doing out there."

"But Milla Jovovich wore the exact same thing for the movie," I said, and he hung up on me.

Anything and everything became an excuse for a photo setup that would be sent to the press. Days like National Bubble Wrap Appreciation Day and Strawberry Ice Cream Day were causes for real celebration. Captain Kirk's birthday got a full sheet cake with his face on it and me making a sexy mess of it in a Star Fleet uniform. I made myself into a human ice cream sundae, and another time a salad with ranch dressing. We even faked a parking ticket once. "Act like you're pissed," Dave directed me as I found the "ticket," which was really a Jack in the Box receipt that I had placed on my own windshield. The headlines spoke of me outraged and fuming the next day, but that I also looked cute in cutoff shorts and my *Doctor Who* T-shirt.

I made Thanksgiving dinner with my feet, and Dave glued leaves on my breasts in a park bathroom in Beverly Hills to celebrate the coming of fall. Entertainment mogul Barry Diller was also in the park, which was awkward, especially when he gave us a thumbs-up when he passed by with his dog. We celebrated Christmas with me dressed as Poinsettia Ivy and the launch of the *Fifty Shades* film franchise with me tied up in rope in a random empty apartment we found open in my building. But it was Super Bowl Sunday that almost got us and two other photographers arrested, when I had to change football jerseys in the middle of the park and the cops got called. Flashing lights and a blaring siren stopped us mid–photo shoot and we were told over the loudspeaker to stop what we were doing and to hold our hands up after the cop car pulled up fast on the grass.

"Were you exposed in public?" the attending officer asked as he examined my license.

"No, Officer," I said with doe eyes, hoping that he might be a fan of

Tom Brady, as I was in an under-boob-revealing Patriots shirt. "We're just celebrating America's game."

They let us off with only a stiff warning.

I needed a redhead to kiss for International Kiss a Ginger Day. A friend of mine knew of a cute lesbian porn star who really wanted to do it. Elle was bubbly and adorable and a fireball redhead. All we were supposed to do is dress in lingerie for a slumber party setup and give each other little smooches to celebrate the event, but it quickly moved into more provocative territory. I could practically see Dave's lens sweating as the kissing got hotter, and we eventually lost all of our clothes.

"You're going to do something in the business one day," Elle said, referring to the world of adult entertainment. I brushed it off. "No, I'm serious," she said. "You're a natural."

On our first trip to San Diego Comic-Con with Dave, I was escorted out by security—again, for the nudity or, rather, the implication that I was nude underneath my costume. "But aren't we all really nude under our clothing?" I asked them as a breeze blew through and hardened my nipples, causing them to shoot out like daggers through the thin material I was wearing.

"We have family standards at events like these," the guy with the walkie-talkie told me as he led me to the doors, right past some violent video game setup where kids were killing zombies with assault rifles, and back out onto the street. "Nipples aren't for families."

"But this is a real costume from the movie *Logan's Run*," I said in my attempt at protest. Dave was documenting the scandal for later release. It was true that my costume was a legitimate knockoff of the one worn by Jessica 6 in the '70s cult classic film. It was also true that it was kind of see-through, but I was wearing panties this time. And you could really see anything only in direct sunlight and head-on, both of which the security detail at the open door were now watching me in. "Learn to keep your clothes on and you can come back in," he said.

I never did learn. But I did get back in.

...

DAVE INTRODUCED ME TO Mary Carey—the former porn star–turned-politician-turned–tabloid headline chaser—and she asked me to a Lakers game. Dave had been instrumental in Mary's publicity and, way back, her attempted run for California governor. Her campaign, armed with slogans like "Finally a politician you want to get screwed by," faced shocking defeat by Arnold Schwarzenegger. When I met her, she was dressed in jeans, talked about wanting to go back to school, and had a bubbly way about her. The game sounded like fun, but I couldn't give her an answer right away, and she didn't seem surprised that I needed so much time to check my schedule. That night, I found myself going back and forth on my decision. Could I—and should I—be seen so publicly with such a well-known porn star? I hated myself for grappling with this question, but I was. Once I finally said yes to her, only twelve hours before we were supposed to attend, I was constantly nervous about it and I couldn't articulate why.

"I know a guy here who will get us right up front and in the premier club," she said, guiding me to a room where wealthy men would bend all over themselves to woo our attention. We were handed courtside tickets and top-shelf liquor from the bar, and one guy even invited us on his private plane for a quick trip to Belize.

"They really treat you well here," I said as we sucked down some oysters followed by washes of champagne.

"It's insane how much guys will give when they know who you are and what you do," Mary said. "They'll fly you all over, buy you a penthouse and jewelry. Sports guys go all out. But politicians and actors too."

Just when I thought I had it all wrong about men and society—that they really could respect someone like Mary, someone who had been paid at some time in her life to perform sex—I sucked back one more oyster and I discovered that I couldn't have been more right.

Kareem Abdul-Jabbar walked in, with an entourage gathered around him. I was starstruck. He's tall and charismatic and looked so friendly as he shook hands with everyone in the place, going out of his way to sign autographs and to take pictures with them.

"Let's meet him," I told Mary, pulling her up from her seat even as she protested. "He's seen me before," she said, apprehensive now and holding tightly to her drink. "I'm sure he'd want to see you again," I said as I pushed us through the gathering crowd.

"I'm such a fan," I said as I reached out for his hand. He smiled graciously and took it and then turned to Mary and gave her a friendly nod. He talked to us for a minute and agreed when I asked if we could take a picture with him. Kareem smiled, tucking us under each of his shoulders while a passerby snapped a shot for us.

"See, he was so nice," I said to Mary as we walked away, though out of the corner of my eye, I saw him motion to a woman in a business suit and point her our way.

"Just a reminder: you can't put that picture up anywhere," the woman said, effectively stopping us from taking our seats. She was also eyeing my phone. I immediately put it into my handbag.

"Why is that your business?" I asked.

"We want to make sure Kareem is always seen in the best light," she said, and she cut a sideways glance at Mary.

"Well, he looks great in the photo," I said, and the woman stared me down. I couldn't believe this was escalating into an altercation.

"If you want to come back here at any point, I'd suggest you accommodate our wishes," she said.

I was about to really give it to her when I heard Mary's light and giggly laugh.

"Nothing is going up; it's just for us," Mary said as she took my arm to pull me away to the bar.

"Why did you let her get away with that?" I asked as she ordered us two shots of vodka.

"It's no big deal. It's just part of it," she said, right before numbing herself with a fast burst of vodka. "When you do porn, it's just the way it is."

I didn't put up the photo. I didn't feel it was my place to make waves and cause trouble for Mary, but I regretted it. And while I could throw stones at Kareem and his handler, and the world for humiliating and passing judgment on my new friend, I would be vulnerable in my glass house. Hadn't I been the one who earlier was afraid to be seen with her too?

All of it made me mad at myself, at Kareem, at society, and at a system where men in high places celebrate sex workers only if they stay in the shadows.

But why was Mary so willing to accept it? Where was the fight in her to say: *I am a person, and I deserve to be treated with decency and humanity?* Would Kareem, or his people, have asked any other fan not to put up a picture with him? Why was it okay and accepted in equal measure by both Kareem and Mary for this kind of thing to happen at all?

This bias that is ingrained in us from childhood runs deep and hidden. We're taught to run away from the bad people, and, somehow, among the kidnappers and robbers and killers, sex workers sit with them on top. The girl who has sex for money is somehow a peer of the man who robs and kills, though her motives shock and confuse us more. Sex workers have always been a favorite of serial killers, to use and to dispose of and to offer up to the voices in their head as sacrifice. Today blood is shed less, but the knife still twists.

If that night serves as one lesson to me, to live by for the rest of my life, it is this: always publish the picture.

AROUND THIS TIME, I began to delve more and more into the world of fitness almost religiously. I became a devotee to Equinox and Cyclehouse, a boutique spin studio. Eight times a week I rigorously cycled and mixed it in with boot camp or boxing. I did it for my mental and physical health, but I was also punishing myself, as always, for never being good enough.

While I didn't have an eating disorder in the technical sense, I was always part of an industry that valued disordered eating. You were applauded if you resisted food and if your ass was tight, no matter how many squats or revolutions of the flywheel it took to get there. If you were thin, you were treated better. But being thin was exhausting. That's probably how they want you so you don't have strength to fight back. Some part of me, ever since my time on *The Bold and the Beautiful* when I was alerted to my weight, has believed that if I am thin, I am good. And this belief system in Hollywood is constantly being reinforced.

I met a girl named Prudence in spin class. We got thrown together one day when Amanda Bynes tried to physically steal her bike. "Can I sit next to you?" Prudence asked, and I nodded. She had a hint of a foreign accent I couldn't quite place. We watched as Amanda proceeded to try and steal another bike, and then another, until the teacher threw her out. I thought "Prudence" was a funny name for a hot blond with almost violet eyes and breasts that never seemed to bounce while in motion, but it somehow worked for her.

I'd watch her on her spin bike, the lines of her body aligning with the bike in perfect form. But she wasn't perfect. She had an ass. I was shocked at how much of one she had and how much I admired the fact that her shorts didn't attempt to cover any imperfections. She just sat there on her bike, cheeks squished and spread out over the seat, her thighs rubbing together at the tops. Why was her body so perfect like this, and why was I always searching endlessly and hopelessly for that elusive thigh gap?

"What do you do for a living?" I asked her one day and she told me, "Oh, I'm in business." That perked my interest. "What kind?" I asked. She laughed. "Mostly wealthy men's wallets."

She was an escort who also stripped on the side. All of it shocked me. While Mary Carey, porn, and strippers were all one thing, escorting was entirely another. This was actually illegal. Yet knowing about it excited me.

"You'd be surprised at what men are willing to pay for," she said over lunch at a restaurant next to the gym. Mary had said that too, though it didn't feel like Prudence would ever let anyone tell her what to do with a picture.

"How do you meet them?" I asked.

"I have an agency," she said, like she was telling me she had a dermatologist. "I also strip and meet people like that."

"Do you ever feel objectified?" I asked, and she casually sipped her pinot.

"I control men's dicks. They should be the ones feeling objectified by me."

Her confidence was unnerving but also making me wet.

"Does it ever make you nervous—" I asked, nibbling at my salad with the dressing on the side, "I mean, to be naked like that in front of people?" I didn't mean so much in a sexual sense but in a more tangible, physical one. I was getting somewhat naked more and more, and I liked it, but I was constantly monitoring my body fat. This was why I did all the spin classes. This was why I ate all the kale. I can't tell you how many times my confidence was destroyed by the dimples on my ass.

"You should come watch me at the club one night," she said. "You'll see what I do."

I WORE FAR TOO many clothes when I walked into the strip club and found a seat. It was one of those places that doesn't serve alcohol, but you have to buy two diet Pepsis up front. I sat there with my two plastic cups, alternating between straws because I had nothing else to preoccupy me except for the man at the end of the row I was trying to ignore. I was highly caffeinated and about to pee when Prudence came out onstage. My jeans, lace shirt, and hobo sweater had me completely out of place and dripping with sweat.

I stripped the sweater off after she smiled at me and gave me a wink. The way her ass moved as she walked was mesmerizing. Each bounce and sway intoxicated the crowd. I noticed she too had dimples on her ass cheeks, but they seemed to have no effect on her confidence or her beauty. Her red stiletto heels marched past me and to a guy throwing out hundred-dollar bills her way. She leaned back onto the black, heel-scuffed stage and wrapped her legs around his neck. He was reprimanded by security quickly when he tried to touch her, but I knew she would let him later—for a price. So did he, because he passed her his number.

I could see what she meant about the sexual power she held over these men. It was her talent, and it was a thing of art.

"When their dicks are hard, they'll give you anything," she said after the show, showing me this man's card, and all the money he had thrown at her for not much more than shaking her tits in his face and demonstrating her flexibility. "If they'd just make what I do legal, all the girls' lives would be so much better."

She turned me on to legalizing prostitution, a concept that was foreign to me. It had been ingrained in me that prostitution victimized women, that they had to be drug addicts or homeless to get to the lowest point a woman could possibly reach—the desperation to sell her body on the street. Prue informed me a lot on the subject—how prostitution itself was actually not the reason women were living in such deplorable conditions, being beaten by their pimps and johns, and suffering in silence. It was the laws in place to punish them that were doing the real harm. They had no voice. And they couldn't even turn to the law when any bad thing happened to them because they risked punishment themselves.

"GIRLS SHOULD BE ABLE to report if a guy beats them up or someone rapes them, or someone steals from them, don't you think?" Prue asked, and I agreed with her, and I wondered if she had been in a scary situation like that. Was she so impassioned from deeply personal experience? So I asked her. "I can kick a guy in the balls before he ever sees it coming," she said, and I believed her.

Model and entertainment personality Amber Rose was hosting her Slut Walk in Los Angeles, and Prue asked me to go. "All these people marching for sex workers is going to be amazing," she said as she fitted me with a T-shirt that said: "Sluts Rights: We Came, We Conquered, We Came Again." I liked how bold the words felt printed across my chest, but I was also keenly aware of the fact that someone could recognize me and maybe they'd think I was some sort of a sex worker too. Did I care? Should I?

"Are you one?" some guy marching next to me on the hot, sweaty streets of Los Angeles asked me, directly referencing the shirt. "A slut, I mean," he said. I didn't know how to answer it, but Prue jumped in with a jubilant laugh, "Absolutely, she is," she said, and she knocked me off-balance when she pulled me into a kiss.

The guy just looked at us and then said, "Cool, because I'm one too."

"Let me be your slut," she said to me that night, with her fingers deep inside me. She had told me we should go to her place to drop off our signs before we grabbed dinner out, but the signs had barely hit the floor and we were undressing each other and then tangled up on her bed. I wasn't really planning on having sex with her, but it just happened.

I told my husband all about it, and again he was encouraging about my need to explore sexually with women, but he was concerned about her secret lifestyle. "Just be careful she doesn't get you caught up in something dangerous."

I agreed—though all of it with her felt dangerous already. That was kind of the point.

"Ken is coming over later," she told me one afternoon as we lay in her bed. "Who's Ken?" I asked. "The guy from the club with the money," she said as she stood up and put on her robe. "You want to watch?"

This made me nervous. I certainly did not want to sit in a chair in front of them, watching them fuck, and I'm sure this Ken guy didn't want that either. And there was no way I was joining in on anything.

"Stay in the bathroom," she said as she readied herself in black lingerie. The strangle of the panties against her flesh accentuated those ass dimples. It was hot. "Just stay in the dark and peek through the door," she said.

I sat down on her toilet, on the magenta furry seat cover, picking at my thumbs as I heard their whispered greetings at her door. I was so nervous I was going to be caught that I almost hit the handle to flush.

I watched as she excused herself to freshen up in the guest bathroom, after he handed her an envelope that she took with her. I guess she was counting the money in there, but I didn't really know how it worked. I watched as he jerked himself off, lying back on the bed as he waited for her. He wasn't good-looking but not bad either. A dad bod with a buzz cut and a farmer's tan. I was amazed at how beautiful Prue looked, in full seduction mode now, when she returned from the bathroom.

It was hot to watch in this front-row voyeur's seat I had been given. I touched myself through the lace of my panties as she lowered her mouth onto his dick, asking what pressure and rhythm he liked. He wore a wedding ring, as I could see the glimmer of white gold as he squeezed her breasts. I couldn't make peace with that, though, so I chose to ignore it. I completely came apart when she lowered herself down onto him and rode him, the dimples on full triumphant display as her ass spilled over his body. He made a few grunts and then it was over. There was no cuddling or real afterglow at the end. He just threw the condom in the trash, gathered his things, and left, telling her he'd call her for another appointment.

"How was that?" she asked me with the stretching back of a cat.

"He was married," I said, surprised it bothered me so much and that I brought it up. "Does she know?"

Prue laughed.

"Sometimes marriages are saved by these things," she said.

I thought a lot about that. How an hour away with a prostitute could give a man like Ken release and relief in order to face the daily grind. His wife would probably have a burst of new energy and vitality if a muscled sex god went down on her for an hour. I had been granted a degree of sexual freedom in my marriage, and it had only strengthened it. I do believe a marriage can be bettered by recognizing it as unique and consensual and your own. What I couldn't come to reason with were the lies.

Prudence moved to Miami at the end of that year. "A new guy got me a condo right on the beach, and I can drive his Ferrari whenever I want," she said, yet this bragging felt less like freedom and more like indentured servitude. She would go where he wanted for a price. But was the price always worth it? I guess that's a question you ask yourself in any job. I guess I wanted to judge her and her lifestyle in that moment because I just didn't want her to go.

"I'll be back," she said, but she never was. She was on Facebook for a while, but when I saw my friend count tick down one day, I knew she was gone. I also knew she was okay, out there somewhere, living the way she wanted to. She had just purposely disappeared into a world that society didn't have light for, and I wished all the more that it did.

I will always be grateful to her. She's the reason I've continued my spin classes and also made some peace with my ass dimples.

I FIRED GLENN AFTER he called me a whore, though clearly not because I took offense at the term. More and more, I liked being known as a woman who goes after something she desires with lust and zeal, and unapologetically. The word *whore* meant more to me than just a body count or a quenched thirst for forbidden lust. It meant unabashed freedom. But in his mouth, it was venom, and I refused to be bitten by his shame.

It all happened shortly after we returned from the Sundance Film Festival. We had experienced a full week of parties and festivities, and all of them made him brood. He liked when I walked the assigned line and followed his itinerary, but he didn't like when I forged paths on my own.

"You're going to embarrass us," he said as we stood next to the ski lift. Adrian Grenier, the star from *Entourage*, had just hopped off, and I grabbed a photo with him, which made Glenn cringe as I posted it to Instagram.

"With whom?" I asked, all the while I was texting someone who could get me into a gifting suite with Lil Wayne and Kellan Lutz. They were giving away top-dollar ski equipment. I didn't ski but it still felt like an opportunity.

"The industry talks," he said.

"So why not give them something to talk about?" I asked.

He hated that I got so much attention from cosplay, and he especially didn't like the risks I was taking when it came to sex. "Michael isn't happy about this," he said, as if that would be the thing to stop me. I was so tired of what Michael and Disney and the rest of the world were unhappy about when I was finally making myself happy. I was tired of everyone treating Michael like he was God—the father sitting on his throne of judgment that the little girl must beg forgiveness of. It's twisted religion, misogyny, and complete bullshit. Anyone who tries to shame you for living in truth and happiness isn't looking out for you. That's a fact that takes too many of us, especially women, far too long to learn.

As *Girl Meets World* continued with production, the talk intensified as to whether my character would or wouldn't come back, and most of it depended on whether I would start to behave. But my pearl-clutching displays weren't the only problem with a possible return to the universe. I was realizing that I didn't want to go back—not just because I didn't want to relive a character that I'd played on *Boy* but because it wasn't *Boy* at all anymore. They were ruining characters and stories left and right, and it was just plain bad.

It broke my heart to see what they did to Trina's character, Angela. What started out on *Boy* as a groundbreaking interracial couple was now diminished to a sad breakup that saw Shawn marrying the expected petite blond bride. Any progress with inclusivity and diversity that was made on the original show was now ruined. It left me with the ill feeling that the pairing we'd come to love was relegated to something rebellious that Shawn did in his youth. A regular white American guy couldn't be seen actually marrying a black girl. But it was totally acceptable for Cory and Topanga to marry at nineteen. This and other sensitive story topics were dealt with so poorly on the new show, and with such little regard to their complicated reality, and who the audience had grown up and whose kids were growing up to be, that it made me uncomfortable. And the fact that these serious topics weren't handled with care or given weight, yet my frolicking around in a bikini with a Hula-Hoop was sheer sacrilege, really proved to me where everyone's hearts and heads were over there.

Still, it was Michael Jacobs who I believe made sure there would be no return for Rachel, regardless of my hesitations or feelings on the matter. He never asked me about that or anything else. We never talked at all. And no, it wasn't because this was a kids' show and I did porn; this was well before any of that. I know it was Michael, in all his fatherly wisdom, who wanted to exert his authority over me this final time. He clearly left a spot for me open in the episode where Jack returns to see Eric, but I knew he would allow me to appear in the episode only if I begged forgiveness from him. He didn't tell me any of that, but I felt it glaringly when I watched, and I'm sure that he knew that. Rachel was talked about as a far-off ghost, an enigma, someone long gone and disappeared. But if I had crawled to him on my knees and apologized to him—for what, really?—he would have placed me in those gaps he'd left open. I know he would say that I owed an apology for my indecency or my audacity or my stunts, which he felt lessened the value of his show and that I owed an apology to my family and to God. But I believe the real thing he wanted an apology for was that I was finally stealing the spotlight for myself.

The cast photo taken for the finale of *Girl Meets World* has every member from both shows posed in it except me.

But that's the photo I'm most remembered by.

That final straw with Glenn came when he saw me dressed in green paint for a San Diego Comic-Con. Let me revise that: when he saw me on the *Daily Mail* having the green paint put on me by men's hands and then washed off my ass in a shower as part of an exclusive story and video. "What are you trying to be—a porn star?" he asked. And I took a moment to pause. Pornography wasn't something I was considering.

Yet.

CHAPTER 12

WHILE THE MAJORITY OF fans of *Boy Meets World* are levelheaded, everyday, rational people, there is another subset of fans who live in the dark while proclaiming loudly from behind their screens they are living in divinely ordained light. That's the group of extremists and fundamentalists who somehow believe *Boy Meets World* was a program sent down to earth through their televisions to proclaim the truth of their biblical God and that I am Judas betraying their Jesus, who I guess is Ben Savage—and all because they saw a shadow of a nipple on my Instagram post.

"Thank YOU for ruining my childhood," one girl wrote on a post where I covered my tits with a hand bra in a shower. Suds obscured the bottom part of me, but you could still make out the shamrock tattoo. "Only sluts do what you do," another wrote, to which I replied underneath, "You mean bathe?" The post was erased within hours by the Instagram police—even though it violated no rules—but not before the woman responded that she was praying for my swift entry into hell.

"You have violated our terms," read every email from Instagram—or Snapchat or Vine; all social media platforms offer the same message of punishment and empty regret. It was happening more and more. As soon as this troop of antinudity slut shamers saw me put up a post with even the least hint of gleeful promiscuity or the possibility of future undress, they'd get on their bandwagon and, much like they voted Carrie Underwood to victory on *American Idol*, report it until it was taken down. None of it dissuaded me, though. In fact, it made me want to enrage them all the more.

I began to think of even more ways I could push the limits and really piss the haters off. This delighted my fans and had them rooting me on like their favorite sports team. If I hadn't had this kind of negativity thrown my way, my fan base might not have grown in the way that it did. My fan community believed they were fighting a good fight with me and that we were all in this together. And that was all true.

My nudity and sexuality would be my online martyr's plight. Joan of Arc was persecuted by these Christians too, wasn't she? *Maybe there's a photo shoot in that.*

I had hired a new publicist named Dax. I'm not sure why I did. I was finding success with Dave and the photo agencies, and I was all over the entertainment sites and blogs, but when I met Dax at an event, he convinced me that I needed more. "You don't want to be known as carpet trash," he said. When I inquired what that meant, he told me they were "the girls who are all over the British press for being ridiculous but never get offered a job."

"Nobody wants to see you be sexy in Hollywood," Dax told me in a way that was supposed to sound helpful, when I told him how my fan base was really growing with the things I was doing. His response? "If they want sexy, they'll find some twenty-five-year-old in a bikini, not you." This was the most glaring commentary anyone had made directly at me regarding my age and the hopelessness of my winning the war for my cause. In my late thirties, I felt far from old, and I was feeling more empowered and sexier than I had ever felt before, but he succeeded in shutting me up. In a matter of moments, he had me feeling hopeless, vulnerable, and guilty for not being twenty-five anymore. Oddly, that made me believe I needed him.

I had found Dax through a friend. I shouldn't have trusted him: he was the kind of publicist who wants to be in all his clients' photos and walks the red carpets by himself, but he appeared to have connections, as he got me into some good events and told me of job opportunities. "I know the guy who got Tara Reid into *Sharknado*. She's a star again," he'd dangle in front of me. In a subtle way, he was letting me know that he was working for me, but that a movie about a shark tornado was the biggest thing a girl like me could hope for.

He called me late one night and told me that *Playboy* was interested in shooting me, which was odd coming from him. "They like the 'all grown-up' *Boy Meets World* angle for a spread," he said, and the way he enunciated "spread" made me uncomfortable.

"I thought you said anything sexy was bad for my image," I said.

"No, it's fine in that magazine. That one is known. It's just not acceptable on your social media for just you to do," he said, and he was slurring. "Look we have to act fast. They just need you to send over some nudes to make sure you look good naked. You could just text them to me now, and I'll send them over to the people."

I looked at the clock on my microwave, which read almost midnight, and could practically smell the tequila coming through the phone. Right then and there, I hung up on him.

That wasn't our end, though. The end came shortly after when he set me up with a potential manager who wasn't a manager at all—the guy who supposedly got Tara the role in *Sharknado*. I came to the coffee shop prepared to talk about what I wanted for my future and my career, but it was clear this guy knew nothing about the business. He didn't even really know about *Sharknado*, as I had attended the premiere and knew too much. He couldn't answer basic questions or give me any real thoughts other than telling me Dax was a genius and that I should just trust him. I knew this guy wasn't a manager, and it was just one of his friends pretending, even before I investigated his name and his firm. They were nonexistent. Dax had sent over information and photos before that weren't even real.

I fired Dax immediately.

The whole instance made me question the long line of toxic professional relationships I had allowed into my life. It all stemmed from the belief instilled in me when I was young that if I pleased some higher-up who knew more than I did, I would be given things and in turn be made a star. Much like how little girls are told to wait for Prince Charming, I was told that someday my chance would come. But for all the times I smiled and performed their tricks and even played dead when they told me to, being a nice, sweet girl never got me anywhere. In fact, it got me passed over and forgotten. And here I was finally succeeding on my own, paving a way for myself that I was told would never work, yet I was still looking for that chance to come and kiss me awake from a coma it put me in.

HOLLYWOOD IS NOT A fairy tale. But they'd all like you to believe that it is in order to keep your attention focused on jamming a foot into that elusive glass slipper.

The only way forward was to bury whatever I had been and hold my own funeral.

I covered my vagina with a panda emoji on New Year's Eve, and that's really what started it all. I wore a black-and-white faux-fur jacket at midnight, with nothing under it, for a live Snapchat party and I covered all the good stuff with the little bear emojis on my phone. I figured they matched the ensemble, and the way I placed their faces, it looked as if they were getting a taste of something good. When the new year struck, I popped champagne all over myself and cried out, "Free the panda!" from my balcony. That became a battle cry for my Wardiors, as they called themselves—those soldier fans of mine that were championing my cause. We all dreamed of a world where one day I wouldn't be censored or relegated because I'm a woman who loves sex and showing her own body. I was doubly inspired when my neighbor shouted out from the opposing balcony, "I'm on the other end of freedom! And what a view!"

"You should sell your content," a fan wrote to me on Twitter, and others chimed in after I tweeted out how frustrated I was that all my photos and videos kept getting taken down. I didn't know exactly what that entailed, but from research, I saw creators making money while being able to post basically whatever they wanted. I saw one girl made $10,000 a month, but that seemed like a lofty goal. I was only planning to do cosplay nudes and lingerie shots. How much could anyone be willing to pay for the possibility of seeing my nipples?

On a whim late one night, I started a Patreon account. Patreon is a platform where artists and entertainers—and even naked bakers—go so their fans can subscribe and be patrons to their art. I didn't know if what I was doing was art, or if the naked bakers were being hygienic, but I went with it and signed up to be an adult creator. I laughed after I made the page. I couldn't imagine people actually subscribing just to see me nude. I closed my laptop and went to sleep, thinking that I'd probably erase the whole thing when I got up. But when I woke up the next morning, I had twenty subscribers and hadn't yet mentioned it to a single soul.

I had 2,800 patrons by the end of the week, zooming to the number one spot for adult creators pretty much literally overnight. What I'd thought might earn me $500 or even $1,000 a month, was sitting at almost $40,000 in less than three days. I kept texting Dave the new numbers as they climbed, and he said, "Maitland, you're going where no one has ever gone before."

And this was true. In the blink of an eye, I had shot up to become Patreon's number one adult star. An account manager wrote to congratulate me. She mentioned how impressive my demographics were and how ardent my base was. My fan base that started growing when I was seventeen had now blossomed into an all-out army that was happily willing to throw down big bucks for my content. Money was never the motivation to try this out—I was just yearning for free speech—but the dollars that came in were so eye-popping I had to keep pinching myself. There was no press announcement that made this a reality, no big moment to pull from. It was, like many of my other great moments, something that just went viral. Was it the *Boy* fans, the cosplay audience, the appetite for provocative content, or me having such a strong social media presence? The truth was that it was all of it. And all of them were ready to embrace me in my new frontier.

Dax was officially wrong: people did want to see me be sexy.

I PLANNED MY FIRST premium Snapchat show meticulously. My husband recorded me walking down the hall in my red high heels. Each clap of the stiletto against the wood would inch the camera up higher to discover my legs and then my ass. I would reach a shower, where I would kick the heels off before submerging my naked body under the water. It was exciting to perform like this, with everyone watching. I finally had the freedom to show my body with no restrictions, and I wanted to do more and more.

I hadn't perfected my art yet or purchased a ring light—the pinnacle of professional illumination that says you're serious about being seen glowingly on the Internet—so when I later masturbated in the dark with my Hitachi, all you could see was the shadow of me gyrating and the sound of the vibrator. "I can't see her vagina but it's still hot," one fan said. I ordered lighting equipment from Amazon the next day. And when I got it, I felt proud that my pussy would always be seen in its best light.

Pirating was huge in the beginning. While I was free to post whatever I wanted, the fans also felt free to post it all over Reddit to nonpaying customers. A subset of even my most ardent supporters had become angry that I was charging money now for all the work I was doing. They wanted nudity for free and felt I owed that to them for the rest of my life. This was an eye-opening experience for me, and something girls in porn and sex work have been dealing with for ages. Some men on the Internet feel entirely entitled to a woman's body and will disparage, demean, and target her when she finds any real success with it. They didn't believe I was allowed to make a living with my own body, especially not such a good one, so it was an endless struggle and fight to keep these Internet abusers and bullies away. Photos had to be watermarked, and only the highest-paid tiers got the really explicit stuff. But the controversy they swirled around me served to broaden and strengthen my brand and attract new subscribers. And to this day, the vast group of them buy every scene I do and every product I make and then downrate them to a 0 just to put the whore in her place.

I FOUND MYSELF A changed person after this all began. I had new confidence and a full-time job, and it wasn't because I smiled for any higher-ups. The validation that I was given, especially after being told that no one would ever pay a dime to see me sexy, was soul changing. I can never thank my fans enough for that.

It changed my confidence out in the broader world as well. For so many years, all I could say was that I used to be on *Boy Meets World* or I was the girl from *White Chicks*. I got numb to amplifying my past while trying to avoid any talk of what I was doing in the present. Even if I was doing a ton of interesting things in my personal life, I was brainwashed into believing that nothing else mattered than a Hollywood job. But with the money I was making on Patreon and the notoriety I was getting, I didn't have to hide anymore or conform. People accepted and celebrated me for exactly, authentically who I was and were excited to discover along with me who I was becoming.

And I didn't need Hollywood for any of it.

Dave and I launched the paid photo galleries by doing sexy cosplay shoots. I'd dress as a favorite character they'd seen at the Cons and then progressively take my clothes off. I used various sex toys. Dave was unfazed by my nudity and anything sexual. "I'm a hundred years old. I've seen it all before," he said, and though nothing shocks him, the fact that I now had a full-time career that paid better than a Beverly Hills surgeon and that had all been birthed from our wild setups did. For nostalgia and by high-volume request, we shot Slave Leia on the beach for May the Fourth that year. The shoot involved my husband in a Darth Vader suit fucking me with a lightsaber on a beach in Malibu at 6:00 a.m. I then posed the way Carrie Fisher did in the waves on the cover of *Rolling Stone*. A true dream realized.

I started following some other sexy girls online—mostly influencers but also some girls in porn—to see what they were doing. While the bikini model types were traditionally hot, they felt stiff and boring to me and entirely too airbrushed. They looked flawless and liked to go out on boats in high-end vacation destinations with sugar daddies a lot, but they never took any real risks, aside from giving their old lovers heart attacks on the open seas. The porn girls, however, were raw and willing to show everything when it came to their bodies and sexuality. This intrigued me; I never wanted to be seen as the kind of creator who would keep it safe.

By popular demand, I brought Elle, my Kiss a Ginger friend, back. This would be the day that I would take my content to a whole new level. "I knew we'd be here someday," she told me between our tongue-twisting kisses all over the bed, right before she parted my legs. When she spit on my clit and her fingers fucked my hole, the reality set in that this was really all happening. Dave shot the photos, and my husband shot the video. And everyone saw me orgasm from another woman's tongue.

My appetite had just been whetted.

I DECIDED TO HAVE sex with a man other than my husband at a hotel in downtown Los Angeles—one of the tall ones with chandeliers and cucumbers floating in chilled water carafes at reception. I hadn't met him yet, though I liked him as soon as I saw the video of him fucking the babysitter while some other woman (I think was his wife) slept. He had a British accent, and his dick was large, but honestly, I was more impressed that he was six-three. He would arrive at four and I would be in lingerie, waiting with a thousand dollars in cash. Lights would be set up and a shade of lip color that couldn't later be confused for shit or blood would adorn my pout. This event would be captured on camera for profit—and my husband would be bedside to press Record.

My interest in performing with the opposite sex hadn't been something I was completely conscious of. It had come to me in dreams and in intrusive thoughts and had spilled out from my pen and onto the paper.

"Wouldn't it be cool if you dominated me with a crop, threw me in the air, and we reverse-cowgirled, and then I projectile squirted all over your face?" I asked my husband one evening while authoring some erotic prose for a bedtime story I would read to my Patreon subscribers. I had been coming up with wilder and more acrobatic scenarios in these pieces, and I wanted us to try them out, but while my husband is well endowed and a giving and intimate lover, being an acrobat or drowned in showers of my unicorn piss while hoisting me into the air and flipping me over his shoulders like a caveman wasn't something he necessarily aspired to. "Don't you have to be athletically trained for that?" he asked.

My erotic stories kept getting more detailed and specific, and the stakes in all these scenarios kept getting higher, almost as if I was challenging myself to go too far. I was fascinated by power-play dynamics, those extremes that I had always been drawn to but was too afraid of. As a younger woman, I would fantasize about such things but with the mindset that they could never really play out. Now there seemed to be more possibility. That frightened me, but in the way a scary movie might. The fear is part of the thrill.

While it's true that these fantasies I was having may have been ignited by the burgeoning success of my new profession, they had always been there, burning slow like a cigarette propped on an ashtray, discarded with the hope that it would eventually burn out—the glowing flame suffocated and then lost like ash in the wind. But they just kept smoldering. And I would find myself waking in the night with my fingers stroking my clit and the bed sopping with my wetness after some forbidden dream.

I wasn't missing anything in my marriage. We were happy and had everything you could want—intimacy, trust, stability, and love—but marriage doesn't bring a person happiness completely. Still, I was trying to escape these intrusive thoughts, the ones I tried to bleed onto the page so they'd be left somewhere and forgotten, but they just kept coming back. Could I go through the rest of my life wanting to do something, and needing to satisfy some deep place inside myself, yet stamp it out because I had everything else that I needed at home? Or would my marriage eventually break because I needed something else, and I couldn't have it?

Still, I had never made any suggestion that I be with another man. I wouldn't do that to my husband. I kept all thoughts of it to myself, which is why it surprised me all the more when he made the suggestion himself on a lazy Sunday afternoon.

"I think you need to try these fantasies out," he said, and he was calm and sure with his words. You could tell he had given them great care and thought—and he said them with bravery. "With other men."

"I couldn't do that," I said. The suggestion rattled me—less because he'd suggested it and more because it was like he was looking inside me and demanding truth from some part of me I had tried to hide since birth. He was good at recognizing these places in me.

"You'll never be happy unless you do all of the things that you want to do," he said, and he took my shaking hands.

"But I'm happy with you," I said, and I meant it.

"But you won't be one day if you're denied this."

I broke down and began to cry, really cry, for several quiet, ridiculously loud minutes. Relief and the terror of being so seen flooded my hands and my lap.

"I see how you love to perform," he said. "You're better than any porn star out there I've seen. That shocked the fuck out of me."

"Me too."

And we both burst out laughing. I reached over and blew my dribbling nose on his shirtsleeve.

"And maybe this is a way for you to do this," he said. "What we're doing now with your content. I don't know . . ." He was searching for the words in the ceiling cracks. " . . . in a controlled and professional way. I could be there. It wouldn't be like cheating. You've taken your fans this far. Why not blow everyone's minds?"

"You would be okay with that?" I asked, and he looked me in the eye and said, "Only if there's complete honesty between us."

It was the most connected I had ever felt with a person in my whole life. I had never had anyone look at me and recognize my twisted-up sexual desires as something valid and real and necessary and as something that had the possibility of being good. I'd never expected that my husband of all people would be the one to embrace the taboo nature of who I really was. But he had shown me before when he recognized my need to be with women, and he was showing me now again. And a good marriage is all about showing up.

My husband is not a cuck, contrary to what the Internet—or you—may believe. Not that there's anything wrong with this particular kink and lifestyle, but it isn't ours. The thing that is especially insulting about the cuck assumption is that my sexual constitution is authored by my husband's desires—that it would be impossible for a woman to do these things on her own—and even more impossible that a husband who wasn't jerking off to it would let her. Even in the most open-minded circles, the immediate assumption is that I wouldn't be doing any of it if my husband's cock didn't benefit in some way.

That really takes power away from a woman's story.

We made a list of all the things we required to be comfortable with the experience. We would choose someone who wasn't after personal gain, could be emotionally detached but also give me a full-blown out-of-this-world experience. He would also have to be someone who followed strict STI testing protocol. We needed a professional porn star. I decided to ask around.

Neither of us saw this as cheating or stepping out, but more of an experiment. I wasn't looking for an affair; I was looking for an experience, and I know that's hard for some people to grasp. Being a performer has always been at my core, and sexual performing is an extension of that. It's who I am, like a dancer is a dancer and an artist is an artist. I'm always asked why Terry isn't afforded the same sexual freedom as me, but he would be if he wanted it. He just doesn't have that need in himself to do it, just as he'd never be an actor or violinist. But neither of us is going out there looking for hookups and dates.

Looking back, it's remarkable how sure and comfortable we were with all this. I know it all seems unbelievable because the most honest things always are, but I truly believe that when you find the path destined for you, it walks itself.

The night before I was to have sex with Danny, we had classy fish and a good wine at a restaurant near the water. We also talked about the ramifications of what was about to happen. Would it change us? In what direction would we grow? How would other people in our lives, especially our families, perceive us if they ever found out? The world at large was getting so much closer to knowing everything. We both felt ready as we finished the bottle of pinot grigio, but how would we feel afterward, when wine and oysters and good intentions weren't making things so rosy? We had sex that night and afterward stared up at the ceiling, holding each other, before making a pact that whatever happened, we'd be okay. If either of us wanted to stop it, all we had to give was the word. The word we chose, probably after too much pinot and seafood, was *tilapia*. Although we were both open-minded adventurers, we knew we were about to experience the unknown.

I HAD MET SOV a few years earlier when I was doing a St. Patrick's Day photo setup. Elle had introduced us. She also worked in porn. We were leprechauns who splashed around in a green tub with green bubbles, all dyed green from the cheap beads we wore and the glittery shamrocks covering our nipples. We remained in casual touch over the years, with the occasional *like* on Twitter, that is, until I started doing content shoots.

Suddenly she was like a groundhog looking for her shadow—or that leprechaun again looking for literal gold.

"You're looking for guys to shoot with?" Sov asked me. "I could hook you up."

And hook me up she did, with a huge name in porn, Isiah Maxwell. That wasn't the only thing huge about him. I had wanted to inch my way into sex with men on camera, and I did so literally with all ten inches of him in my mouth. It was the first time I had ever choked on anyone that deep, and in that way, and it was so thrilling that it later demanded cough drops.

"There's a bit of a slut in you," Sov said, with a strange envy as she watched me gag on Isiah's dick. The slobber and the mess had her rubbing herself but also shooting daggers as she sat on the bed's edge. Like the slut in her was jealous of the ferociousness of the slut in me. We were like lionesses in the wild, two competing animalistic sluts in heat, only we were both on birth control, a fact Sov later commented on, saying that the lack of danger in a creampie—an internal cum shot in lay terms—had made her vagina depressed.

She tried to grab the dick away from me to share as I gagged on him, and saliva ran down my chin. We both sucked him for a moment, competing to see who could deep-throat him the filthiest, until Isiah threw me on the bed and proceeded to eat me out. Let me tell you, there is nothing like an award-winning professional going down on you. I screamed so loud security came to check on us.

Isiah was nice and funny and had me and my husband, who was recording all the footage on an iPhone, at ease as soon as he walked in. Isiah was also Black, which I didn't even think about until both Sov and Isiah warned me that there would be racist fans out there who would try to make an issue of it.

"I can't imagine any of my fans would be like that," I said.

But they were right. When I posted a simple smiling photo with Isiah on my social media, the vile, hateful comments flooded my timeline.

"You've been ruined by a black bull now," a man with Confederate stripes on his profile pic said; another told me I needed to get down on my knees to apologize to my daddy, and I think he meant him. My husband was an immediate target and called terrible names. "Cuckboy can't keep that white pussy satisfied. A black man's gotta give her that baby," one guy wrote, and there were others who echoed that. I lost followers over it. These types of people, if I can even call them human at all, get off on degradation and shame and this antiquated racial fetishism and misogyny. They love to watch white women get destroyed by Black men, like the women are meat and the men are animals all performing for them. But when they fire at you, they expect you to cry and run away. But I wasn't crying or running, and I never would.

"I think I might date him," Sov said, referring to the Brit I was now about to fuck in the hotel room. She had set me up with him too. Sov was becoming my headhunter of sorts. I figured that since she was in porn, she'd know how to navigate these things, and since this was going to be a full-blown, full scene of penis-in-vagina sex, she'd also help document the event from different angles. She'd be a sort of pussy cam. Sov really wanted to be a porn director. I think she also really wanted a boyfriend. "He dates a lot of the girls in porn. He married two. I think we have a connection."

Danny, my British-porn professional, arrived on time, just as Sov opened two Asahi beer bottles. "What the fuck does this hotel think, it's a fucking sushi bar?" she said before chugging her longneck. Danny was clean and shaven and surprisingly polite for a man who was about to throw me on the bed and fuck me senseless while my husband filmed us.

"Don't worry, he's okay with it," I said to Danny about my husband, clutching my own longneck and fully realizing I was just moments away from clutching his.

"Well, I hope so, or he might clock me in the middle of it," he said, and we all had a laugh, which served as a good icebreaker.

He and my husband had a chat about football, both American and

European. Sov then popped my boobs out and played with them, while she filmed a bouncy little intro to the video I would sell later, before butting into their conversation with some story about how she was a direct descendant of John Hart and some people in Scotland with a castle. "*The* John Hart?" Danny asked her, and she gave him a nod and a sultry grin.

Within fifteen minutes of meeting him, Danny had carried me to the bed, which checked two fantasy boxes of mine: to be fucked immediately by an almost absolute stranger and by a man with the arms of a beast to carry me places.

It was all a whirlwind from there. We jumped around from position to position, with him guiding all the action toward the camera, which was something foreign to me. "Open up your right leg, so the camera can see your pretty vagina," he said. He was really in charge of our scene here, and I loved that I didn't have to think. I just followed his lead in this sexual dance. I was able to lose myself in everything and let completely go. During the whole thing I kept waiting for the nerves to kick in or for my husband to shout out "tilapia!" but it never happened. I was okay, and so was he. Society had pegged the whole thing wrong.

And society wonders why so many marriages end in divorce.

Right before Danny put his dick inside me, Sov whispered to me, "Are you ready to show the world you're no longer a Disney princess?" I looked up at her and then at Danny—who looked confused as hell as to why she was asking me this and also reaching over to tug on his balls simultaneously—and then, most important, to my husband. There was a moment of heartfelt and soul-searching eye contact, something deeper and more connected than anything we had faced before. I nodded to him, and then I said that I was ready because I really was. I was ready to give that young, frustrated, terrified young woman inside me her voice.

And she had waited a long time to scream this way.

The whole thing was fun and freeing, and none of it felt like infidelity. It was a performance, but it was also the real me exploring a side to myself that I needed to get to know—and my husband had seen and recognized that. And just as skiers feel exhilaration as they race down a hill or a singer feels exuberance hitting that perfect note, my orgasm came from these heights and that landing. And then it came again, and then came once more.

"How do you feel?" my husband asked as we sat there in the room afterward, taking turns drinking from the last bottle of beer. The rest of the world would expect us to be broken, but we were fine.

"Like myself," I said with a smile. "Finally."

And I knew that the path I was now traveling was my own.

MY FANS NEARLY HAD heart attacks when they saw the footage, and people were racing to steal and post this video. I had such satisfaction that all the naysayers were completely shut up too. Those people who said I would never push any boundaries or take any chances were speechless. "She'll just shake her tits around for a few months and then she'll take off with everyone's money," one Reddit user had said. The truth is, no one believed a Hollywood actress would have sex on tape without having to pretend it'd been stolen and then cry in utter shame about it—because that's what EVERYONE who has a sex tape does. But there I was, happily fucking a man for all to see, and I had no regrets.

I realized something important: no one can shame you when you regret nothing.

The truth is nobody can leak a sex tape for profit. It's federal law that any sex tape that's on shelves or on pay sites must be accompanied by a signed document authorizing permission from those involved and two forms of valid identification. So, no, I don't believe Kim Kardashian and Paris Hilton were terribly wronged when those sex tapes were leaked. It doesn't take a brain surgeon to figure out that those were probably big-money deals made ahead of time and used for the sole purpose of gaining fame and profit with them, which they did. Everyone in the porn industry has to provide permission on camera and those two forms of identification for every single scene that they do. While scandal and weeping regret create headlines, and also a way out for celebrities from owning the fact they fucked for fame, these tears they cry are crocodile.

When I later asked Danny what he remembered about that first time, he said that he thought that I'd be nervous and was surprised that I wasn't. "You just jumped in there and immediately gave it your all."

And for a porn star with almost fifteen years of experience to say that to a girl on her first time, that takes something unique.

I would later shock myself with the realization that maybe porn was my God-given talent.

I BEGAN HAVING SEX with both Danny and Isiah regularly for content. Every month we'd think up new scenes, my husband would shoot them, and my subscriber list would grow. I was having a lot of fun and living out my fantasies, but I was learning from them too. I didn't realize it at the time, but this was my training ground, and these were my teachers. They were patient with me and caring as they taught me valuable techniques and tricks of the trade. If I hadn't been so lucky to find such nice, respectable men to work with right off the bat, things may have turned out differently. I may have given up or quit. And I certainly wouldn't have had such a master class in the art of porn.

I really have to thank Sov for her guidance too and for setting me up right.

I loved using the holidays and comic book themes for our scenes, much like I did in my former press setups, only this time I would be holding Santa's sack in a whole new way. And instead of me making Thanksgiving dinner with my feet, a big-dicked Pilgrim would just eat it off them before stuffing my turkey.

For Christmas, Danny played Santa Claus, and he gifted me with a camera guy and makeup artist to up my game. "You need to make it all really professional looking now," Danny said. "You're ready for it."

I got along with Cammy, the makeup artist Danny provided, immediately. She wasn't what I expected of an adult industry makeup person. She was sweet and bubbly, and she felt like someone you could trust. My robe kept slipping open as I sat in her chair because the silk was slippery and my tits kept falling out. And I kept apologizing, to which she responded, "Don't worry. Being naked is nothing to apologize about." So I finally stopped. And she was right.

I spoke at length to Cammy about where I envisioned my career path doing adult content might lead. "I want to make something where I can act and have sex," I said while she was applying eyelash strips to my holiday gold-glittered lids. "Something people want to watch for the story but that has really hot sex in it too." Cammy stood back, waving her hand over my eyes to help dry the lash glue, and thought about that.

"You should talk to Bree Mills," she said. "She's a film school–trained director and she's got a whole Adult Time channel over at Gamma, which is a big porn production company. They're looking for more scripted porn, and they could really use good actors. You'd be perfect with her."

I was taken by the fact that not only was there genuine interest in quality writing and acting in porn out there, but there was a woman at a big company wanting to make it happen.

At the end of the shoot, she texted me Bree's information, and I added it to the contacts on my phone. I would pull it up time and again, preparing myself to pursue a meeting with her, but I didn't. I looked at all the stuff that she had done and I was impressed, but something just stopped me from going any further. Maybe I was nervous, or maybe it just wasn't my time yet.

Or maybe I hadn't met the right person.

Sov set up a threesome with another girl, Marley, for my birthday. While I was getting made-up, they were talking about the AVN porn awards weekend they had just been to. "Lansky just signed Kayden Kross on to launch a new brand," Sov told the girl.

I didn't really know what they were talking about, except that Greg

Lansky was the creator of Vixen, a high-end porn site that I had been a casual fan of, but I found myself intrigued to listen.

"Yeah, and she won director of the year," Marley said. "They're calling it 'Deeper.'" Sov looked at her with the curious envy of a woman who would love to be in the position that Kayden Kross was now in. "I bet they're planning to do something big with it," she said.

I didn't know at that moment that the *something big* was going to be me.

CHAPTER 13

"**H**OW AM I GOING to put that thing inside of me?"

It was a question I asked myself when I first met Jason Luv on the set of *Unprofessional* for the website Blacked—the scene where I would make my first big professional porn debut. Jason, my costar, introduced himself to me while stroking his cock. It wasn't creepy, though; it was just part of the job. He had to be hard and ready to plow me from behind, in front, on top, and with my leg stretched straight above my head from the side, and that took preparation. Jason was tall and robust with tattoos covering him and a grill in his teeth that made him fierce yet adorable when he smiled. But it was the massive organ in his lube-slicked hand that had me wondering that if by the end of it all, I'd have entered orgasmic nirvana or I'd finally know what childbirth was like. I went to shake his hand but when I did, I accidentally smacked his dick, and what's worse, I embarrassingly apologized directly to it. "It happens a lot," he said with a shrug and then the production assistant handed me my bottle of douche.

They call it "doing girly stuff," which basically means they send you to the bathroom to douche and clean yourself with baby wipes, so that everything smells clean and nothing falls out unexpectedly. This is also a time you can "warm up," getting yourself aroused and lubed up and ready for the scene. "Your pussy will look prettier if you rub one out," I was told, and encouraged to masturbate. "And you'll have a natural glow." As I stood bent over a bathroom counter with a window view overlooking Los Angeles, sticking a baby wipe a half inch up my asshole to make sure nothing alerted anyone to the fact that I was a human who shit, I heard a truck blasting Talking Heads' "Once in a Lifetime" outside, and I too wondered, *How did I get here?*

Vixen, the Lansky-helmed production company that owns Blacked—a site dedicated to high-class, high-glossed, interracial porn—had been following my story on social media and also watching my content with Isiah who was one of their site's biggest stars for some time. Some weeks earlier, they had called to see if I was interested in making my professional porn debut.

I first took note of Vixen a few years before when I saw Tori Black, one of its biggest contract stars, in a photo shoot where she hung out of a helicopter above Los Angeles. There she was, classy and in control, as she flew over the city, dangling her red-soled shoes out over the edge, almost as if she was daring the earth to steal her back from her place soaring next to the sun. It was both terrifying and exhilarating, and the photos belonged in the center of a fashion magazine.

Shortly after, I watched one of Tori's feature films with the company, and I was impressed with the script and quality, as well as the cinematic depth. I could've been watching anything on Showtime or HBO, except for the hard-core fucking scenes that served as raw, sexually impactful tentpoles to the story. But there was actually a story, and it was good. I didn't know at the time that the blond girl smoking a cigarette in a bathtub scene was also the writer and director of the piece. I didn't know yet that it was Kayden Kross.

"Should I do something this high profile?" I asked my husband as soon as I got the call from Vixen. I was hesitant. Sure, I was making all my own adult content, but this was professional.

"Isn't this what you've been talking about? Taking it up a level?" he asked.

He was right. How many times had I spoken aloud my dreams of filming something on a professional level—something big and beautiful and filthily grand? While my productions were hot and fun, they could take me only so far. I didn't have a film crew on hand, just a guy with a camera and a few borrowed sets. Plus, I wouldn't admit it to anyone, but I knew that I needed to do a professional scene for my own bucket list. I never wanted to look back and say that I was good, but I was too scared to go all the way.

"If you're going to come out big, this is the way to go," Isiah told me when I went to him for advice. He had worked with them for years now, and he had been a manager for talent in the industry before he was a star, and I knew he would never steer me wrong. "They're always professional, and it's like you're on a film set."

A film set in porn is what I'd been looking for, but somehow, I still couldn't give my firm yes.

Ricky, an agent in the industry, also approached me about a professional career around this time. "There's such interest in you out there. We at the agency can really make you shine." I didn't know much about porn agents or who Ricky exactly was. I did know that the owner was an ultrapopular performer whose career path was impressive—she had taken her MILF star status and turned it into a branded empire. Half the time she was an award-winning sex star, and the other half she was a married mom in Michigan. Porn had afforded her both lives. "We'll take small steps, as fast and as far as you want," Ricky said. This sounded good to me, so after giving it some thought, I agreed to try them out.

"Why should I let you do porn?" the girl we'll call Kat, who I had been having semiregular sex with, said as she pounded me with her strap-on. We were experimenting with power-play dynamics. Dominance and submission were extremes that had intrigued me for some time, as had the world of BDSM, and Kat really got off on dominance. "You're mine now," she said.

"But I already shoot with guys. And other girls. I'm married," I called out as her nails dug deep into my hips. My hands were bound behind me with thick rope so I couldn't move. My husband was fully aware I had been seeing this girl and encouraged me to have fun with this experimentation, but I wasn't sure I was having fun now. It felt like a sexualized version of my grandma waving that golden-framed Jesus picture in my face. I shook my head and closed my eyes. I didn't want to imagine Jesus or my grandmother wearing a strap-on.

"Yeah, but that's different," she said. And she punished me more with her rubber dick.

This girl, a mainstream actress people would probably know if they saw her, had direct-messaged me on Instagram. We had met some years earlier at a charitable event for the homeless, and I thought she was hot with her wild hair and intelligent yet rebellious nature, but her message in my inbox surprised me. She had seen a few shoots that I'd done with a tattooed girl for content, and they'd turned her on.

"Your girlfriend is beautiful," she said. "But I have a longer tongue." She ended it with a winkie-face emoji—the one with the tongue sticking out so you know that it's sexual but could also be played off in the aftermath of rejection. I wrote her back and told her that the tattooed girl wasn't my girlfriend, just someone I use for shoots, and then asked her if she wanted to have lunch.

I chose a place out of the way, by the beach, as I didn't want any paparazzi taking our picture. I needed to discover her before anyone discovered us. She was there before me, drinking some amber liquor over a large block of ice in a lowball glass. I ordered an Aperol spritz as I never like to drink too much in the daytime and I thought it looked classy—like it belonged in the hand of a girl with windblown hair on the coast of Capri. "I guess I'm the alcoholic here," she said with a laugh. I watched the way her lips hugged the glass and that long tongue she bragged about licked the rim. When the ice knocked up against her, she didn't flinch.

"So we came here to fuck, right?" she asked as she put down her second drink. The ice clanked against the glass and liquid sloshed out. Mesmerized by her boldness and the nipples I could see piercing through her Guns N' Roses tank, I just nodded my head in agreement. Everything about her mesmerized me.

And fuck we did. All afternoon we lay in her bed pleasuring each other. She had so many sex toys, I wondered if she had a side business. "I love this clit vibe," she said before she hooked it on her tongue and used it on me. My whole body shook as the hum rolled over my clitoris. And it didn't stop the whole time I was with her.

"If you want to explore BDSM, we could do it together," she said, and she told me all the experience she had. Her whole bedroom felt wicked and as if it could be converted into a dungeon if she pressed a hidden button. "I want to bring you to your knees in submission." I told her I'd like that too.

"VR Bangers wants to shoot you," Ricky said on the phone. "They called this morning." By this time, it was late afternoon. Ricky rarely woke up before one and usually fell back asleep after two-thirty. If you wanted anything from him, it was best to call Mr. Furley's Bar in the valley after ten at night and have them shout out, "Your cat is on fire!" so he'd actually come to answer the call.

VR Bangers is a virtual reality porn site—one that requires the viewer to wear a headset to feel as if they're right there and part of the action. The guy's face is never shown, only the dick, so the fans can imagine that they have a nine-inch schlong they're satisfying you with. VR Bangers was open to me doing whatever I wanted, and I have to say I was intrigued by the concept. It was new technology that was becoming more and more popular. I thought my fans would love it, so I agreed.

My husband dropped me off to the first shoot. I knew it was on the up-and-up, but I still wanted him to know where I was, how to get me if someone tried to kidnap me and sell me into sex slavery, and for the production assistant to be warned that a man was aware of my last whereabouts. "He'll be back in a few hours," I told the production assistant in a firm, loud voice. "He knows the way up here and he's going to be waiting very close by for me to be finished." The PA just smiled and said, "Your brother can watch if he likes."

They didn't seem swift enough to be kidnappers, so I sent my husband on his way.

"I guess you're the one my dick gets to act with today," my scene partner, Will, said as he introduced himself with a hug and a smile. "Well, it won't be the first time my costar is a dick," I said, and we both laughed. Will had been in the military but had an injury that led him to pursue stunt work, and then mainstream acting, and then, suddenly, on a dare, he did porn.

"Mainstream and porn are really the same thing," he said. "The guys in mainstream just don't have dicks they want to show off." I laughed because I knew firsthand that was true.

We talked about metaphysics and jujitsu and video games, all while only partially clothed. I couldn't believe I was having an intellectual conversation with a man who was caressing his manscaped balls. During the scene, I was to speak directly into the camera—and also the little ASMR ears attached to the sides of it—while doing whatever I wanted with this man's headliner. They had me read erotic stories as a dirty sex therapist, much like I did for my content on Patreon. It was fun and quite empowering. He was stuck there behind this giant metal VR contraption that required a team of strong-armed professionals to free him from as I made him explode onto my reading glasses.

"You know they're just using your name to get viewers," Kat said as I lapped her pussy with my tongue, collared and leashed, on her black satin sheets the next evening. I sat up and looked at her. "Well, yeah," I said. She just shook her head and then pushed my face down to her pussy to pleasure her again.

Kat was complicated for me. While I was becoming more and more of an independent and give-no-fucks kind of person, I also became more and more reliant on her dominance and reprimand. There was still a place in me that equated my happiness and freedom with the need to be punished for them.

I couldn't figure out why I couldn't let go of that, but I started to get hints.

"Don't you ever want to work as an actress again?" she'd ask me, usually after telling me of some great audition she'd landed or invitation to an industry party or festival she'd received. And I never knew how to answer her. "Maybe, if the right opportunity comes along," I would say. But sometimes, after I left her, that question would make me cry.

"Vixen called for you again," Ricky said one evening, just before he left to have martinis with himself. I had been avoiding making this decision, but I knew, like Ricky does at 1:58 in the morning, that this was last call. "I'll let you know tomorrow," I said.

"Okay," he replied, "but make it after one."

"YOU CAN'T BE AN actress ever again if people see a dick shoved in your mouth," Kat said to me over dinner. She was shoving pasta into hers, something she never did because she always wanted to lose five pounds and was never out of control.

My possibly becoming a porn star was really pissing her off.

"But they've seen it," I said, slowly sipping some water, watching this limp noodle massacre. "And I thought you said what I do is hot."

"Nobody even sees what you do now," she said, and I put my glass down. "I mean pervert fans but not like executives or anybody up top that matters. And when people do find out, you can act like all those girls do. You can cry about it and say you were at a low point and on drugs or something."

Like those girls who cry the crocodile tears.

She was dismissing me, and everything I now was, and this wasn't part of our experiment. More and more she was trying to purposely hurt me. I could only hold on to my rage and sadness by imagining each of her drippy, white noodles attaching themselves directly to her thighs.

Why was I continuing to accept this from her? Why was I sitting there and forbidding my tongue and lips to move so that she could continue to speak over me? Because she was a "real" actress and I wasn't anymore? Because she had a big agent who got her big meetings at big studios and big networks, and I had been cast out? With all the success I had found and all the work I'd put into it all that nearly bled me and broke the bones that had me now, finally, standing tall, why couldn't I just let her be gone?

But I still just couldn't.

Looking at her there, with her judgment and reprimand and her need to dismiss and yet still control me, I realized what attracted me to her in the first place: she was the complete personification of Hollywood. And I needed her to like me.

"I'm doing the scene," I texted Ricky in the car, before I drove home. And while I couldn't let her be gone just yet, I needed to do this on my own and prove something to myself.

"I'm proud of you," my husband said as we climbed into bed the night before my shoot. I was nervous but looking forward to it. "I think it'll be okay," I said.

"Are you kidding? You're going to knock their socks off," he said just before we fell asleep. "Nobody beats my girl."

It was 9:02 a.m. when I walked onto the set of filming for the Blacked site. The penthouse was stunning, and a man met me with a robe and bottled water. It was exactly like any other mainstream film set I had been on, only we had to hold our IDs up to our heads, while being recorded, to give our consent to fuck on camera. There were several dozen pink and white roses waiting for me in the upstairs bedroom with a card thanking me for being part of the Vixen family. Chanel tweed suits and Louboutin shoes were laid out on the bed for me to try on. It felt like a dream. "They do a photo shoot just like *Vogue*," the wardrobe girl said. "Downtown may smell like urine, but it'll feel like you're walking in Paris."

I was playing a married real estate agent who was tasked with selling a massive penthouse to a sports hero, played by Jason, my cock-stroking new friend. Of course, after the successful sale, I make a proposition. "Everything is included in the deal" was my line, as I pushed him against the wall, felt up his hard dick through his pants, and then the scene would go from there.

His dick didn't make it into me on the first several tries. "Damn, you're like the tightest girl I've shot with," Jason said. "And that's saying something." He laughed, and I said to him, "Can you quote that on the box cover?" I began to panic that my porn career was over before it began, but then I wondered how a vagina in porn can be fired for being too tight. That might actually up my street credit. I could see the headlines now: "Maitland Ward's Vagina Is Too Tight for Porn." But all my worry and headlines of legend would prove to be preemptive. After we kissed and warmed up a little, and he poured lube onto himself, my vagina gladly accepted the length of his entire shaft—thick and hard and pulsating.

I think they expected me, unsure and new to all of this, to be timid and shy. They didn't expect the beast in me to be unleashed.

"Yes, yesssss! Destroy that cock! It is your destiny," the French director screamed out as I rode Jason to pleasurable destruction. We fucked in every position; hard and fast, slow and passionate. I had never experienced such a large dick in this way. The sweat was dripping, our hearts pounding. Jason's dick was stretching me in such a glorious way that I wanted more and more of it. "Take it all and speak the filth that comes from your soul," the director said, and boy did I give them filth. I became a wild woman, completely untethered in the throes of this cinematic passion. "Fuck me until I don't know my name," I said at one point and Jason obliged. We joked afterward that I would now forever be known as Marissa.

"That was what dreams are made of," the director cried out, right after Jason came all over me. I knew we had shot something special, but what really floored me was the compliment that came next. "You're such a good actress!" he said. "We never have those."

I hadn't acted in anything on film or television for thirteen years, and I think a part of me was resigned to the chance that I never really would again. But porn had just made me an actress again.

I left there with a smile on my face, holding the vase of my flowers in the town car ride home. The cast and crew had made the day enjoyable and professional. I had been on a real set again, and that made me proud. The director said he hoped I'd come back for butt sex or maybe a gang bang. "You would be fantastic being plowed by six or seven really monster-cocked men," he said. And it was the nicest thing I'd heard in a while.

Amped from the wildly successful shoot, I agreed to film a scene with Brazzers two days later. "They're doing something super special for you because you're a star and they really respect this agency," Ricky said. I wasn't sure if I respected this agency, and I didn't know why a whole conglomerate actually would, but I was excited to fuck and act again.

I wasn't given the scene until I got to the set, which I thought was odd, but I guess it isn't in porn. I sat in the makeup chair, eager to get to my lines, when I realized I didn't have any. None. Zip. Zilch. I didn't even say *hello* to the guy before we had sex. I just swam in a pool, walked inside, and got fucked.

"This is a mistake," I muttered to the makeup artist, but she didn't seem fazed when I showed her the page—it was a generic scene pasted together and photocopied, which included sketch art of a girl in a bikini doing various things that would entice a man for sex. I later would find out they had to put in drawings so no one would have to bother to read the words. "Oh yeah," she said. "That's one of our go-to scenes."

I would see this exact same scene play out multiple times, with different talent, in the coming months.

While this was not a scene that would harm or demean me, it was just stupid, and it made no sense. They had a trained actress there. Why not throw a few lines together or have me ad-lib a story? And at least give me an original scene, preferably one without pictures. I brought this up to the director and he just laughed it off. "We're not making Oscar films here. This is porn."

Brazzers and its parent company, Mind Geek, are arguably the largest distributors of porn in the world. Their brands, including Pornhub, have such a reach in the market that they are responsible, whether we're fully conscious of it or not, for how we view porn—both literally and as a more metaphorical whole. My thinking is that Mind Geek has realized that people love to masturbate and they love porn, but their formula also follows the belief that these same people are uncomfortable with the taboo of watching it—or rather admitting to watching it, so why not make it all a mindless joke and laugh all the way to the bank? By dumbing down everything for their audience, their profit margins increase, even as the perception of porn's value as anything more than mindless jerk-off material plummets. If you watch any of their scenes, it's all big-eyed expressions and over-the-top ridiculous setups. I could never see how anyone could be turned on by a guy making wild googly eyes straight to camera, while a girl in a cock-eyed nurse's hat slobbers all over his cock-eye, but the model has obviously worked extraordinarily well for them. Just like McDonald's feeds our nation, Brazzers feeds our need and our fear of sexuality by leaving us full and yet still empty.

Now, is it wrong to enjoy a hamburger? Absolutely not. But is it wrong to think that cuisine can't possibly exist beyond hamburgers? Absofuckinglutely.

And when you eat a big, juicy steak, isn't that more satisfying?

When people tell me, "but it's just porn," my response is: Why does it always have to be?

My scene on Blacked came out on a Saturday, and the site crashed from the traffic. For thirty minutes, fans were sent messages telling them that they were working on repairing some technical difficulties and that the scene would be up in its entirety soon. I hadn't alerted any press to the event, and to this day I'm shocked that TMZ never caught wind of it. Just Barstool Sports said, "Everyone was hung up on Topanga, but Rachel is clearly the one making the statement here." Other than that, it was a completely grassroots, viral event, driven by my following—both my fans and my haters showed up in droves and droves. The scene broke all records for the site and all its brands and will go down in history as the site's most searched and sought-after scene on release day. Greg Lansky personally sent me a note thanking me for my work and for choosing the Vixen family.

I was on cloud nine.

That same Saturday, Kayden Kross was beginning to film her first big feature film, *Drive*, with Deeper. For months she had worked on the detailed script, planning all the shots and formulating her directorial vision, even after having been warned by everyone at Vixen that it was too soon. The brand had only been around for four months; she had another year before she needed a release of this depth and scale, but she wouldn't hear it. It had to happen now.

They were already under the gun. It had to be finished by the end of the month. All the planets had to line up.

Drive was set to star porn superstar Angela White and a temperamental starlet who told Kayden and the crew that day that she would complete this first scene only once her medication arrived. She was stressed by the high floor they were filming on and by a mass shooting that happened the day before. Only Vicodin and her weed-laced vape pen could quell her anxiety and pain enough for her to blow the task in her hand. Of course, the drugs didn't come right away, so she held the cast and crew hostage for four hours. While it started off fine, the scene began to devolve quickly. Her eyes began to roll to the back of her head, and she became incoherent. At one point, it looked as if her head was going to roll off her body, and the scene was stopped. No one in the company, especially Kayden, would tolerate this kind of behavior, and they knew they couldn't expect her to last for a lengthy and time-sensitive shoot—especially with all the dialogue Kayden had written. Kayden had to get rid of her, and she did so immediately, but it isn't easy to replace a star in porn, especially one who can deliver a somewhat believable line.

Kayden went to Vixen that Monday, after a weekend of my Blacked scene's record-breaking success, and told them her ordeal. "I need someone for this role, or we have to shelve it," she said. She expected that they'd tell her to call it quits and to wait until the following year, like they had before. She didn't expect the words that followed.

You need to talk to Maitland Ward.

I GOT THE CALL from Ricky on that Monday around noon. Kayden had been trying him all morning, but he had been sleeping off some binge. "I don't know where this came from," he said, and he sounded excitedly shaken. Like the president was on line two and he wasn't sure if he was getting the Medal of Honor or the red button had been pressed. "Kayden Kross called me. She wants to meet with you about doing a feature film with Angela White and her husband, Manuel Ferrara. It's for the new brand at Vixen—Deeper."

Kayden Kross—the one Sov and Marley had talked about.

We were to meet at a Starbucks that afternoon in the Valley.

I read the script as soon as it was sent over, and I actually pinched myself after I was finished, not believing it was a real thing. This was a mainstream-quality script with real words and characters—and, thankfully, one that didn't include pictures, though I could see the vivid descriptions so clearly. I was floored by the depth and complexity of this full-length feature, and even more so that it was penned by a woman—this woman whose name kept running parallel to my journey in whispers, and it literally fell into my lap.

I GOT TO STARBUCKS just before the hour and ordered coffee. As I waited, I grew more nervous, and my heart was racing. Maybe it was the coffee, but honestly how many coffee meetings had I been on in the past when I didn't get the role?

My career before porn had consisted primarily as a series of blue balls. But maybe that was the point. Maybe literal ejaculation was the key to my success. I pondered on that as I sipped my drink, telling myself that I was my own woman now and calling my own shots. People were obviously responding out there. The Internet literally broke over my scene. Maybe this time would be different.

Kayden Kross walked in moments later, the little bell on the door alerting me that she was there. She was dressed in Lululemon pants, with her long blond hair pulled back tight in a ponytail. She was effortless in her beauty, and I was intimidated when we sat down with our coffee. She wasn't like anyone I had met in porn so far. She had an intelligent assuredness that was as striking as her looks. While I fiddled with my hands and my coffee and an errant straw wrapper discarded by the customers before us, she didn't seem nervous at all.

She opened a notebook as soon as we sat down, and I suddenly feared being graded. I was relieved when I saw that she wasn't taking notes on my appearance or personality; it was just the script we'd be going over along with shooting dates on a calendar.

"I loved the script," I said to her, though I tried to play it cool, but you can only be so cool while nervous sweat from your ankles drips into your ballet flats. Her green eyes lit up. "You read the whole thing?" she asked, and as I nodded, I wondered why she seemed surprised.

Oh, that's right; there are girls who are used to reading picture scripts.

I didn't want her to know that this was the kind of acting role that I never thought I'd ever be offered and also a part for the actress inside me that I thought mainstream had left dead. I didn't want her to see me as some rotting Disney Princess corpse brought back to life and whose entire survival depended on the consumption of human cocks. I wanted her to see me as more than all of that, and it really felt like she did.

"I changed some things to suit you better and added some dialogue for your character," she said. "You're a real actress. We want to use you to the best of your abilities."

I smiled, beaming as I bit my lip to control its quiver. Fuck Hollywood and its continued dismissal of me. Fuck those picture scripts. Fuck those who shunned me and kicked me aside and told me I would never be a performer, or a success, or an actress again at all. Fuck everyone who made me think or made anyone else in the world ever think that you can't be everything that you are.

"This is what I've been looking for," I said to her, and I felt tears welling up in me that I knew I'd cry later.

"Well, that's what I want too," she said, and I think there were some unshed tears in her eyes too.

We arrived there that day as two women who traveled on much different paths for different reasons and wanted to prove something to a world that refused to take them as seriously as it should.

We left there as two women about to make a movie.

CHAPTER 14

NEARLY GOT MUGGED AT a stoplight right before turning into the warehouse we were using to film *Drive*. It was near a homeless encampment in downtown Los Angeles, and there was a constant whir of helicopters overhead. "We'll gate your car in," the production assistant, Marc, said as he directed me to a spot. "And if someone knocks a window out, we have insurance."

This was a far cry from the luxurious penthouse where I'd filmed for Blacked. I figured it was an aesthetic choice. After all, we were doing a pounding sex club scene where I would play the physical embodiment of Angela White's sexuality, leading her through chaos on a chain. We were spiraling into the dark unknown. I wasn't selling real estate anymore.

"You can go to wardrobe first and then makeup," Marc said. He was gruff, had an eye patch over one eye, and emptied packs of Marlboros all day with calloused fingers.

"Which are those rooms?" I asked as he led me through the warehouse. The paint was chipping on the walls and the pipes made noise. With a cigarette hanging off his lip, he nodded to one single room that housed a worn director's chair, an empty clothes rack, and a mattress with only a flat sheet. "You could sit on the bed," he said. "No one has used that one."

What happened to the Chanel box coats and array of Louboutins? This was a Vixen production still, wasn't it?

I didn't yet know that Vixen didn't fully believe in the box office potential of these scripted projects and that Kayden had fought tooth and nail to get them to film it that year at all. I did have an inkling when she told Ricky that her budget was so tight that she could only pay me half my going rate, which arguably was the highest in the industry. And I accepted it because I wanted to do this project so much.

But this set felt demeaning for her and for what we were setting out to create.

There were a lot of girls there that day. The sex club required numerous bodies and extras. Watching them all gather and chatter made me feel like the new kid at school, but not one from somewhere like New Jersey or Arizona—rather, someplace far away and exotic and whose language they didn't speak. "Are you one of the extras?" some young girl in thigh-high white boots and feathers for earrings asked me. I just shook my head.

Kayden showed up with a suitcase full of wardrobe, and she fit everyone at once in this little makeup/wardrobe/dressing room setup that was really just the largest room there. The whole thing reminded me of a fashion show right before all the models take to the runway: chaos and activity and the designer pricking her fingers with pins and cursing the bent clasps on the bras. Kayden was definitely stressing out. After introducing Angela and me to everyone as the stars of the film, she had to run out of the room to take care of an electrical problem. We hadn't even really said hello to each other yet.

I held Angela White on a dog collar and chain almost as soon as I met her—the designer kind that looks both expensive and dangerous. She was gracious and kind as we walked onto the set, thrust into taking photos for the DVD box cover. I had been nervous to meet her, an icon in porn. I wasn't sure how she'd react to me suddenly being the costar of her film, but she greeted me with a warm hug and her comforting Australian accent. "Well, if I could choose anyone to be my inner sexuality, I would choose you," she said with bright blue eyes and a smile, "even though you kill me in the end." She and I shared a laugh, and as the flashbulbs went off, she told me I could tug harder on the leash.

In no way was this a glamorous job. The setting we were working in was gritty and uncomfortable. There were no dressing rooms or craft service tables. Any dreams of mainstream star treatment I had to immediately leave at a door that once you walked through, sealed you away from any humanity or light. I curled up most days on an old, ripped couch in the corner of the warehouse, going over my lines. Like a trained studio brat, I'd sometimes get teary over this boot camp I was experiencing. I had a stark realization that so much of what Hollywood had been to me was now ripped away, and yet something was being reborn and given back to me too. I was being gutted and hollowed down to bare flesh and bones and the lines on the page. In the past, as an actress I had been caught up and consumed by the flashes and the stardom and the thrills. I hadn't realized that so dramatically until I sat there alone, with nothing but my lines, on that couch.

"You don't have a dressing room?" Kat asked me over the phone. I had called her on my break. I felt the need to check in with Hollywood.

"Porn is different. There are no real dressing rooms," I said, and I was trying to whisper as I spoke to her in a bathroom with a chain flush and creaking pipes. The rust stains on the walls denoted trouble. "Besides, I've been on a bunch of indie film sets. None of them are glamorous."

I could practically hear her rolling her eyes, but luckily the pipes were louder.

"It's so nice to have a real actress," the cameraman, who also worked in mainstream, said to me as I stepped onto the set to film my first big pieces of dialogue. "The girls with a lot of lines usually have to have them fed to them or taped to their partner's chest."

In my entire career, I had never been thanked for my work and my talent. And to be called a real actress now, after I had been doubting I would ever be one again, really hit me. How many auditions or jobs had I been on where no one cared that I'd stayed up all night to memorize the lines or stressed to make the lines good? I felt acknowledged by the cameraman in that moment and smiled and thanked him genuinely for a compliment I hadn't known was so necessary.

Kayden and I didn't speak much as she tied me up into my corset or gave me direction on set. I could tell her mind was in a million places. I had imagined us collaborating as director and artist, sitting down over martinis and pages and applauding ourselves for all our great ideas, but she was up to her chin in stuff I had never seen any director be responsible for. "Tell them to slide the cheese off the pizza if they're vegan," she yelled out to Marc when faced with that pressing dilemma. It was a solution, and I could see that's what she worked all the time at doing—solving the problems and solving them fast. I didn't know if she could risk the time to sit down and talk about anything. And even though she could use one, she definitely couldn't afford to be tipsy on a martini.

The stage was quiet and filled with lights and haze when I stepped out and began to speak. I was nervous that I wouldn't have what it takes anymore. It had been sixteen years since a movie camera filmed me for *White Chicks*, and though I thought I might be rusty, the moment Kayden called action, those words that she'd written for me fell from my tongue, and they all fell into place.

"That was so wonderful," Kayden said after the scene was done and wrapped. She was quiet for a moment. I don't think she expected to hear her words like that. Most of the girls who read her words don't really say them. But I brought them out from a place that was deep, from the gut, and somewhat jarring. And I think that was confronting for her. It was confronting for me too.

"How was it?" my husband asked when I got home that first night. I flopped back onto the sofa and let our two dogs cover me with kisses. "I thought the windows of my car might be knocked out, but I loved it," I said.

He looked confused.

"I'm not sure if she really likes me, though," I said, referring to Kayden. "I mean, I know she's stressed and busy, but we don't really talk. Maybe a part of her misses the other girl."

I don't know why these thoughts weighed on my mind, but they did—probably because she was so cool and wound up around me all at once, and I didn't know how to process this. I couldn't tell if that was the truth or my insecurities talking, but they were jabbering in my ear all night. Maybe it's because I sat on a torn couch all day and listened to the weeping of old pipes. Maybe I've never been forced to sit in one place and really listen to that.

Just like Kayden hadn't really been forced to listen in any true way to the words she had been writing. No one had ever really delivered them.

"Your call time for the second day is at ten," Ricky said on the phone, while I was actually driving to the set on day three, and then he dropped the phone. I could tell because I heard a crash and then him wrestling with his cat. This became a running joke that Ricky couldn't get any messages to me, and that Marc should just bypass him and give me the call times himself.

"He's always visiting his dying mother at a hospital with no reception," Marc said to me as he smoked his cigarette outside the warehouse on a break. "Except sometimes it's his sister."

Marc, though a bit gruff, resembling a lifelong pirate and on the razor's edge of a fight with nearly everyone, had taken a liking to me, and I to him. I'm sure he thought I would be this diva actress coming in, but by the end of the first week, he had softened to me. He wanted to help. "Ricky's a disaster," he said. "You shouldn't put up with him. You're too good for a guy who gets liquored up with his cats before hospital visits."

The day I was to film my big sex scene for the film, a stool our photographer was standing on to adjust the lights collapsed, and his leg was crushed under it. The guy was immediately sent to the hospital for stitches. I still remember the screams and Kayden yelling for towels saying there was "a lot of blood!" And then Marc telling me in detail about this guy's protruding bone. I didn't witness anything firsthand. At the time I was practicing taking a banana down my throat. There was a special shot where I would be doing this; it wasn't particularly sexual, though a banana always conjures up those images. I wanted to take it down deep and relatively sexy, and without choking on the stalky end. I discovered I was good at this trick.

Amid the chaos, the set dresser had canceled on Kayden at the last minute, and she was hanging up all the draperies herself. The place was supposed to look like a speakeasy boudoir. Burlesque. "He told me at ten o'clock last night he'd be here to take care of everything," she said after I asked if there was anything I could do to help. She wasn't going to cry—already I knew that of her, but I know that she wanted to.

My period decided to start about three thrusts into my big scene, but I hadn't noticed. I was notified there was an issue when Kayden yelled, "Cut," and moved to us. I was having sex with her husband, Manuel, at the time, so I feared she was angry. Images of her slapping me, pulling my hair, and throwing me off his dick flew through my mind. "I saw blood," she said, standing over us. I looked down at his giant member and saw it for myself. In my haze of panic and sex, I initially didn't process what was going on and said, "Did he cut himself?"

Razor pussy was a joke in some circles for a while.

"I have a bag of makeup sponges in my tool bag by the Lysol cans—under the electrical tape," Marc said as he moved to rummage through it. I was handed a triangular cosmetic sponge and instructed to put it up my vagina. That's what the girls do when they're on their periods. It's shockingly effective at catching all the blood up there while no one is the wiser when the act is going on. Then if the guy's a gentleman, he'll help you fish it out at the end. I just hoped that whatever I was putting up in me hadn't lingered too long with the Lysol cans.

While I kept fearing a gusher of blood might be set off with how intensely he was pounding me, the scene went great. It was passionate and raw. He was the kind of performer who challenged me and brought something real and tangible out in my performance. He was that rare performer I connect with in this way. I worried it might have been a little too raw. This was Kayden's life partner. I knew she watched him have sex with women all the time, as does my husband with me, but I also felt she saw me as an outsider still. A girl who had gone on vacation to the Great Barrier Reef only to wet her toes.

I QUICKLY DISCOVERED THAT the difference between mainstream Hollywood and porn is the eyelashes. In the entire history of my career in mainstream, I can count on one hand when I wore false eyelashes. Usually, it was for some fashion show or big event. I think I wore them in the 1940s episode of *Boy Meets World*. But in porn, even if you're lying in bed, in a coma, and possibly deceased, a strip of imitation minks will be adhered to you. Eyelashes in porn are the equivalent of your mom's warnings to always wear fresh underwear. You don't want to get hit by a car and possibly die or be fucked without them.

"Do you think I really need eyelashes?" I asked the makeup artist. She stepped back, a tweezer holding one end of the fluffy strip, and looked at me like I was crazy. "If you're Angela's sexuality, then you probably need two rows."

I lay on the hood of a car that night, seductively eating grapes for a scene with Angela where I try to lure her to her edge. It was nearly two in the morning and the streets were silent but definitely not considered safe. We had different crew guys positioned around to keep watch for anyone trying to start any trouble, but we were still three women out there on our own.

"Who is that guy across the street in the car?" Angela asked, pointing to a man just watching us, parked in an old beige Datsun.

No one knew.

Angela and I moved to tell one of the crew guys to go check it out, but Kayden had already started to walk over to him first.

"Kayden," I called out to her, but she kept walking forward.

"She better be careful," Angela said, and I agreed.

As I watched her cross the street, this petite blond woman, who was beautiful and would be categorized as being too vulnerable by men who like to shelter these kinds of flowers, barreled her way over there with this attitude of "You're not fucking up my shot, whoever the hell you are!" I could see this fire and determination in each step, her sneakers bouncing with purpose and a worthy goal and also because reliable sneakers do those things on uneven pavement and potholes. It struck me how this whole walk and confrontation was a metaphor for so much of what was required of her to be a success. To break out of this mold that we as women and performers and public personalities create for ourselves to find a solid place in the world to cling to when we are young.

And it's wise to create a rock to anchor yourself to then, but it sure as hell is a bitch to get rid of the shackles that hold you to it.

Angela and I watched as the window to the car rolled down and Kayden's voice echoed through the mostly abandoned streets. We watched the car start up and pull away and Kayden march back, satisfied.

It turned out to be one of our crew, parking there because he was told by Marc to watch over us while looking like an extra in the shot. Marc forgot this happened.

"You were so brave," I said to Kayden when she came back, laughing now and readying my bunch of grapes for the next shot.

"You can't lose a staring contest with a guy in a beige Datsun," she said.

And those were words to live by.

The last day of filming, I was to drive Angela to suicide by falling out of her hospital window. My character had also driven her to her hospital bed, so I was there, dressed as a nurse, to finish the job.

"Death and orgasm are really the same thing," Kayden said as she taped an IV to Angela's arm. The phony monitors kept beeping. It was an affordably rented bed. "Once you get there, there's no place else to go but to fall."

I hadn't thought of sex in that way before. An ascension and then a falling. Of course, that's all it is: a reaching for something and, if it's good, a sense of loss for it but also the satisfaction that you touched something rare.

That reminded me of living at the end of extremes and how that once terrified and tempted me; now I was brave enough to face them head-on. Isn't the height of orgasm the extreme, and the end of it another extreme, which is the fall? Moderation, the seemingly wise choice, is not the lack of striving for a great beginning (everyone strives for that, and a lot achieve it); it's the never searching for the fall and the crush of any great end.

And isn't that fall and that end really the thing that forces us to be reborn?

"We did good," Kayden said after the last shot of the production was finished. I smiled at her, and we sat alone on a little tattered bench at the corner of the room, by a slit of open door.

"We did," I said as I unpinned the nurse's cap from my head. "But you always knew we would."

"No, not always," she said, and though she was smiling, I could see how these weeks had been stressful for her. "But I think it'll be something special."

I told her I thought so too.

"ARE THEY DOING A press release? Did anyone take photos on set? Why didn't I take shots to send out?" Dave asked me a few weeks before the premiere, and the truth is, I didn't know the answers to any of his questions.

Some press was on set, but mostly AVN and XBIZ, which are the adult industry trades. We didn't have a media day or press junket like most film sets have. I don't think they were planning on getting any photos to Getty or Wire Images, where news sites and blogs could pull from.

"I'm not sure they're planning for any real press at all," I said to Dave. And I wondered why they were missing such a golden opportunity to show the world a really impressive film that also shows Rachel from *Boy Meets World* doing porn.

Aside from the head of social media, Anthony, who was a millennial die-hard *Boy Meets World* fan who knew it would sell big, the marketing department at Vixen seemed clueless.

"We'll be covered big by all the industry news," a publicist there said when I suggested that we talk to some major outlets. The publicist wasn't being dismissive; I think she was genuinely baffled at the prospect of reaching out to anywhere beyond what they normally did. But I was shocked at how nobody, including Kayden, saw this as some major opportunity.

"Mainstream never really covers porn, and if they do, they can be cruel," Kayden told me when I shared with her some of my ideas for a media blitz. She encouraged me to reach out to anyone I knew but warned me, "Just be careful. I don't want them tearing you apart."

None of that dissuaded me. My entire career had been built by headlines.

P. T. Barnum may have put it best: "I don't care what the newspapers say about me as long as they spell my name right."

I just didn't know that the circus was coming to town, and it was about to explode. But they sure as hell would know how to spell my name.

CHAPTER 15

I BEAT BERNIE SANDERS'S HEART attack on the day the news went viral. I was the number one Google search that day, with three million searches alone just for my name, while his near-death was number two. The wounded ticker of America's progressive grandpa was no match for the shock headline: "Disney Princess and *Boy Meets World* Star Is Now Doing PORN!"

"You're beating the Bern!" Kayden told me as we texted back and forth, sharing article after article headlining my story after the word got out. And let me tell you, once the word got out, the word got on horseback and shouted like Paul Revere. Over 180 news outlets carried it—and it made television shows like *E! News* and *Entertainment Tonight*. It had all the ingredients for a viral event if you think about it. Your favorite childhood sitcom featured an actress who now rides dick for artistic purposes. But she didn't go into porn to give up on acting. No, quite the contrary: porn was now giving her better lines and better roles. In the end, when comparing the two major headlines of the day, the question was posed: Did Maitland's news actually give Bernie that heart attack?

"I have a story idea for you," I said to someone I had known for years over at *In Touch* magazine right before the big release of *Drive*. We hadn't really talked since I began doing adult content, and because of what Kayden had said to me, I wasn't sure how she was going to react. Sure, they had run stories of me in bikinis and cosplay before, but this was now different. Once I had given the pitch and sent the trailer over for the film, I feared the reporter might tell me the magazine couldn't write a piece on porn, but I hoped that she'd at least do it for the shock and awe value and also not tear me down. I nearly fell over when she set me up with one of their top entertainment reporters for an interview.

"You can't talk to them," Kat texted me after I told her the news. "They'll murder you."

"But she was so positive," I texted back. "She said they loved the story."

But inside, I wondered if the press would judge me harshly.

"Be careful what you say to them," I was told repeatedly by those around me in porn and mainstream. It was the one thing both packs could agree on: the press was evil. All this had me on edge before the call, but as soon as I got on the phone with the reporter, Jaclyn, I could tell I was in good hands. She was friendly and positive and genuinely interested in my story. She was also a *Boy Meets World* fan.

"So how did you make this life-changing and female-empowering decision to switch career paths?" she asked right out of the gate. It stumped me for a moment. I had been armed for a battery of questions where I'd have to prove I wasn't on the precipice of a 5150 mental health hold, on drugs that altered my sense of reality, or that I didn't owe money to a guy who looked like Marc. But this was a great question with a depth I wasn't ready for. To put everything that had happened along the way to bring me to this place in one quote felt impossible to me. "It's just my authentic journey," I said. And that's all that it's ever been.

She interviewed me thoroughly, took all my quotes, and wanted to time the piece for when *Drive* was coming out. What I was most taken with was the care and respect she gave this film and me. She didn't have to, but I think she saw this for what it really was: something more than just a story about sex. "This is going to be a fantastic piece," she said, and I could tell that she genuinely meant it.

"From *Boy Meets World* to Adult Films: Inside Maitland Ward's Authentic Journey into Porn": that's what the headline read. No mention of shame or degrading words. No talk of desperation or depravity or aims to tear me down. She used the word *authentic*! And the piece inside was thoughtful and came across as a story about a woman taking a liberating march.

"I've never seen any headline about porn like this before," Kayden said, her mouth slack as she read the piece over and over again. "And they put the website right in the story." She pointed to the name of her brand, her finger drawing an invisible line underneath the print. "You have a mainstream article celebrating you and directing people where to buy your porn. You have no idea how monumental this is!"

People were reading it. The hits on the news site were going through the roof, and subscriptions to Deeper were climbing. And that was just the beginning. None of us realized at that point how far and wide that reach would grow.

"The story just broke in the *Sun*," my husband said as we got into bed. He was on his phone monitoring the Google alerts. "You mean in the UK?" I asked, and he nodded. As we were about to go to sleep, the UK was just waking up to the news. We both knew that was a really big deal. We had history with photos and stories going viral, and it's the British press that breaks them wide open. "Maybe it'll get a little more attention," I said before I dozed off. "That would be cool."

The next morning, I thought an alarm was waking me, but instead it was the constant buzzing of my notifications. My phone was vibrating against the wood of my night table in bouncing excitement. Everyone I ever knew was texting me: friends, coworkers, even my dentist, though that had to do with a cleaning. Huge news outlets were trying to reach me for more comment. When I went to get coffee, some paparazzi followed me, and TMZ interviewed me outside a lunch spot later in the day.

"The site is crashing with subscriptions," Kayden texted me. "There's so much traffic to see this!" I loved how excited she sounded, and surprised. This film and this site were her baby, and she had put so much work into it. I didn't know at this time just how much blood, sweat, and tears it was all made of, but when she scrolled down on the computer and saw how many people were going to see her film, I could hear a joy normally assigned to Christmas morning, tossed graduation caps, or a child taking breath for the first time outside the womb. "I can't believe the trailer is playing on repeat on the *Daily Mail*."

It was the kind of news piece that isn't just a news item. It's something you send to your sister, or your coworker, or your high school friends who tuned in weekly to TGIF. It's the kind of story that bleeds into every corner and facet of life.

A publicist I had known long ago contacted me once he saw the headlines and all the noise surrounding me. I knew him from my early Disney days, and he went on to work at one of the big-time firms that didn't have time for people like me, but suddenly, it seemed, all that had changed. "You know this kind of attention and press is only reserved for big stars," he said. "People can't get enough of this. It's like you're promoting a Marvel movie here."

When news reaches absolutely everyone, the only trouble is that it reaches absolutely everyone. And the everyone I was especially worried about were my parents.

"I saw a story about you in the *New York Post*," my father texted me that morning after the news had reached him. I gasped. I didn't know what to do. My mother was calling me too. I didn't answer. This was the only moment in my life where I thanked the heavens my grandmother was already dead. Of course, my parents could probably still drop dead from it. I had already given Bernie a heart attack; I didn't want to be responsible for more.

I knew the time had come, and I needed to sit my parents down and talk to them.

I hadn't had to talk to them about all this before. They knew I did "content" online but more like dressing up in cosplay or lingerie and taking photos and making posters, and even that was too embarrassing to send them evidence of, but they never demanded it. I was so caught up in my success, first with Patreon and now with porn, that I never put any real thought or planning into telling them, and I certainly didn't want to. I thought maybe one day I could ease them into it, possibly when they were ninety-seven, in a nursing home, and had to be reminded that I wasn't their childhood aunt Sally. I never expected that day to arrive with a marching band, floats, and a grand marshal in the form of Harvey Levin.

My husband and I drove out to the house, and we all sat down in my childhood living room. There was an awkward silence as my husband picked off chocolate almonds from my mother's crystal dish. I'm not sure what I was expecting. Murder, perhaps? Certainly some part of me would have to be sacrificed. It was odd that I was sitting in the house I never uttered a word about sex in about to tell my parents that I wasn't just having sex; I was sex's biggest new star.

"Mom, Dad . . . I've been working really hard." Bad choice of wording. "I mean, I'm now doing something that I love doing." Even fucking worse! "Something that's been inside of me for a long time." Oh God, kill me now!

I looked up at the Precious Moments crucifix on the wall—the one with the little angel children, all big eyes and halos. First, I thought how creepy it was all those little porcelain kids were dead and flying around over us, blessing our gardens. Then I imagined them turning on me, their doll eyes exploding with hellfire and then me being stricken down and used as their fertilizer. Maybe the Precious Moments gardens were just charred bodies of the sinful. I also imagined how all that would be a welcome relief.

I took a deep breath and tried to gather my thoughts, but my mother knocked all of them out of me, hard and fast, with her next sentence. "We're so proud of you," she said.

What?

"You are?" I squeaked out. Did I hear her right? Was this a trick? Why is my husband so obsessed with those fucking almonds?

I looked to my father, who just sat in his big easy chair, flipping the channels on his television to nowhere in particular, and then back to my mother again.

"Dad's family never did anything this exciting, so he's quiet because he's not used to such big, unusual success," she said, and she looked at him pointedly. He remained quiet, though I don't think it was because Uncle Newman on the farm never made it as a businessman. "We'll just have to let Dad get used to all this success *alone* and with his *mouth shut*." She looked pointedly at him again. She had definitely had a word with him before we came.

"You're not mad?" I asked her.

"Mad at what?" she asked, and I was surprised when her eyes got weepy. "You sound so happy in that article we saw. You haven't been so happy about your work for such a long time."

I sat there floating in some sort of out-of-body space, above myself, watching my life down there as both an adult and a child. A repressed child who thought hiding herself and everything she was made her a good one. An adult who felt the same. And I finally saw a mother recognizing that pain.

I immediately broke down crying. My mother handed me a tissue from a crocheted box.

Acting and all its failures had made me miserable for so many years. Week after week and year after year, I kept losing. Losing auditions, losing status, losing years, until I had nothing more of me to lose but the shards of me on the ground. Hollywood was my toxic relationship. I was wooed by it and charmed, and when I was young, I was told such sweet things. But I was fooled and then broken and then left, and yet I accepted the cycle of this treatment again and again. If I could tell my younger self, that girl inside that woman sitting on the couch, one thing, it is that it was never about making people like you so they will give you things. It's about claiming your own space. You have to go out there and find your own happiness, and you're the only one who knows what that looks like.

"I *am* happy!" I said, and I hugged my mom. This woman who used to be embarrassed to say the word *masturbation* was congratulating me for having a successful porn career.

My dad sat there for a minute, still quiet and brooding, staring at a marathon of *The Andy Griffith Show* reruns.

"Well, I'm not happy!" my dad finally said, and we all turned to him. "My friends keep asking me questions."

"Well, Bob, they're old and all half-senile anyway. They'll forget," my mom said, which gave us all pause to laugh.

My dad gave me a hug that day, longer than either of us was prepared for, and he told me how he never wanted to know about anything I did but he was proud of me for making my own way in the world. "I knew you were special the moment you were born," he said as he held me and rocked me like his baby. "As long as you're safe and careful. Maybe you'll do something that's never been done."

I got my mom alone for a moment before we left. "Thank you, Mom," I said as she packed up some snacks in the kitchen for us to take. She stopped what she was doing and stood there for a moment, thoughtful, as she looked out the bay window and onto our front lawn. "I was scared for so many years to do the things I wanted," she said. "There was always a reason not to. Someone to not make mad. Some feathers not to ruffle." She sighed. "But when they tell you not to do something, they don't mention how you'll feel when time is gone and you don't have a choice in the matter anymore at all."

She didn't share with me what choice time and all those people stole from her, but she didn't have to. I knew what it was like for someone to take away your *yes*. I just hugged her and sat with her there a moment.

As I walked down the hallway to leave, I caught a glimpse of that gold-framed Jesus, still sitting in the same spot in my room that it did when I was a kid. But his eyes weren't following me now. And they seemed kinder somehow. Maybe they were never really judging me for anything. Maybe they just wanted me to take notice of things.

And I think me doing porn really did make Jesus proud.

It certainly had my husband feeling that way. "You did it," he said as we drove back home. And he lifted my hand to kiss it. "I don't think the realization has hit you that you're starring in a movie with sex and acting that's getting major attention. It's what you've always wanted."

And he was right. It hadn't hit me yet.

I ALWAYS THOUGHT HOLLYWOOD, or anywhere else really, had an entrance and then a staircase. You'd walk through the front door and take the steps assigned and necessary to get to the top. One by one, or if you were especially ambitious or had generational wealth and privilege, you'd take them by two. But success is not a front door. It's a brick through a window or a kicked-through exit. Sometimes, as was the case for me, it was an old key that I had to scrape and polish and manipulate through a rusted keyhole. And it took years and decades, and nights, propped up against the door, crying out to the sky to open it, until finally the key was ready to turn. And the room you enter doesn't look like anything you ever thought, but that's okay. It's up to you to figure out what you're going to do now that you're inside.

"You broke all records for sales on Thursday and then broke your own record on Friday and Saturday," Kayden told me as we monitored the subscriptions for the site.

"Your site and this film are the reason I could do this," I told her.

"You're the reason all these people are seeing my site at all," she said.

We were both quiet for a moment, taking in the scope of what all this meant for us as individuals but also together. Neither of us had ever had to deal with a formidable woman like the other before. Everything about that was jarring and alive and terrifying. And all of that would be realized more fully in the weeks and months and years to come. But now was a time to purely celebrate.

"I thought that I had to do this all on my own," she said. "And I had to do everything—and it was all that I wanted it to be, but it was so exhausting." She looked to me with teary eyes and a smile. "The great surprise of my life is how you took a thing I only dreamed of over the finish line."

"You've done the same for me," I said.

Kat called me, desperately wanting to see me. I had only spoken to her a few times since that dinner, and I hadn't seen her since doing porn, but I went to her house in the afternoon. I needed to come face-to-face with Hollywood.

"You're a fucking genius," she said as she offered me some chilled white wine and a variety of cheeses on a platter. She had taken care in making this presentation. "I thought you were crazy, but I see what you're doing here."

I picked up a cracker and spread on some soft brie. "What do you mean?" I asked.

"I know I was a bitch when you said you were going to talk to that magazine," she said as she plopped down next to me. "But seriously, I was talking to my agent today, who saw everything. He's like, holy shit, she's going to get a lot of offers now." She leaned over and kissed me. "He wants you to call him. He says you have real possibilities."

Hollywood always likes a front-runner.

I thought about possibilities while I sat there and ate her cheese. My life was now, because of this viral moment in time, suddenly full of them. Just days before, I was told by everyone that this moment would destroy me. That I'd be crying in my room for all the names I'd be called and all the daggers the world would throw at me. That I would be done as an actress, and yet here I was being offered the number of an agent.

I had been told a lot.

"Here, take his number down," Kat said.

I looked at her a moment, so desperate now for me to like her. Now that I had made something of myself on my own. But I didn't care if she liked me anymore. In fact, I wanted her to hate me as I walked out of her door. Or at least feel remorse.

"You know what, I think I have other plans," I said and then I left, after discarding the rest of my cracker on her tray.

I picked up my phone that night and texted Kayden: "Let's make more movies!" She texted back some excited emoji face and said she was forging a plan.

I imagined Kat and my toxic relationship that was Hollywood commiserating somewhere, depressed and alone, and throwing darts at my headlines.

That's an image that helps me sleep at night.

KAYDEN AND I GOT married in Las Vegas—well, our equivalent of matrimony. Just hours before the AVN Awards, we stood facing each other in floor-length gowns on the balcony of a hotel penthouse overlooking the Strip. A ceremony was conducted, photographs and video were taken, and Kayden recited vows from her heart before placing a solid gold lock with the word *Deeper* inscribed on it around my neck. It was the first and only of its kind. On the back it read "Mistress Maitland," the name that had so quickly and powerfully become synonymous with my persona and the brand. I now held the only contract ever for the brand, and I was bannered as its face. "The dedication you've given to us, we're going to give back to you. We're with you as long as you'll have us," she said as she secured the heavy piece around my neck, the gold firmly weighted over my heart. In tears, we embraced, and our union was met with applause.

It was an arranged marriage of sorts, as there was no courtship or time spent dating. It went from coffee to picking out a china pattern in a matter of weeks. We dove in headfirst not knowing if we would hit a cement bottom or swim in blue water, but we had faith in the water. Any high dive is really just a held breath and toes courageous enough to peel from the board. Much like a couple who heads to Vegas to elope, we had become close and intertwined so fast and profoundly that we really didn't know each other yet; we just both knew we wanted to be there. This greatness was very much thrust upon us, but we still had so much to learn. Newlyweds metaphorically living together who had to suddenly, yet enthusiastically, figure out which side of the bed we get and how much closet space.

"I bought you a whole new wardrobe," Kayden said right after I signed my new contract. No longer would we be filming in a warehouse; we would now be in a mansion, and I'd be wearing designer threads—a testament to how profitable and game-changing *Drive* had been.

We began filming the eponymous feature series *Mistress Maitland* some months before our ceremony in Vegas. This persona whose name Kayden would later have imprinted on the gold lock was assured, smart, and wealthy in her own right, though the husband she keeps as a deviant partner in actual crime also drips with dollars and, more impressive to her, a thirst for taboo. "I want to play a new game," I say to him in the first scene. It's a play on *Cruel Intentions*—that famed nineties film where two sexually charged stepsiblings dare each other into provocative high-stakes challenges—wagering bets that make us question our own moral compass and how far we're willing to go. But the stakes are higher here. When you lose, you lose everything.

But I always win.

The first girls I worked with—who looked like any young women you'd see on a college campus or a spring break beach—were giggly and excited just to be there. They were also *White Chicks* fans, who had followed all my headlines and they wanted to know everything.

"You make me believe that I could really do both porn and acting one day," one of the girls, who had come from Colombia to pursue her love of sexual performance and film, told me. "Before, it just didn't seem like it would be possible. I think now everything is changing. And that's so much thanks to you."

It really hit home to me that these girls, and other performers I was meeting, were looking to me to be a voice to those who wouldn't listen to them but might to me, since I had been on their TV screens and to forge ahead some new path. But I wasn't sure I knew what that path was yet. I loved the work and the performance, and I found satisfaction in being unapologetic in my truth, but I didn't have a map. No new frontier ever does.

But I did believe that I was put in this place and in this time for a reason bigger than myself. I had been given a spotlight when I was dropped into porn, this world of real people—moms and dads and daughters and sons and also people who had been rejected or marginalized and cast out—some who turned to sex work because they loved it and some because they didn't know where else to go. Every story is different and real, despite what you've been told. Porn doesn't have to ruin you; porn can save you. And in many ways, it saved me. I know that if people could see the people of this industry as I have, they wouldn't dismiss them. They would listen to them, as human beings, and they'd hear a different story from the one they've always been told.

And maybe telling a new story is the path ahead.

"THE ONE THING YOU need to know in this industry, is that everyone is obsessed with awards," a journalist from one of the porn trades told me early on. I thought he was joking until we arrived at awards season and everyone suddenly started acting like Black Friday shoppers at a Walmart, grabbing for the last TV. "There's XBIZ and XCritic and everyone ends the month of January at the AVN convention in Las Vegas. And let me tell you, watch out for those best new starlets. They'll eat their own."

"You're going to win for your acting in *Drive*," Marc told me on set one day while he was pumping Cetaphil face wash into a device that would later be used to spray pretend splooge. Cetaphil is a little-known trick in the industry to amplify men's loads, especially in photos. But all spunk aside, I wasn't sure I believed him. I had been fed these honey-laced lies before back on the soap for that Emmy.

Was it all just splooge and mirrors?

"I don't know, I'm pretty new," I said, trying to brush it off like I didn't care, but I really did. "I don't even know if I'll be nominated."

He laughed as he sealed the fake jizz inside the receptacle. "I've been in the business for over twenty years. If you don't get nominated, I'll sell my balls to science."

Marc seemed pretty serious about science and his balls. I wondered if science was where his eyeball went.

"Listen, I forwarded through all the sex in that feature and when I got to the end," he said, "I didn't miss the fucking. Like not at all. I had just watched it like a real movie. That rarely happens in porn."

But it was happening in porn more and more, and it was remarkable to me that it was by and large happening because of women. Unlike mainstream Hollywood, it's the powerhouse female directors and writers of the industry who are creating the projects that take home the top accolades and are moving the industry forward. Jacky St. James, Casey Calvert, and Joanna Angel were contenders, as was Mason, who rarely shows her face. And I mean this quite literally. She wore a burka to an award show one year, not because of religious reasons but because it was the only thing that would cover her face completely. It's rumored she was a child star on *Little House on the Prairie*. Voices of queer women, women of all shapes and sizes, and women of color were being heard now and celebrated. Aubrey Kate and Natalie Mars were breaking down barriers for trans women, and body empowerment icons like Karla Lane and Sophia Rose were now formidable forces in the evolution of how we view sex and the female body. Shine Louise Houston, a filmmaker celebrated for her ethnically diverse, queer, and feminist porn, was making an impact beyond the industry, bringing marginalized groups to the forefront and in a real and exceptionally crafted way. But it was

Bree Mills—the one I almost contacted way back when—who would be Kayden's chief competitor for Director of the Year, and the film she'd made based on the story of her coming out, *Teenage Lesbian*, would be the competition for *Drive*.

"You will absolutely be nominated," Kayden said, offering me assurance. She also offered me some insight into the importance that these award shows play in an industry whose creative work is far too often dismissed as nothing more than jerk-off material. "They validate the work that we do, and no one out in the world recognizes us publicly for anything good."

It made sense. As an outsider, I had been completely unaware that so many of these creative, story-driven projects were being made. I knew of XBIZ and AVN, but I never conceptualized what these shows meant to the industry and its people.

But what did these awards mean to me?

One morning, when I held my soaped-up shampoo bottle in my hand, I found myself standing there, imagining an audience and a speech I'd make and how the gold felt in my hand.

Hadn't I done that too when I was promised that daytime Emmy?

"What are you doing with that shampoo bottle?" my husband asked, startling me out of my fantasy as he brushed his teeth at the sink, watching me through the glass.

"Oh, I was just checking for sulfates," I said, pointing to the label. His smile told me I wasn't deserving of any award for that line.

Over the course of two nights, XBIZ and AVN host nomination parties, and anyone and everyone in porn attends. This year, XBIZ served wine and filet on the rooftop of a hotel in Hollywood, while AVN hosted a party packed wall-to-wall at a hot nightclub.

After all the breakout success I had, and now being the contract face of the Deeper brand, I had hoped that events like these would be a way to connect with the industry and make new friends. But I had been sheltered in my new home. I was a treasured little goldfish in a bowl with coral and a sandcastle and all the pretty rocks, now being scooped out with a net and thrown into the ocean. Sure, there are a lot of pretty things in the water, but there are also large fish with teeth.

People were watching me everywhere I went. The scale of reaction ranged somewhere between *Oh, she's cool*, to *Who the fuck does she think she is*, to *I am witnessing a rare beast being released from captivity, out into the wild.*

"Don't be so nervous," my husband told me, as I succeeded in making nail marks through his wool sports jacket and shirt straight onto the flesh of his arm.

I had assumed that everyone would suddenly accept me or at least talk to me. But not many people were, except the ones I already knew. I feared they all hated me. I had made a big splash in this pool, but I guess I didn't fully grasp how much room I took up in it, and none of them knew me yet.

"They don't know if they can trust you," Kayden said. "You have to remember that the industry is always on the defense with people from mainstream. We've never known anyone like you. They want to be friends, but they fear if they reach out to pet you, you'll attack."

But I'm a goldfish!

In the months ahead, I would witness more and more instances and hear stories about just how persecuted performers are out there in the world, and it helped me better understand. There's a history of mainstream celebrities coming in fast, getting whatever they want out of the industry—be it for their sex tapes, or nude photo spreads, or even dating a porn star for the value of shock and awe—and then leaving it in the dust. And no matter what, it always involves reinforcing the stigma that sex work is a shocking, degrading, bad thing.

When the industry is constantly being lit up for controversy and then forced back into its place in the shadows, it's looked upon as something scary and evil, and that gives society permission to attack. Sometimes with words, often with actions, and sometimes those actions can be violent and even deadly. Marginalized groups have it the worst. Women of color, queer performers, and any group that challenges the puritanical societal norm are hunted and mocked. And when things do turn violent, society rarely hears about it. It's not even a blurb on the news if a sex worker is killed. And if it somehow is, because it's exceptionally gory or heinous, it's a shrug of the shoulders and a question asked, "Well, what did they expect?"

Porn stars are used to casual discrimination too. The sideways glances, the whispered remarks. Social media removing them just because of their profession or being refused an apartment because of where their paychecks come from. It wasn't that long ago that a porn star couldn't get a bank account, and banks often still close accounts for no reason or make up excuses to refuse to cash checks.

"I was on a flight to Miami and a couple next to me found out I did porn, so they switched their seats," a young female performer told me. "They weren't even casual about it. They made sure everyone knew I was a whore." She laughed it off, but I could tell that it really had bothered her. "Karma got them back. They were stuffed into seats in the middle row." But she didn't tell me what it felt like to be sandwiched between the weight of two empty seats.

Kayden had her own experience when she was picked up in a town car to do a radio show gig. She and the host were supposed to travel to another location together. The guy had begged her for the interview, and she agreed, even though she would be missing an event where she would've been paid well. "Who's in the car in front of us?" she asked the driver as she settled into the back seat and he told her, in no uncertain terms, "Oh, that's the show host and his girlfriend. She says she won't breathe your same air." And he had the audacity to punctuate it with a chuckle.

I wanted to make sure that performers out there knew that wasn't me or anything I was trying to be about. I may have come from mainstream, but I had also been discarded by it. And the only things I wanted to tear down now were walls.

Kayden and Marc had been right, though. I did get nominated and nominated well. I was told no other performer in the industry's history had been recognized for such coveted awards so quickly out the gate. There were, of course, the nominations for my acting, but what surprised me most were the ones for my sex scenes in *Drive*. "It's a huge deal that they're recognizing you for both," Kayden said.

To be recognized was really something.

And in the weeks that followed, I found myself clinging more and more to my soapy shampoo bottle.

THE *TAMRON HALL SHOW* called and asked me to be a guest. "You're just so sex positive and it's really something fresh and different, plus people know you from Disney," the showrunner said, and I immediately agreed to it.

"You're actually going to be on daytime television," my PR rep said after we set it up. I'd be flying to New York to do two segments on the live broadcast. "Do you know how huge this is? They're going to be talking about porn on a major network in the middle of the day!"

My husband accompanied me on the trip. The show filmed at the ABC studios building in our old neighborhood, on the Upper West Side of Manhattan. "Did you ever think we'd come back here like this?" my husband asked as we made our way down Central Park West by town car, and I shook my head. I tipped my forehead against the glass and looked down the edge of the park I used to walk through when I was discovering new things about myself. I would get so lost in stories I was writing on those benches where the horses would clop past.

Everything about the ride was idyllic, until all the pipes on the Upper West Side blew and the streets started to flood. That should've been my first warning.

"We're moving the questions around a bit," the showrunner told me, scrunching her nose as she escorted me to hair and makeup. "We had to condense a few things. Oprah is on today!"

"Is she here?" I asked with a gasp of excitement.

Another scrunch of the nose. "No, it's recorded. But her personal echo is powerful."

The stage was hot and bright, and my name was illuminated in gigantic letters behind me.

Tamron smiled and shook my hand before we settled into our seats. Everything was glossy and beautiful, especially Tamron. There was an energy to the crowd; a few fans even shouted out my name. I felt positive about this—until we went live and my gut sank into the feeling that I had been set up.

"Can social media lead to sex trafficking?" was the question she posed straight out of the gate.

What? She thinks that porn automatically means sex trafficking?

Here it was, that negative media moment I thought had been avoided. I had to keep my cool.

I told her it was a concern, of course, for young people to be coerced out there, but this had nothing to do with my story—or legitimate porn. She looked stunned as I spoke of porn as an industry of hope and empowerment and liberation. She kept asking me questions and it felt like she was trying to find some negative angle. But honestly, I think she just didn't understand. She had never met anyone like me. A sex worker who was happy and positive and not ashamed. And I can't blame her for that. I was seeing firsthand how the media can manipulate the image people hold of a sex worker by twisting words and phrases, pointing questions in certain directions, and highlighting bad things instead of good, all to give the audience at home watching a negative perception. But there I was, smiling and in bright lights, telling my story.

And I thanked her at the end for the opportunity to do that.

· · ·

THE FOUR LONGEST WORDS in the English language are, *And the winner is . . .*

When I heard them being read at the XBIZ Awards, they were muffled and underwater as if I could either swim in them or drown. The award for Best Actress was delivered early, which I wasn't prepared for. Kayden was on one side of me and my husband on the other, and each clutched one of my hands. As I was holding my breath in the water, they were holding me steady.

When my name was called as the winner, it was like I was in a dream. Kayden stood up next to me, a fist in the air, and yelled, "*Fuck yeah!*" My husband's arms crashed around me, and then someone helped me all the way up the steep stage steps and to the podium. And there I cried, because I had really won something.

I would go on to win two more awards that night—Best Feature Sex Scene and Crossover Star of the Year. And each time it was the same reaction.

"I think you're the only person to win Crossover Star who went the other way around," I was told as I held tight to my trophies. My husband then shot a photo of me with the trio of golden statues balanced in my arms. I would look at that picture over and over again, and I would see a woman who was happy, who had dared to dream big but also work hard, and who had truly been awarded for that. It took a while to wrap my head around the fact that that woman was really me.

And while Kayden took home Director of the Year and Deeper best new brand, *Teenage Lesbian* beat *Drive*, setting up a dynamic that would continue to play out in Vegas for AVN.

"I saw you on *Tamron Hall*," one performer said as she stopped me in the ballroom. "You really stood up to her." She seemed giddy about it and surprised.

She wasn't the only one to mention this to me; in fact, people were coming up to me left and right to talk about it. And everyone was treating it as if I was riding in on some horse and gathering the troops, and that I had announced my march forward with some battle cry. I hadn't expected this kind of reaction.

"You were so confident," a woman in sparkling gold said. "You didn't even break a sweat. Most everyone folds to them"—*them* meaning the outside world and mainstream.

I took that to heart.

We all took off for Vegas and AVN that following week. Dave begrudgingly followed us there to document everything for press and my content. I never have to worry about him charging movies to his room or racking up room service, because he always chooses places that don't have a working television and have vending machines that can be emptied with a swift kick. "This hotel is fantastic," he told me. "It's right next to a Seven-Eleven and a White Castle." And he was serious.

The Hard Rock Hotel was overtaken with porn stars and fans. Vixen hired bodyguards to accompany us everywhere in case anyone got threatening or overly enthusiastic. I had never seen a convention so wild and outrageous and of such epic proportions—both in crowd size and in breasts. And if you had breasts of any size, you were sure to draw the crowd.

I hadn't realized how popular my breasts really were until that weekend. I know I have a good rack, but I never imagined people would know such details about them like the ruler length of my nipples and that my right one has a freckle. The freckle on my asshole, which I had only discovered while filming myself inserting a butt plug for a content shoot, was also given its respect. It was anointed by my fans with a name: St. Baxter's Cathedral.

I had my vagina molded in a penthouse on the Strip the morning after we got there. It wasn't the same penthouse Kayden and I got married in, but the views were equally stunning as I lay there with my strip facing the Vegas one, waiting to get plastered by a man in a flannel who was in constant search of Red Bull.

My vagina—and my asshole, because they were molding that too—had finally arrived.

I was going to be a Fleshlight Girl.

Becoming a Fleshlight Girl—a chosen one of the industry whose lady parts are molded for coveted sex toys—is comparable to getting a Lifetime Achievement Award at the Oscars. Only the most select group of stars ever get them—to this date, there are only about fifty out of the thousands and thousands who have performed in adult films. And this would be even more special because I would be the brand's first mainstream celebrity pussy and asshole.

It isn't just the status of having one; Fleshlight supplies an incredible income for the performers. From each Fleshlight sold, you get anywhere between 12.5 and 17.5 percent of the profit, which means the most popular models are easily taking home a good five figures a month. I know of women who have started businesses, bought properties, and developed new projects, all from the proceeds of their Fleshlight toys. "I financed my early films with mine," Kayden told me.

Fleshlight, legend has it, was started by a man in Texas over a quarter century ago when his wife, who was having twins, was put on bedrest and told to abstain from all sex. Nothing leads a man to ingenuity and invention quite like the prospect of having to ejaculate into a sock every day. *Hey, why not make it a rubber vagina-like sock!* Of course, the technology of the products has come leaps and bounds over the decades, and it's now arguably the top-quality product made, but it was that first Fleshlight that made it possible for my holes to be available to the world.

"This is for you," the guy said as he handed me a Hitachi massager still wrapped up in the box. I thought it was a gift at first, until he told me to open it and use it to get myself aroused. Only in this industry was this a casual, legitimate request. "Oh, but don't come," he said. "We want you to look ready, not done."

The idea is to bring blood flow to the surface, to open you up, so when the warm, gooey plaster is poured, your vagina is at its most turned on and inviting. I didn't really feel turned on as I laid there with the massager on my clit as the guy stirred up the plaster, and I worried it wasn't plumped up and fluffy enough. They had given me one of the stronger devices—one of the old-school ones that were used for heavy back pain with the plug in the wall. So it was extra strength and I had to stay in one place on the corner of the bed while I did it. And every time they asked me a question about something, I answered in the rhythm of a jackhammer.

"I'm not sure I'm getting aroused enough," I said, and the buzz of my voice lingered.

He looked over and said, "No, you're ready now! Your flower is perfect!"

Getting molded is sort of like a combination between getting a wax without the hair-rip and a gynecological exam without the Pap, though more casual and with your makeup and hair done and a nice catered lunch. Aside from the gloppy gunk, a computer scan is done with a wand to ensure every nook and crevice is accounted for. "Nobody will ever know your vagina better than us," he said.

Well, maybe the fans now.

THE CONVENTION FLOOR WAS covered when I made my way in to sign autographs. Kayden and I were doing a Twitch show with Manuel and fans mobbed us, eventually being pushed back from the ropes by security and then forming a solid wall around to watch. Dave was there, amid all this madness, snapping shots, when some guy came up and said, "Aren't you the dude who puts on her clothes?" Dave mouthed that he would kill me later when he had to sign an autograph for the guy.

"Everyone ends up with the AVN flu," porn superstar Riley Reid told me as we posed for pictures and fans thronged us.

And I was surprised how up close and personal the girls really do get with the fans. All the hugging and kissing and talking really is a breeding ground for germs. "I want the fans to have a weekend they'll remember," Abella Danger said as one fan kissed her cheek.

I won that night too, and the words again were muffled and underwater and the two people championing me the most were again holding me.

As I marched triumphantly up to that massive stage, it was one of the proudest moments of my life. The weight of that golden statue made the moment solid and real. I looked out onto the crowd of so many good and talented people who are so often marginalized or ignored or, worse, treated as if they don't exist at all. These people, in this place and on this night, were recognizing me. And I think they really knew me now. I made a promise to everyone in my speech that I would make it my life's goal to knock down all of the walls.

"I've never been prouder of you," my husband said as he embraced me there on the floor as the audience was clearing. And I held on to him for a really long time.

I also won for my sex scene, and I was so proud to be acknowledged again, not only for my work as an actress but also as a sexual performer because I am both. But my work with Deeper wasn't the only thing that I was awarded for that night.

"Hey, Dave, I won for Best Cosplayer," I told him just after the show. "Who would've thought all the crazy stuff we did would win me an award?"

"If you would've told me a lot of things, I wouldn't have believed you," he said. "But, hey, I discovered you." And though Dave is never one to get emotional, that night I thought I saw a tear. He'd say his eyes were irritated because of all the idiots smoking in the hotel, but I could tell he was proud.

Drive didn't win. But Kayden did pull off another Director of the Year. Bree's film about her coming out as a teenager deserved the accolades. It was a real story, about a real person, and it had a voice aimed at something higher. I was disappointed we didn't win but it was exciting that both of these films were now art that porn had to offer the world.

Everyone went up to the company suite to eat and celebrate. It was pretty low-key for a bunch of porn people, but it was pretty special too.

"Next year, we'll have a really big film. With a huge story and budget. It'll be a showcase for you," Kayden said, already mapping it all out.

And as we sat there in the hotel suite at nearly four in the morning eating french fries, the world to us was bright and the future endless with possibility.

But things changed quickly in the world.

Kobe Bryant died later that morning, and the coronavirus was looming.

CHAPTER 16

I WAS BEING FITTED FOR a black latex catsuit in downtown Los Angeles on the day before the world shut down. Kayden and I were planning a cosplay vignette where I'd play some cat-o'-nine-tails version of Catwoman—with whips and chains and collars for the kittens, who would lap milk, and other things, up at my behest. We were in a rush to perfect this costume, fitting it precisely and exact so it hugged every curve of my sleek, shiny frame. I kept refreshing my phone as a guy measured me from neck to toe and nips to hips, for any new developments on the Covid front. Every time I did, the news got bleaker.

The threat of Armageddon was also a period of intense planning for my future with the brand. Kayden and I were discussing scenes and promotional campaigns, and we were putting serious thought into what our next huge feature film project would be after *Drive*.

"I want to make commentary on the state of our vapid modern world," she said to me one night, and then she sent me 750 pages' worth of books on the plight of early man. "We don't face the same obstacles that they did. We have the luxury of walking through our everyday lives without real, credible threat to our survival."

And then, all at once, the world shut down.

I think we jinxed ourselves.

I started thinking a lot about survival like everyone else was, but not so much for myself. I worried about the people in this new industry of mine—one where they are all too often forgotten about as being human and deserving of anyone's real help. Veiled attempts at helping sex workers get out of sex work is not the same thing. I wondered how some of the new girls in the industry would survive without the money they relied on from porn site work. Everything had happened so fast that nobody really had time to get a grasp on things. And the sad fact is, no one wants to say they helped a sex worker remain a sex worker.

But I felt it was important that I did.

"Maybe I should masturbate for charity," I said to my husband, and he was encouraging. "I just think it would be sad if someone had to crawl back to somewhere they left for a reason, just because they couldn't afford groceries."

I decided to put on weekly cam shows through Cam Soda and also on my OnlyFans Live—a streaming service for the platform, which allowed me to talk and perform in real time for a paying audience. There they could ask me questions, we could play games, and they could group jerk off to me riding a rubber dick attached to a rubber torso that I nicknamed Quarantine Man. He had no head, so I joked he was the perfect partner because his dick was always at attention and he could never talk back. Anything that was made on these shows would be donated to the Free Speech Coalition, an industry help organization, and would be distributed to those most in need. I wasn't trying to be this savior; I genuinely wanted to help and lend any voice I could. I knew what it was like to be young and trying to make your way in the world and for things out of your control to stomp your dream out.

I tried to make these live shows fun and upbeat, and they served as a place of real human connection for both me and my fans. We'd have nude baking parties, showers where I'd demonstrate how to wash your hands and all your parts safely and effectively—I even bought penis-shaped soap to do it. We had a dance party where I'd change all the song names to reflect our current state. "My Corona" and "Don't Stand Closer Than Six Feet to Me" were favorites.

These platforms not only provided the necessary sexual relief we were so missing in these times of aloneness and isolation, but they were a way to find connection in our humanity. Not only was it impossible to date, hook up, or even steal a kiss in some corner of a dark bar, you couldn't even meet your most platonic friend for coffee or even see your mom. The connection between my fans and me in this way helped me as much as it helped them.

I can't tell you what an odd yet exciting feeling it is to know that all the people watching you ride a headless dick man are masturbating into your smooth silicone sex holes. It's intimacy like no other.

"Can you make a video of us on a date?" a guy asked on my OnlyFans.

"You mean like we go home and have sex after I've seduced you?" I asked. Simulated sexual situations were typical requests that I'd get for custom orders—personal videos bought by individual fans, which range anywhere in price from $200 to $500 a minute. Usually they're just solo masturbation videos, but they can also involve costumes and specific story points. I do dozens of these a month. "No, no sex," he said. "I just want to talk to you at some bar. I really miss bars."

I hadn't really gotten this before, but I would get it more and more as the weeks and months dragged on.

The girlfriend experience was what people were craving during this time locked away. To be flirted with, talked to, and to experience something we all thought was so attainable and ordinary before. "Just smoke a cigarette, wear a low-cut blouse where I can see just a trace of your bra, and call me by my first name," another fan asked. "If you blew smoke in my face, that would make me come so hard."

Some months into the pandemic, something happened that shifted the trajectory of the entire adult industry and made all performers' futures more secure.

The rise of OnlyFans.

Although I already had a massively popular account, it grew exponentially during this time. I found myself consistently making six

figures every month. That hasn't stopped, and it hasn't stopped growing. Other girls, even the ones newer to the business, were also hitting
financial windfalls. And they were discovering that they didn't need the
big studios like they were conditioned to think. When the world finally
sat still and those corporate voices were quieted, girls were discovering
that they could do it on their own.

"It's so sad and desperate she's on OnlyFans," I saw a guy tweet
about a young woman who had just financed a BMW and was bragging
about doing it all on her own. It made me laugh, though. I guess if she's
desperate to make $30,000 a month as a twenty-three-year-old while
barely leaving her apartment, it would be sad for him.

A new term was coined; instead of sugar daddies, there were OnlyFans
mamas. The hot girls no longer had to rely on a man to supply their lives;
they could throw around their cash to boy toys.

Mainstream celebrities were also joining the platform. Cardi B,
Blac Chyna, and Tyga are just a few names. Bella Thorne caused a stir
when she signed on, angering sex workers who had built the platform
up from its inception, when she was sort of dismissive of them. Headlines blared that she had made a million dollars overnight, supposedly
promising nudes, but she didn't deliver, which caused her to get massive
charge-backs. There was a rumor that because of this, the rules would
change and limits on how much you can charge would hit, but nothing
happened. There is always a constant rumor that porn will be kicked
out in favor of a cleaner mainstream image. But sex just makes too much
money. That was proven later, when OnlyFans tried to say it was going
sex-free and then changed its mind a few days later. I was interviewed
by TMZ about it, right before they announced their decision reversal,
and I predicted correctly that they couldn't survive without sex workers.
But it's still unnerving they even tried.

I don't think it's necessarily a bad thing that mainstream wants a
turn at OnlyFans, as long as sex workers are celebrated and accepted too
and in equal measure. It's another reminder that porn and mainstream

are no longer running on different tracks; they're now racing parallel. And to normalize them side by side is always a good thing.

But money was never the reason I did professional porn. I could retire away to a little island with umbrella drinks and toes dipped in water and white sand and still have my empire keep running. My fans would probably like to see me masturbate on the shore of some tropical seas. But Deeper—and porn—was always about so much more to me than that. I wanted sex to be a cinematic experience, and Kayden and I had made so many plans.

I had begun to doubt that a feature, or any scene at all, would happen that year, but as we edged toward summer, there were rumblings that we might be able to return to set in some capacity. But a feature film was such a big undertaking.

"Our feature this year can't be on horseback in Europe, but I promised you a feature, and dammit, I'm giving you a feature," Kayden said on the phone one night and my heart leaped.

And I continued reading about early hominid man, in the faithful hope for humanity that she was right.

Can pornography be art?

This would be the question posed by my character to her students in our feature film *Muse*. It was also a question that Kayden and I were trying to answer ourselves with this project. Could we make a piece that could be all things at once—something that could provide both sexual gratification and something that you carry with you after?

A penthouse—the largest in the city—was secured downtown to film our big feature. Unlike a studio space, this was a controlled environment where no one could get in and out without Covid protocol checks and daily test clearance. Los Angeles was opening up again, and we were ready to hit the ground running. But this deadline would be strict. We had no idea when the world could shut down again.

"None of it seems big or important enough," Kayden said as we were spitballing ideas for the script over the phone some weeks earlier. The one in question had me and a neighbor in a sexually charged war during lockdown. Adriana Chechik was sent a rough draft of that script. "Let me sleep on it," Kayden said, and we said our good nights.

She didn't sleep because she texted me at midnight, "You are my Muse!"

I thought that was sweet and replied with a few blushed-face emojis.

"No, you are *the* Muse!" she texted back. "I'll talk to you when I'm finished."

Four days later she delivered a script called *Muse* to my inbox.

My character in *Muse*—who is based on elements of my own real-life persona—is a sexually empowered professor of psychology whose high profile in the world as an author and filmmaker, as well as a fierce advocate for sex workers' rights, makes her a polarizing figure who is both vilified and celebrated and tragically never feels a sense of real love because of it.

The subject of women, and who is deserving of true affection, is something my character grapples with, as do we all as women. We go from daughter to mother to grandmother all in a straight line: women in a drill of succession; a stepping-stone march to the pedestals they have been assigned. But the one who does not deserve it, or the honor of any of these roles, is, as my character states, "the sexually demanding, unapologetic woman who fills her own place first."

But isn't freedom better than the love you get sitting on any pedestal? Pedestals are often far too close to the sun, and to escape them, you have to crush your bones.

The scope of this script would be an undertaking that even in the most stable of times would prove vast. It was the biggest script to date; my character alone spoke over 600 lines. There were sets to build and special effects. For anyone who says, *Oh, it's just porn*, I have a three-page monologue I'd like you to learn in a day.

I loved that I could be seen as a beacon for sexually empowered women but at the same time be real, and tragic and broken in that power. And feeling all of that as a woman is real and important. Sadly, the women on pedestals don't feel anything but love.

I did get worried we might not achieve our lofty goals when Adriana came in the first day, saw my classroom set, and said, "Wait, I thought we were doing the movie about the psycho neighbors."

Being back on the set after being isolated was thrilling. It felt as if we were entering our own little beehive each day, stealing away from the world, and making something we could be proud of. Every morning we'd stand in line to get our Covid tests, and the following morning we'd get our results and be tested again for the following day. The rhythm and the cycle of it was comforting, as we had just lost half a year in the endless days.

And all the while, mainstream was still scrambling to film anything.

My first sex scene has two guys running up to me and treating me like meat, all because they've seen me sexual and naked. I don't wither in this misogynistic treatment; I duct-tape them up in my apartment and threaten their balls with scissors to teach them the meaning of respect. I am a teacher, after all. At the end I take one's cum and smear it on the other's face. He's forced to swallow it. It's the revenge fantasy that so many women want after dealing with men like this.

BY THE END OF it, we were exhausted and exhilarated, but I think we really left the audience with a resounding *yes* to answer the previously posed question. Porn *is* art and we made that. And the film we never thought we would be able to make in a time of world-changing chaos was done, and the shoot had been a success.

I was gifted a Gucci handbag that belonged to the wife of actor Aldo Ray, who had, by some accounts, been pushed out of mainstream after he did an acting part in a pornographic film.

"Take it to the Oscars with you one day," Kayden said.

I took it to AVN that year and won Best Actress with it—where we also won Best Feature and swept everything—and that felt just as good.

CHAPTER 17

"**Y**OU SHOULD START LIKE half a week before, because it'll take forever to clean all of it out," Adriana said to me when I asked her advice on performing my first anal scene in a continuation scene for *Muse* called *Continuum*. By "all of it," she meant exactly what you'd think. All. Of. It. While it did seem believable that humanity collectively has three and a half days' worth of shit in their gut at any given time, I didn't understand why it takes so long to get rid of it. "It sticks to your ass walls," she told me. "And if you're keto, forget about it."

She told me about the science and precision of a metal rod you could install in your shower to conquer the stickiest corners. She pulled up photos of it on her phone. It was a long, skinny metal rod with a nozzle on the end that shot water out—or rather up—with force, thus completely removing the contents of one's colon with relative ease and professionalism. But I still didn't get why it took so long. Surely a gadget like this would expedite delivery. It sounded like the anal equivalent of Amazon Prime.

"I hadn't cleaned out for the entire pandemic," she said. "That's why it took like hours for the water to shoot out clear." I grimaced. I hadn't cleaned out in my entire life. How long might it take me? Realizing I was behind the timeline, and had only three days until my scene to do this properly, I mumbled to myself, "Oh shit," and it felt universally appropriate.

Anal scenes are a big deal. The asshole is the holy grail of porn. Huge money is negotiated for a star to deliver her first, and since I'm Disney and mainstream, my asshole is especially golden. It was negotiated months before in my contract that I would be performing my first for the Deeper brand. It was also a true first for any mainstream actor. Anyone can leak a sex tape, but the back door was still too taboo to be considered survivable. And MTV reality star Farrah Abraham doesn't count. *Backdoor Teen Mom* was a disaster.

Everything was discussed in laborious detail. The scene. The setup. The dick. I was presented a lineup of reliable talent to choose from— "reliable" meaning they get hard, stay hard, and know how to pretty your gape. By the end of a scene, you want your hole to look an aggressive but not too angry shade of pink, yawning wide and right into the camera. Believe it or not, this is some men's specialty. I wanted those men. There were so many options of makes and models laid out in front of me, I felt like I was purchasing a car. I guess on some level I would be taking it out for a spin and parking it in my garage.

"If you choose a small one, nobody will respect you," one girl warned. I was told of the plight of a girl who had accidentally done her first one during what was supposed to be a regular scene. She can only blame herself, though. In the middle of it, she screamed out, "Fuck my ass," and he did. She said she didn't even really feel it because he was so small. She lost out on a fortune. "Do a massive uncut one. It's dramatic but they have nice padding."

Extra flesh for a more pillowy entrance was a sought-after thing for the assholes of porn.

When I mentioned this massive padding idea to Dave, he said, "Fuck that; you're Rachel from *Boy Meets World*! Anything up your ass will cause mass hysteria. You have a pass."

But I didn't want a pass. I wanted to prove myself as a big deal who could take a big deal and earn street credit.

"I absolutely refuse to take a small one," I told Kayden in no uncertain terms as we were paying for our coffee at Starbucks.

"Why not Manuel?" she asked, pulling her card from the reader.

Manuel was a logical choice as we were already star-crossed, volatilely passionate sometime lovers in the *Muse* universe. We worked well together, and I could trust him. Plus, he was uncut, massive, and on the regular made girls' assholes look pretty.

It was decided then and there, celebrated by a crumble of blueberry scone and one of those carb-less egg bites. I guess the barista behind the counter overheard my earlier size proclamation, because I got a venti handed to me that I didn't order.

As the time approached, I wanted to make sure I did this right. I knew about hosing and padding, but what else? Surely there had to be more to this than what sounded like basic gardening.

It's one thing to have anal sex in your personal life, which I do enjoy immensely, but to be doing it on a full production is a different story. My fear was less about the act of it and more the terror that something errant and brown hanging from my starfish would be preserved on the Internet for the ages—or, worse, TMZ for the moment.

I needed a solid plan for the removal of my solids.

During my time of inquiry and investigation, I came to discover that girls treat their anal prep as sacred and varied as one would religion— each ritual and rite performed in a different way but moving toward the same dogmatic purpose.

First, there were the girls who swore by fasting. The ones who took no chances. Their primary philosophy was that if there's nothing there, then there's nothing there.

But how long do you starve for? An hour? Six? Two, maybe three days? Has anyone ever died for clean ass sex?

"Eat some corn and then see how long it takes to show up in your stool," Angela, my *Drive* costar and anal queen, told me as the dishes were collected from our meal and they were readying us for dessert at this industry dinner. The guy with the crumb rake was awfully observant. "Once you see it, then you'll know how long you'll have to go without eating," she said, sipping tea from a proper cup. The fucker was still raking. At this point he was collecting lint. "Monitor your system using the corn as a marker. That way you'll be sure nothing makes an appearance on set." I finished my cappuccino, a bit queasy as I stared into the brown froth and collection of grounds at the bottom. Was this my future? The raker dumped his lint and immediately offered to fill my cup.

There were girls who didn't starve themselves but organized their food choices. These girls often viewed themselves as scientists. Their diets consisted mostly of chicken broth and gummy bears in timed-out portions. Gummy bears were popular because they give you a sugar boost, fill you up to an extent, and take forever to digest. Win, win, win!

"Don't eat beets," one member of this food portioning sect said as she waved her arms in an X shape in front of me, like beets would be the absolute worst decision I could ever make. "Everyone will think your ass is bleeding!" That was a valid point. "And nothing yellow either. No mustard or turmeric, and for sure don't go absolutely crazy with saffron."

I couldn't think of a scenario where I would go absolutely crazy with saffron, but that too was noted.

Then, like the ones who conform to no religion and follow no god, there were the stars who gave absolutely no fucks. Well, it depended. Porn legend Stoya is chief among them. She's said that the entirety of her preparation comes down to one thing—sticking her finger up her ass, and if it comes out clean, the scene is a go. If not, it's a wrap.

I aspire to that kind of anarchy.

I didn't limit my investigation to fellow porn stars, though. I decided to seek the advice of digestive movement professionals in other fields as well. The girl at the juice bar; my friend who recently had a colonoscopy and offered me her instruction materials if I promised to give them back; Reddit. The Reddit thing got weird, though.

My yoga teacher told me I should do more twists to encourage productive movement and to drink some kind of herbal tea blend she gets from a man in Van Nuys. "You shouldn't shock your gut with any sudden activity or angry manipulations." She twisted her body on her mat, demonstrating poses that I was to copy. "It's more of an opening, an ease. An invitation to a journey. Don't push it, or you'll never make peace with the exit." It all felt like good advice for some long-held trauma, but I wasn't sure I could embrace taking my waste on a spiritual journey.

I did do a lot more twists, though.

When it came time to purchase the necessary materials, I decided to get all my supplies at Amazon. I didn't wish to stand in line at a store with a basket full of enemas, Vaseline, and frozen corn.

I was preparing to eat my corn, watch my shits, and then starve when Kayden called me.

"Please don't do that; you'll faint," she said. "Just eat lightly. Do an enema tonight and one in the morning, and then just fill the douche bottle with warm water and keep gently washing out."

But what about the hours and hours of cleaning? The beet juice? The corn?

Hearing her talk, it all sounded so simple.

"Most girls don't understand basic biology," she said. "If you eat a banana ten minutes before the scene, it doesn't just fall out your butt."

This was true. I don't ever remember a banana just falling out my butt before. Possibly some hot wings or a fiery mole sauce, but not a banana. Of course, I never checked. What if it was just up there inside lurking?

Stoya's finger test was sounding smarter by the minute.

On a side note, I found out some interesting information. The number one reason a girl cancels an anal scene the morning of is because she's cut her butthole while shaving it. I took that under advisement and got a wax.

So, the night before, there I was on the bathroom floor, asshole bare, petroleum jelly–slicked, and up in the air, instructing my husband how to give it to me so I could really feel it deep—the enema, that is. Although my fingers did flirt with the "buy now" slider on Amazon, I didn't feel professional enough for that shower nozzle yet. I needed to run this race first (with no runs!) before I merited equipment.

"Just stick the plastic tip all the way in and squeeze," I said to my husband as I flicked off the top to the enema bottle and passed it to him. The little green tip bounced on the tile, serving as an alert that this was all actually happening. The gates were open, and it was time for the horses to come out.

"It says on the box most people need about half," my husband said, while actively squeezing the gushing fluid downward, filling up my rectum. "But I think you're going to take the whole thing." He laughed.

He knew.

It's a well-storied fact in my family that my father's side of the tree has large shits. Yes, I said it. It's not pretty, but actually, in a Guinness book, far corner of the Internet kind of way, it's sort of impressive. It's a family joke that my dad always clogs a toilet good. In fact, my mother has been known to banish him to fast food or medical building restrooms if he's preparing to deliver an especially large load. I don't have that problem. I've never had to run to a Denny's or anything, but let's just say my capacity for fitting voluminous material up my asshole is impressive.

And, yes, I took the whole bottle.

After a few minutes of lying there on the bathroom floor, with my hole blinking up for mercy at the ceiling fan (they instruct you to remain in this position on the box), I began to feel a rumbling, a gurgle. The pulling back of the wave before the crash. I ran for the toilet. And while my yoga teacher may not be happy with the drama of this exit, I made my family proud.

I followed instructions and did another the next morning, and then continually cleaned out with the water enema in the shower. I was surprised that it only took a half hour before the water came out so clear I could drink it if I wanted to. I briefly wondered how much this water, all bottled up and labeled nice, would sell for. That one girl sold her bathwater for a small fortune. I'm sure my butt water would garner a much higher price point.

I took a deep breath, smeared some lube on and in, and then inserted my butt plug. I'd been wearing one pretty steadily all week, so I'd be nice and opened up. It was a strange yet not unpleasant sensation to wear one to the grocery store. It sort of makes you walk like you're on grass wearing high heels.

I texted Kayden and said I was ready—and I was. She replied immediately with a YouTube clip of *Pulp Fiction*. I laughed at the song.

"Girl, You'll Be a Woman Soon."

CHAPTER 18

IT WAS IN MY second year of porn that I started noticing the full circles—those times in life when the beginning of one journey is a conclusion of sorts, but also back to some start. I never really saw the value in them before. Coming full circle felt repetitive and endless, and not going anywhere but around and around. A straight line had always been my focus, that staircase, that trajectory upward, something far and away from somewhere you'd already been. But, in that year, I discovered the power of circles.

Muse launched a second season. Following monster success and winning all the awards, it was made into a continuing series. It was a bold move and the first of its kind to marry porn and mainstream in a serious way. "If you cut out the hard-core sex, it would be Netflix," Kayden said while we were on set for the scene where I have sex with superstar trans performer Aubrey Kate and where we also discuss the harm of colonialization and religious oppression.

I vowed this year to push my boundaries and to challenge myself. The fantasies I used to write about were now all coming true. There were threesomes and foursomes and more and more anal. But it was during my gang bang, for the grand finale scene of the series, that I was joined by my old friend Danny again.

"Well, look who's here," I said as I tackle-hugged him. I hadn't seen him since before the pandemic and only once or twice since I had been at Deeper. This reunion was a long time coming. How wild it was to be on a big set with him like this. That experiment he was part of back in that hotel room, when I didn't know where it could possibly lead, led to this.

"Look at you, superstar," he said in that British accent of his. "I told you, you were a natural."

"You did," I smiled.

Will, from my VR Bangers shoot, was there too. "You just exploded out there," he said, referring to my successes and being now the face of the brand. But I, of course, kept it light. "Well, you'll be the one exploding today." He laughed.

And explode he did, four times to be exact! He has a considerable talent in reloading and unloading again. It's an art.

The scene had me tearing through a sex club after reaching an emotional place of despair from a world that was trying to wrong me. I identified with this raw and primal means of escape and then rebirth. I ravaged my way through this circle maze, pulling anyone and everyone to me and then throwing myself onto the center of a bed. A swarm of men and women crowded around while four men filled my holes. This kind of ravaging tears your soul from your body. At one point, you float above it all and watch yourself—this ravenous, insatiable whore who won't apologize for it and whom you're proud of.

Navigating so many dicks in so many ways is more difficult than you may expect. To give all of them equal time and attention takes athletic skill.

"Bite it," one of the other guys told me, and it took a few moments to compute that he meant that I should actually bite his dick. When I nibbled it, he called out, "No, really bite it!" So I really did. And it's an animalistic and liberating feeling to actually tear your teeth into a foot-long dick.

I was a sweaty heap of a mess at the end of it. I'd lost two earrings, my right eyelash strip, and all my breath, but there was applause from all the crew. "Better make room for more trophies," one of the guys on set told me and I thanked him while I was still covered in cum.

Mistress Maitland also had a second season, and this time, the history and depth of my character and my persona were fleshed out. I stood at an old Hollywood microphone in front of an audience and told them my story, flashing back to all the parts of my life that made me who I was. As I left the stage, I thanked them for watching, and I disappeared into the darkness and haze while they applauded my exit.

Isiah joined me for the grand finale, which again brought another relationship to some full-circle moment. It was an *Eyes Wide Shut* type of setup with a *Phantom of the Opera*–like pianist and a room of people in robes and masks. The girls would all fall to their knees at my commands because I was now their mistress.

This scene also just happened to be filmed on the second anniversary of Kayden and me meeting at that Starbucks. "I baked you a mulberry pie," she said as she handed me a little box with a tin. "And I picked the berries myself."

We found ice cream in the fridge and ate our pie on the set after everyone had gone. "This past two years has really been something," she said as she spooned some berries and ice cream into my mouth.

"Do you ever think you'll do mainstream again?" my friend Michael Maloney had asked me over lunch. He's a journalist I have known since I was a teenager, and he worked for *Soap Opera Digest*. I gave him my first interview, and he's one of the few who knew me through every stage of my career and life. It was fitting that he was sort of interviewing me now, again.

It was a question I got a lot, actually, especially since I was gaining more and more of a profile in the world. XBIZ and the *Daily Beast* had me penning articles about the industry, and the press would all come to me when anything in the world of sex work or porn came up. I liked being a voice people would listen to—someone they could trust because I had been in their living rooms before I was in their bedrooms. I thought

I'd never want to go back, but the world was shifting and changing. I hoped that everything we had done at Deeper and everything I was sharing about my story was a real part of that shift.

"I guess if I had control over it," I said, "and if I could create something special."

Not long after, I got a message from a production company on my Twitter account. "We'd like to talk to you about a potential television project," it said, and when I investigated it, I found that it was completely legitimate.

Rob, the head of Leaving Normal Productions and the executive producer of a new sitcom project about life in the world of porn, introduced himself on a phone call. "The writer of this show brought your name up in our meeting. You were the only one she wanted for the part." He added, "I mean, you have experience that no one else has in this world, and you're also a celebrity who's worked on sitcoms—you would be such a vital piece to the puzzle we're trying to put together."

When I later talked to the writer, Zerelda, she told me this had been a passion project of hers for the past three years, but she felt now was the time, partly because of my success, to make people out there look at the industry in a different way. "I used to pitch this idea, and everyone told me a lighthearted comedy show about porn would never work," she said, and there was real passion in her tone. "And a few months back I was talking about it again, and the guy said, 'Well, Maitland Ward is a porn star now and she's legitimate.'"

Who would've thought that it would take becoming a porn star to finally be considered legitimate?

Although I loved the pitch, I wasn't sure about it. I hadn't read the script yet. Would it really be something other than the stereotypes and archaic tropes that Hollywood had peddled before?

The Big Time, as it was given to me, was about a virginal aspiring filmwriter who finds himself down on his luck, so he answers an ad for a writing gig on Craigslist. He meets a leggy, scantily clad actress and enters a strange studio world where half the people are naked and nobody seems to notice, but he doesn't ask too many questions until he's offered the job. "You'll be writing porn," he's told, and he nearly collapses.

While the situations weren't entirely realistic and the setups and characters could use work, I found myself smiling after I read it. This wasn't the same bullshit Hollywood tries to feed us—that porn is a scary, mixed-up, dangerous world where you'll end up on drugs, destitute, and probably dead. It was a hopeful story, full of light and fun. It needed some work, but it was good.

When I got back to them, agreeing to star in it if they would be open to my suggestions, they jumped at the chance. "Come on as a producer. You would add such value to our project and our team," Rob said, and a new role for me on the project—and in my life—was born.

Over the course of a few months, I spent my time helping to retool the script. We completely changed the character of the virginal screen-writer to a virginal superhero lover whose comic book ends up in my hands. I would now play a top porn star who hires him to revive a studio that is struggling by helping us make something that's big and bold and revolutionary: we would make superhero porn. This really played to my fan base on all levels, and the comedy aspect was taking me back to my roots. In addition to helping develop the story, I was tasked to look at location photos for our upcoming shoot in New York, cast actors, and do everything a producer and star of a show does.

I would be going back to New York again, as a sex star and a writer and a producer, but also as an actress.

"You have to be in this!" I told Isiah. We needed an adult actor in the story to legitimize it and connect the worlds—and also to show his dick, which also connected worlds, though in more of an implied way in this project. I knew Isiah was talented with comedy, and we had done a lot of superhero porn of our own for content.

"I've never done anything in mainstream like this," Isiah said.

"Well, when I first worked with you, I had never done anything in porn," I said, and he was smiling, like I was, when he agreed to take on this new challenge.

THE NEWS OF MY return to mainstream in this sitcom went far and wide, and it spread like wildfire. The interest and excitement people had over the prospect of my returning to sitcom television, and in a show about the porn world, was overwhelming. Everyone from the *New York Post* to the *Daily Mail* and TMZ covered me that week. Even Perez Hilton at some point tweeted, asking if he could guest on the show.

"I can't believe so many people want to see me on TV again," I said to my husband. I really was floored. "Of course they do," he said. "But," I continued, "I don't know if I can do it. To be on a sitcom again. It's exciting but I'm scared I'm going backward, and I might lose myself all over again."

"This is your show now," he said. "You call the shots. You can do mainstream your way this time."

Muse 2 got a billboard right in the heart of Hollywood. There, my face and my name and the project we created to marry porn and mainstream were atop the city that once shunned me, and they were up there in lights.

"We did it," I told Kayden after the press had flashed photos of me beneath it. She smiled proudly.

That night, we took it all in, and I realized that what I had told her was really true: we had done it. That journey that we had set out on two years prior, to show the world that we could make a movie with sex and acting and story, was complete. Of course, we talked about making new projects together, but we also knew that what we set out to do was done. Deeper was a success now. We had won every major award, we had made movies that meant something, and now we had a billboard too. But in order to move forward, we needed to recognize our circle's end. Our circle deserved that.

"You know, everyone always says you opened a path, but I don't think that's true," she said as she looked at me with emotion in her eyes. "That path closed up right behind you because you're the only one who could ever walk it."

"Well, I hope someone tries to walk it, or what we did never mattered."

"Oh, what we did mattered," she said.

I LEFT FOR NEW York City to film *The Big Time* in the spring. It was the first time I had been back on an airplane since the Covid lockdown, and the first time I would step foot on a mainstream sitcom set in fifteen years. The last time I had touched down in either of these places, it was a different world.

The city had definitely changed. Covid lockdown had taken away the daytime business rush and the nighttime theater and dining crowds. None of the restaurants or bars were open in my hotel, and this was in the middle of Times Square. When I looked for a late-night dining experience when I first landed, I was pointed to the all-night Krispy Kreme.

New York City, it seemed, was trying to find its feet again after a long pause. My mainstream self was trying to do the same.

While I knew how excited everyone working on the project was from our Zoom meetings, I could never have anticipated the reception I got from them when I walked onto the set. I'll never forget the cheers and arms waving as my car pulled up.

"We're finally here!" Rob said, and we all dove in for a group hug.

For months we had been talking and planning and working to make a moment like this happen. All of us were coming to this with some dream that hadn't been realized yet. Most people don't get the chance to step back into familiar shoes and to walk in them on a new road. I was twenty-one when I walked onto that *Boy Meets World* set, and now I was forty-four. And here I was with the dream of doing it differently this time, and simultaneously all again.

"I just want to say that your story inspires me, and it's really helped me come out of my shell," one of the young actresses told me. "I watch your stuff on Deeper all the time. It's fucking brilliant."

I knew everyone on set would be porn positive; they were working on a show about porn, so they would kind of have to be, but I was overwhelmed by the reception I was getting, and the questions and the compliments and the sheer rush of positive excitement, especially from the women, about what I do.

"Your porn actually tells stories," one of the girls on the production team said. "I can't get off on that silly porn. My mind needs to be turned on before my body." And she smiled at me with real gratitude and, dare I say, hope in her eyes: "I don't have to be ashamed to watch it, and everything out there made me feel ashamed for too long."

I had been hearing this a lot—primarily from women. Finally, there was porn they could watch with their husbands or boyfriends and also really get off. They were tired of being force-fed the kind of scenes that don't take themselves or the performers or the audience seriously. "I just can't get turned on by a pizza boy who gets paid by the slice with blow jobs."

Isiah had the first scene up with the adorable virginal superhero writer we cast. He would show the new guy the ropes, welcome him with open arms, and tell some funny jokes, all with his dick out. I had forgotten that mainstream sets don't have large, bare dicks casually hanging around, because as soon as Isiah took off his pants, half the women and a quarter of the men were in love.

"I've never seen anything like it," Zerelda told me. "This is a whole new experience!"

Isiah and a few others were my superhero squad. And we all wore jokey pornographic-themed costumes. Labia Man was my favorite. Isiah had a shield covered with condoms, and when he held it out, he said, "WaCondom Forever." Everyone laughed and Zerelda said, "We're using that!"

I was so proud by how prepared and funny Isiah was. I knew he'd be good and that people would love him because he works hard and he's a gentleman, and he has such talent—but everyone absolutely adored him. "I never knew a mainstream set would be so friendly," he said. "But maybe I should try to do more of this."

And I smiled. Mainstream and porn had met, and they became united in superhero costumes.

While I had been nervous, finding my rhythm in comedy again came easy to me. It was like riding a bike, but a bike ridden again after walking in those old shoes I talked about for a lifetime on an unpredictable road. But the shoes were really mine now, and it was better this time because of it. I was confident now, and I was not afraid of everything that had held me back as a girl.

Porn gave me that.

MY LAST SCENE WAS with me and my bodyguard, a gruff man of battle who was in love with me but couldn't admit it. We sat there with this sweet, raw emotion between us. I spoke about my failures and my dreams and how all of that seemed to be so up in the air.

"You know when you think you have everything figured out and it feels like you can actually make a difference? But then life throws a curveball at you and suddenly it's all just a pipe dream?" he asked, and I nodded. And then I asked him, "Do you just move on to option B?"

The question sat between us for a moment, before he looked me straight in the eyes, and gave me an answer that I, Maitland Ward, had spent my entire young life trying to find.

"Burn the ships," he told me, and he leaned in to share with me life's secret when backed up against something that there seems no good option to win. "In the Spanish conquest of the New World, Hernán Cortés showed up outnumbered. Instead of retreating to option B, he burned his own ships. No retreat. No option B."

My character takes this advice to heart and decides to take a chance and hire that nerdy comic book writer to create superhero porn with her. But this line felt more personal to me. Hadn't option A failed for me? And hadn't option B seen me somewhere I didn't want to be, doing something I didn't want to do and never really discovering who I was born to be?

So I burned my own ships.

And I stood there, in the flames that my passion and vision, and, yes, my drive lit as they threatened to set fire to me.

Instead of burning me to ashes, I let them light my path.

ACKNOWLEDGMENTS

I WANT TO THANK FIRST and foremost my husband. If it weren't for him, and his love for me, I wouldn't have had the support or encouragement to live out the dream I know now I was meant to accomplish. My mother and father for loving me unconditionally and always encouraging me in my acting and art. Your support has always been immeasurable, especially on this unconventional path. To my grandmother, you always said I was a tall reed meant to stand out. I hope you're proud of me up there now.

To Dave, my photographer, I could not have made this journey without your wit, sarcasm, or ability to sew me into the tiniest costumes. To my agent, Stephanie, thank you for believing in me and seeing a story that needed to be told and always fighting for it. Thank you to Michelle, Atria Books, and everyone at Simon & Schuster for giving voice to a woman finding freedom in her sexuality and trusting me to write this book, as a first-time author, all on my own. Though I couldn't have put it all together without this wonderful team.

To my friend Michael Maloney, who has been my breakfast date and confidant since we were both sixteen. I couldn't ask for better than you. And thank you to everyone in porn who has welcomed, helped, and guided me along the way. You are members of an industry who are not recognized enough for your love, grace, and generosity. I have received that firsthand.

To my fans, my Wardiors, who I couldn't have done this without.

And, of course, Kayden Kross for taking a journey like no other with me. What we did definitely mattered.